L.D.

Mayor Louis Taylor and the Rise of Vancouver

Daniel Francis

ARSENAL
PULP PRESS
Vancouver

L.D.: Mayor Louis Taylor and the Rise of Vancouver
Copyright © 2004 by Daniel Francis

ARSENAL PULP PRESS
103 - 1014 Homer Street
Vancouver, B.C.
Canada v6b 2w9
arsenalpulp.com

The publisher gratefully acknowledges the support of the Canada Council for the Arts
and the British Columbia Arts Council for its publishing program,
and the Government of Canada through the Book Publishing Industry Development Program
for its publishing activities.

Design by Solo
Edited by Stephen Osborne
Cover photography courtesy Vancouver Public Library, VPL 12604, VPL 4658

Printed and bound in Canada

National Library of Canada Cataloguing in Publication

Francis, Daniel
LD : Mayor Louis Taylor and the rise of Vancouver / Daniel Francis.

ISBN 1-55152-156-3

1. Taylor, Louis Denison, 1857-1946. 2. Vancouver (B.C.) — Biography.
3. Vancouver (B.C.) — History — 20th century.
I. Title. II. Title: Mayor Louis Taylor and the rise of Vancouver.

FC3847.26.T39F73 2004   971.1'3303'092   C2004-900680-0

Acknowledgments

Along with the many librarians and archivists at the Vancouver City Archives and the Vancouver Public Library who have been so helpful in dealing with my requests over the years, I wish to thank in particular three individuals without whom this book would not have materialized. Roy Denison Werbel is Louis Taylor's great grandson. If Roy had not decided to contact me about his great-grandfather, the project would have been stillborn. And if he had not kept the boxes of family documents that had come into his possession, L.D.'s story would be missing many of its most interesting details. Roy welcomed me into his home and gave me access to his archive without once trying to influence my opinion of his great-grandfather and without placing any restrictions on how I might use the material. He also shared with me family memories which were clues to hidden aspects of L.D.'s life. I hope Roy feels that in return I have done justice to his great-grandfather's story. My friend Howard White suggested to me, back in the mid-1980s, that Louis Taylor might be worth investigating. That was the first time I had heard L.D.'s name. Over the years Howard patiently listened to my evolving theories about Taylor, and offered a few of his own. And Stephen Osborne, friend and editor, has helped me to find my way to what I wanted to say about L.D. and the city.

Special thanks to my wife Quita. For the several years that Taylor lived in our home she never failed to be a gracious hostess, but I know that she is happy that he has moved out at last into the pages of this book.

Mayor Taylor was at the height of his political power when this photograph was taken in the living room of his apartment early in 1927, shortly after he had won his sixth term in office. Leonard Frank, who took the photograph, was Vancouver's leading commercial photographer during the inter- war period. VPL 6464

Prologue

One evening in February 1939, a reporter for the *Daily Province* newspaper came across Louis Taylor sitting alone in the lobby of the old Hotel Vancouver. It was after a political meeting at which the former prime minister of Canada, R.B. Bennett, had been the featured speaker. Bennett was retiring to England, where he would live out the rest of his life, and he had come to the West Coast to say his goodbyes. Louis Taylor was out of place at such a Conservative gathering. At eighty-two years of age, he was still embroiled in local politics where he was known for his progressive policies. Some even called him a socialist, others said he was a crook; whatever, he was the furthest thing from a Conservative. But Taylor had come along to say hello to R.B., whom he knew from his days as the city's mayor. As the reporter approached, he saw that Taylor was holding a small autograph book, and as they fell into conversation the old man showed off his collection of signatures gathered from celebrities met during a long career in public life. "In a casual way he began to yarn," said the reporter, whose name was Ronald Kenvyn, and who started to think that he might have a story.

Kenvyn suggested to Taylor, who had been mayor of Vancouver more times than anyone before or since, that the veteran politician allow him to write his "reminiscences." "Do you think they might be of interest?" Taylor asked coyly, and together they embarked on a sixteen-part series of articles which appeared in the *Province* between February 27 and March 16, 1939. In a modest way, Kenvyn became the old man's Boswell. His articles, which cover Taylor's early days in Vancouver as well as his ten years as a newspaper publisher and his eleven years as mayor, are the closest thing there is to an autobiography of Vancouver's most successful local politician.

Readers of the series in the *Province* would not have needed any introduction to Louis Denison Taylor. To most of them it must have seemed like he had been around forever. His eight terms as mayor spanned three decades of the city's history. When he arrived from Chicago in 1896, Vancouver, population barely 20,000, was still rebuilding atop the ashes of the disastrous fire that had occurred ten years earlier. Forty years later the population had grown to 250,000 people, making it the third largest city in Canada, and the tiny milltown on Burrard Inlet had become a major seaport, the economic engine of an entire province. The international airport, amalgamation of Vancouver with Point Grey and South Vancouver, the eight-hour day for civic employees, a juvenile court, the city's first planning commission, industrial development in False Creek: these were some of the initiatives that Taylor had championed during his years in government. Vancouver had grown up under his care. For many voters, their feisty mayor, with his trademark red tie (he asked to be buried in it when he died) and the ubiquitous cigar clenched in his fist, was as emblematic of the city as Stanley Park or the North Shore mountains. As Ronald Kenvyn put it, Taylor "has certainly carved a deep niche for himself in the hall of municipal fame." And he wasn't finished quite yet. At the time that Kenvyn's articles appeared, it had been four years since the old warhorse had occupied the mayor's chair, but nine months later he would run for election again, gaining just one percent of the vote and finishing dead last. It would be his final attempt at public office.

For such a successful politician, Taylor cut an unremarkable figure in person. He was short and slight, with a grey-flecked moustache and, as he grew older, fewer and fewer strands of hair scraped across the top of a balding head. Photographs show that aside from the red tie, his usual costume consisted of a pair of round, owlish glasses, a heavy three-piece suit, and a pair of stout leather shoes cut above the ankle. People who met him were surprised at how softspoken he was, which contrasted so dramatically with the combative politician they knew from the election platform. He had the appearance and manner of a kindly school teacher, or the bank clerk that he had been in his younger days. To everyone, friend and foe alike, he was known simply as L.D. (Denison was his

L.D.

mother's maiden name.) But Taylor was no milquetoast, as his political opponents learned at their cost. He was the outspoken friend of the average voter and the implacable enemy of large corporations and other vested interests. Any campaign in which he took part was guaranteed to be a contentious one. He loved to conjure up dark intrigues by unnamed conspirators who, he charged, opposed him because he stood for the common man. As mayor, L.D. did not sit on his hands. He wanted to accomplish things, to make a difference to the city. As a result, he was never far from controversy.

Readers with long memories would have found it ironic that the *Province* chose to publish his reminiscences. It was the *Province*, after all, that had carried on a bitter war of words with L.D. over the years, opposing him in every election and doing its best to dig up fresh scandals to scuttle his chances. Questionable land deals, police corruption, extortion of favours, pandering to the city's underworld: all these charges and more clung to L.D.'s reputation like the smell of cheap perfume. But everyone loves a fighter and, like the city he governed, L.D. was notorious for rising from the ashes. If he won more elections than any other mayor in the history of the city, he also lost more. Sixteen to be exact: once for license commissioner, four times for alderman, and eleven times for mayor. But he always bounced back, refusing to take no for an answer. Sixteen months before his death, when he was eighty-six years old, he announced that he was going to run in the next general election in Britain as a candidate for the World-Wide Political Party, an obscure group dedicated to bringing world peace by doing away with political partisanship. In the end good sense prevailed (or maybe it was poor health) and he did not run, but even in his eighties he still had the fire in his belly. And his tenacity went beyond politics. Three times he almost died. Once, on a trip down the Parsnip River in northern B.C., his boat overturned and he had to be pulled from the freezing water. At another time, he was struck in the head by a whirling propellor at the Vancouver airport and the newspapers actually declared him dead. And then, in the summer of 1931, he was hospitalized with a mysterious ailment and had to take a sabbatical from the mayor's job while he recovered. Even when they were voting against him, Vancouverites found it difficult not to admire L.D.'s gumption.

I was born the year after Taylor died and grew up in the city he had governed for so long. Yet I did not hear his name mentioned even once until I was in my thirties. That was the first thing that intrigued me about L.D. Despite the fact that he was Vancouver's most successful politician, he is mostly forgotten in the city. There is no monument with his name on it, no biography or statue. The only landmarks are a short street at the edge of Chinatown and, because he was a supporter of the creation of Garibaldi Provincial Park, a dilapidated hikers' cabin in the alpine meadows below the Black Tusk. When I asked oldtimers about him, the most they could recall was the red tie and the cigar. The "deep niche" Kenvyn thought L.D. had carved for himself in the municipal hall of fame was empty. I wondered why. When I came across the series of articles in the *Province*, my interest was further roused. As presented by Kenvyn, L.D. had an appealing lack of pomposity. There was a sly twinkle to the stories he told. What's more, he was a mayor who had been proud to identify with the city's workers and to promote policies that would improve their lives. He seemed to represent a radical history that had been suppressed, or at least forgotten. At the same time, and just as appealingly, he was obviously skating around the truth of his own life. Like most autobiographies, L.D.'s was revealing for what he left out. To begin with, his account of why he came to Vancouver did not sound plausible. What about his wife and children? Where did they fit into the story? And why was he so neglected by a city he served for so long? I became seduced by the secrets that I suspected were there to be discovered.

When I set out on the trail of Louis Taylor, I discovered that a full biography was impossible. Too little is known of his private life, especially the half of it that he lived before he came to Vancouver. As far as anyone knew, there were no private papers surviving in libraries or archives, no letters, diaries, or scrapbooks. Still, he lived much of his life in the public eye, as both politician and publisher. This part could be reconstructed with some thoroughness. Furthermore, his career encompassed so much of the history of Vancouver, more than four decades from the time he arrived until his final defeat at the polls, that he seemed to offer a unique window through which to view the evolution of the city during its first fifty years. So I decided to undertake a "life and times": a book as much about Vancouver as it would be about Louis Denison Taylor.

This didn't mean that I didn't want to find out as much as I could about the man himself, however, and to this end I attempted to contact surviving members of his family. I knew that he had had two sons. Both of them lived in the United States and both had come up to Vancouver for their father's funeral. I tracked down the death certificate of the eldest son, Ted, who died in Los Angeles in 1963. This document listed Mrs Mary Werbel as an informant about the deceased. Suspecting that this might be Ted's daughter – that is, L.D.'s granddaughter – I wrote to the California department of motor vehicles requesting her address, but the department refused to give out the information and the trail went cold. Time passed. Then one evening my home telephone rang and a voice at the end of the line identified himself as Roy Werbel calling from California. Roy was phoning to tell me that his mother Mary, by then deceased herself, was indeed Louis Taylor's granddaughter. Unknown to me, the motor vehicles office had forwarded my letter to her. She had not been interested in my project, but Roy was. He told me that he had grown up hearing stories about his great-grandfather, the "Red" mayor of Vancouver, and would love to be of help. It turned out that Roy was keeper of the family archive, dozens of boxes of material assembled by Ted who, Roy said, had been something of a packrat. Twenty of the boxes related to L.D.

When I went down to California to sift through the material, I discovered that the boxes contained a mass of dusty newspaper clippings, scrapbooks, photographs, mementoes and, most importantly, family correspondence. Thanks to these documents and the stories Roy told me about his great-grandfather, I went from knowing almost nothing about L.D.'s private life to knowing enough to fill a soap opera. Bigamy, embezzlement, drug abuse: it turned out that Louis Taylor was not only Vancouver's longest-serving mayor, but also by far its most "colourful."

I had enough to begin.

Making a Civic Politician 1

L ouis Taylor arrived in Vancouver on Sunday, September 8, 1896. He had left his home in Chicago several days before, travelling by train via St Paul, Winnipeg, and the Canadian West, heading for Seattle. He was thirty-nine years old, an accountant, and married with a newborn son. But he was abandoning the life of a respectable business and family man to set off alone, as he put it, "in fulfillment of a boyhood dream" to visit Alaska.

When the train reached Mission, a small farming village in the Fraser Valley about seventy kilometres east of Vancouver, L.D. gathered his baggage and prepared to switch trains for the last leg of his trip to Seattle. At this point, fate intervened in the shape of a baggage handler who also turned out to be a Vancouver booster. Why not continue on to the end of the line, he asked? Vancouver was booming. It deserved a look. The accommodating porter even offered to change L.D.'s ticket for him. L.D. did not know for sure where Vancouver was located, but he had some time on his hands and a desire to see more of Western Canada, so he threw his bags back in the luggage rack and settled down in his seat to enjoy the run through the Valley out to the Pacific Coast.

L.D. arrived in British Columbia a fugitive from justice. His head may have been filled with dreams of the Klondike, but his trip was not a voluntary one. Back in Chicago, L.D. was wanted by the courts. A business venture had turned sour and he stood accused of embezzlement. Like so many other newcomers who were flooding into the city, L.D. came to Vancouver to escape the past and discover a new life for himself.

L.D.'s mother Amy (left) and sister Kate, in 1898. COURTESY ROY WERBEL

i

Louis Denison Taylor was born in Ann Arbor, Michigan, west of Detroit, on July 22, 1857. Almost nothing is known about his father, Gustavus Taylor, and almost as little about his mother, Amy Denison. He had one sister, Kate, who married Eugene Cooley and lived, at least for a while, in Lansing, Michigan. At the end of her life L.D.'s mother was living in Lansing as well. He visited her there in 1901, apparently because she was ill. She died in 1904. Judging from Louis's correspondence and his reminiscences, his father had by this time either died or left the family, probably the latter. Louis makes no mention of him in any of the surviving documents, while he speaks often and warmly of his mother. On one occasion he credited his support for women's suffrage to the influence of his mother's example, leaving the impression that there was no father around the house from the time he was a small boy.[1] Nothing is known of L.D.'s Ann Arbor boyhood except for a few memories that he shared many years later. On these occasions L.D. gave a strong impression of family poverty. In a biographical memo he wrote for the Vancouver City archives during his final term as mayor, he said that as a student he had had to borrow books from other pupils or earn his own money to buy them. During his political career L.D. was known for always wearing a red tie; in the same memo he explained the origin of this habit. "I adopted the colour as a youngster, when, due to a distinct shortage of money, my mother invariably knitted me a pair of red mittens with a cord to go around my shoulders for a Christmas present. Incidently, this was the only present I received on many a Christmas. Since that period of my life, red has been my favourite colour."[2] On another occasion he told of going fishing in a local stream in an attempt to get food for the family supper.[3]

L.D. credited his interest in printing and publishing to this period of his life. The father of one of his friends owned the Ann Arbor *Courier* and the two boys used the newspaper's print shop to make simple calling cards which they sold to earn spending money. Following high school, L.D. went to work at the library at the University of Michigan. Later, in the mid-1880s, still living in Ann Arbor, he appears in the city directory as a teller at the First National Bank. Around the same time he was a partner in a bicycle sales business and a truss company. L.D.'s interest in politics dated back to his Ann Arbor days and to the same newspaper publisher who had urged his entrepreneurial ambitions. This individual, a Mr Beal, was an active Republican who encouraged his son Julius and young Louis Taylor to take an interest in local politics as teenagers, introducing them to the backrooms and filling them in on party gossip. Later, L.D. attempted to launch his own political career in Ann Arbor, and ran unsuccessfully for alderman. It would be another couple of decades and in another country before he eventually would achieve electoral success.

In 1891, L.D. moved from Ann Arbor to Chicago to work for the Wabash Railroad. The Wabash was one of the principal railways of the American Midwest. It had expanded into Chicago in 1880, and L.D. joined the company as assistant to the auditor. By this time he seems to have left his impoverished background behind him to become a successful mid-level business executive. A year after arriving in Chicago, on May 26, 1892, he married Annie Louise Pierce, the daughter of a successful architect, Osborne Pierce, and his wife Caroline. Annie was twenty-five years old, ten years younger than Louis. The marriage was not a happy one. Apparently Annie's father recommended against it and years later, after they had separated, Louis speculated that he and Annie had been temperamentally incompatible from the start.[4] In Chicago, L.D. began to display a pattern of restlessness that marked the rest of his life. His sister Kate described this impulse in a letter to Annie. "It is high time this dreadful restlessness in him is conquered so he will not be continually striving after big things and losing his gainings. There seems to be a desperate enemy in him which makes him lose his head. . . ."[5] Louis left the railway and joined a lumber company as an accountant, but before too long he left this job as well, ostensibly because his employer asked him to work on Sunday, a request that offended his strict Congregationalism. "I then tried several 'business opportunities'," L.D. later recalled. "None of them turned out successfully and . . . I thought I had better start for Alaska before my savings disappeared."[6]

Actually, the story was a bit more complicated than that. In August 1896, L.D. was partner in a bank, North & Taylor, located on West Madison Street in Chicago. At ten o'clock on the morning of Tuesday, August 11, a notice appeared in the window of the bank informing depositors that North & Taylor was closed, its affairs in the hands of a receiver. "Rumors flew up and down West Madison street all day yesterday," the *Chicago Tribune* reported. "Depositors gathered in groups in front of the closed iron gates at the bank entrance and discussed steps to recover their money."[7] It turned out that a few days before, North had withdrawn from the partnership and the bank had been renamed L.D. Taylor & Co., but most depositors had not been told of the change, which made them all the more nervous. In an interview with a *Tribune* reporter, L.D. explained that North had run into personal financial difficulties and had withdrawn from the partnership in order to protect the bank. L.D. said that he had hoped to carry on but that he had failed to gain an extension on his margin of credit, "making it impossible for us to meet maturing liabilities."[8] Angry creditors, however, asked pointedly why some of their deposits had been accepted at the bank when L.D. knew the business was insolvent. Apparently some of them believed rumours that North had been investing money in chancy mining operations. Whether or not this was true, North bolted for Mexico.

On Friday evening, police arrested L.D. at his home on a charge of receiving a deposit of $785 while knowing the bank was insolvent. He spent Friday night and much of Saturday in jail before a judge released him on $2,000 bail. No sooner was L.D. on the street than another depositor charged him with embezzlement and on Monday he appeared in court once again, where bail was continued. At this point, L.D. went into hiding somewhere outside the city. According to press reports, he had repaid some depositors and was trying to repay others. But as disgruntled creditors met to consider their options, and with further criminal charges hanging over him, L.D. decided to follow his partner North into exile and left for British Columbia.

ii

Disembarking from the train in Vancouver that September afternoon at the small wooden CPR station at the foot of Howe Street, L.D. was not impressed by what he saw. A thick pall of smoke produced by clearing fires around the edge of the settlement hung in the air, irritating his eyes and throat and obscuring the view. The Sunday streets were empty. In 1896, Vancouver was a frontier town with pretensions. Just a decade earlier a fire had spread out of control and reduced the newly-incorporated city to ashes in less than an hour. The conflagration began on a Sunday afternoon in June 1886, when sudden gusts of wind blew sparks from clearing fires on the north side of False Creek into the adjacent underbrush and remaining stands of timber. From there the blaze did not so much spread as explode. In a matter of minutes it had pounced upon the cluster of humble wooden buildings that then constituted "downtown" and devoured them. "The city did not burn," said W.H. Gallagher, who was one of those who tried vainly to put the fire out, "it was consumed by flame; the buildings simply melted before the fiery blast." There was no chance of stopping it; one could only run for one's life. "The fire went down the sidewalk on old Hastings Road so rapidly," recalled Gallagher, "that people flying before it had to leave the burning sidewalk and take to the road; and the fire travelled down that wooden sidewalk faster than a man could run." Residents, some of whom escaped with little more than the clothes on their backs, fled south across False Creek or north into the waters of the harbour. One group tore up a wharf and used the planks to make a raft, on which they paddled to safety. Others clambered aboard the sailing ship *Robert Kerr* which had been blown by the gale from Coal Harbour down off Hastings Mill where it took on refugees. As the flames bore down upon the Mill, the wind suddenly dropped and shifted direction, veering eastward, and the fire petered out. It was over in less than an hour, but in that time more than twenty people died. Most of the bodies were burned beyond recognition. The corpses of a mother and child were discovered in a well where they had hidden, then suffocated when the fire passed over them, sucking all the oxygen from the air. The bartender from the Balfour Hotel was incinerated when he tried to dash to safety through a wall of flame. Another man was seen watering down his woodpile with a tin can of muddy water as the fire engulfed him. When evening came, Gallagher described "a mass of glimmering lights in the darkness of the night, smouldering embers and smoke. The city had been swept clean. . . ."[9]

Vancouver began its rise from the smoking ashes before dawn the very next day. "The fire was a tragedy, but it was not a defeat," declared Donald McGregor, an early historian of the disaster. "At three o'clock on Monday morning teams were delivering lumber on the ash-strewn streets, and by daybreak the city was rising again."[10] Ten years later, when L.D. arrived on the scene, the city had been reborn. Residents were proud of the imposing stone office blocks going up along Granville Street, the palatial homes of the wealthy in the West End, the new

20

L.D.'s predecessors on city council had to hold their meetings outside this makeshift tent in the days and weeks following the Great Fire of 1886. CVA, CITY P.30.N.7

electric street railway, the half-laid sewer system, the Opera House where Sarah Bernhardt had performed. Buildings sprawled across the downtown peninsula and were climbing the southern slopes overlooking False Creek. "The forest vanished and up went the city," observed the writer Ethel Wilson, who arrived at about the same time as L.D.[11] The population in 1896 was approaching 30,000, and a banner strung across Granville Street predicted: "In 1910 Vancouver then will have 100,000 men."

Still, it was not Chicago, where L.D. had been living for the previous five years. Chicago had skyscrapers that towered sixteen storeys into the sky. It was a megacity of more than a million people, the railway capital of the United States, home to giant steel mills and vast stockyards. In 1893, it had hosted the World Columbian Exposition, and almost certainly L.D. was among the twenty-seven million people who visited the famed "White City" where the fair took place. It was the greatest exhibition of modern technological achievement ever assembled and affirmed Chicago's place as America's "second city" after New York. (It is tempting to imagine L.D. touring the replica village of cedar plank houses occupied by a group of Kwakwa̱ka'wakw people brought to the fair from British Columbia, perhaps his introduction to the province that would soon become his home.) No, Vancouver was not Chicago, and as L.D. made his way down Hastings Street from the train station to his hotel he was dispirited by the city, with its board sidewalks, dirt streets, unpainted, wood frame houses, and somnolent air. And, of course, the choking wood smoke. "I felt the need of consolation," he later recalled, "so I decided to go to church."

At this point, L.D. was still a tourist, intending to move on when he had exhausted his curiosity about Vancouver. But in church he ran into old friends from Chicago, George Bessell and his wife, who had settled in the city and were full of optimism for its future. They invited him home after the service and, discovering that he was somewhat rootless, convinced him to give Vancouver more of a chance. Unfortunately for L.D., he arrived on the West Coast in the middle of a recession. A decade earlier the first transcontinental Canadian Pacific train had steamed into town, touching off a frenetic development boom. In just five years, the population jumped to about 15,000 people. Land values skyrocketed; in 1890, lot prices tripled in just six months. The real estate speculator was king. Construction boomed, fuelling a heavy demand for lumber from local mills. The CPR's rail and steamship operations stimulated the expansion of local business. Ocean liners arrived from around the world. City boosters crowed that Vancouver would soon become "the London of the Pacific," the "Constantinople of the West." But booms do not last forever, and when this one collapsed in 1893 Vancouver's dreams of glory collapsed with it, at least temporarily. Construction slowed to a halt. Stores closed. The street railway teetered on the brink of bankruptcy. Lineups of unemployed sought a warm meal at church-run soup kitchens.

The day after he arrived in Vancouver, L.D. wrote to his father-in-law, O.J. Pierce, who was his mainstay during this period. He told Pierce that he had received advice immediately upon his arrival that his crime could only be characterized as a breach of trust and that his was not a deportable offence. "Hence I shall not need to go to Alaska."[12] Still, he worried about his situation, going so far as to advise Pierce to address his mail to "L.T. Denison." "That will be the safest way, although I am known here by my right name."[13] During the first few weeks of his Canadian "exile," L.D. was optimistic that something could be worked out to allow his return to Chicago. He devised a plan to ask the bank depositors if they would agree to make a partial settlement directly with him rather than going through the courts, and even suggested that he might sneak back to Chicago to orchestrate negotiations. When this plan proved unworkable, he accused his lawyer, Porter Coolidge, of incompetence, and worse. "I don't think he is acting in good faith," he wrote to Pierce, "and I think that these rumors of mining speculation emanate from Mr Coolidge. I dislike to think so, but I believe that for some unknown reason he was mighty anxious for me to leave Chicago."[14] In a letter to his mother, he explained that the problems at the bank resulted from the poor economic times "and not through any gross mismanagement on our part," but he despaired of being able to convince the depositors or the courts.[15] Very reluctantly he came to the realization that he was going to have to make a new life for himself in British Columbia.

Years later, when he was firmly established in the city, L.D. recalled his early days in Vancouver for a journalist who was interviewing him for a magazine article. "It often happens," he said, "that the man who comes to Vancouver begins to think, after he has been here a month or two, that Opportunity is somewhat slow in getting around to his door. He expects too much; he is too impatient; he has not yet got into sufficiently close touch with British Columbia life to become a part of its onward movement."[16] L.D. was speaking here from personal experience, recalling, no doubt, his own introduction to the city when jobs were scarce and the insistent rain wore out his patience. He wrote to his father-in-law: "I think if it is necessary for me to stay here this winter I can do a little something and perhaps get a position, though that is hard at the present time. . . . I don't know as I shall like the climate. The rainy season is now due and it will rain until about April 1 they say almost every day. I have not seen the sun since I came on account of the fog and smoke which hangs over the city all the time. . . ."[17] Desperate to make some money, L.D. went in with his friend Bessell who had plans to buy a load of tree bark on Hernando Island, about 150 kilometres to the northwest, for resale in the city. The partners took a steamer to the island, but the promised bark was not there and the deal collapsed. Back in Vancouver, L.D. was relieved to receive a money order from home, but was still pessimistic about his prospects. "There is no chance of getting a salaried position here," he complained in another letter, "as this seems to be the stopping point of all people without money."[18] One day he mounted a bicycle and pedalled out Granville Street past the city boundary at Sixteenth Avenue and through South Vancouver toward the Fraser. What was then called the North Arm Road was a narrow dirt track through the forest. The only regular traffic was the daily stagecoach from downtown. "I remember the hills," L.D. later reminisced, "there were a lot of them, I went up and down each one, and it was hard work too." And all for nothing. There turned out not to be any jobs at the shingle mill at Eburne or the canneries at Steveston. For a few weeks he tried prospecting for gold at Harrison Lake, but by mid-November his spirits had bottomed out. "This weather gives me the blues," he told his father-in-law. "I am so anxious to get to work . . . I wish some one could suggest something that I can do. It is so hard to pass days and days idly. I never had such a time before."[19]

At this time Vancouver newspapers were giving glowing accounts of mining opportunities in the interior of the province. "British Columbia . . . has at length come definitely and decidedly to the front as a gold mining country," the *News-Advertiser* informed its readers. "After a long period of unmerited neglect, the whole district has begun to resound with preparation, and every hill is covered with its knot of prospectors, anxious to be early in the race."[20] But without a grubstake, L.D. could not outfit himself with the necessary supplies. He decided to go to the

L.D.

southwest United States to look for work, and sunshine, hoping to make the money he needed to get to the goldfields.

Early in the new year L.D. travelled to California, then on to Texas and Colorado. It might seem odd that someone who was wanted by the authorities in the U.S. should choose to return there, but given the state of border security and communications at the time, it is not likely that he was taking much of a risk. In Colorado Springs, he got a job soliciting subscriptions for a local newspaper. When spring arrived, he headed back north to British Columbia to try his luck prospecting at Harrison Lake and in the Cassiar District in the far northwestern corner of the province. He failed to strike it rich and retreated to Revelstoke, a CPR divisional point, where in July 1897 he found work as a baggage handler with the railway.[21]

L.D. clung to his dream of finding gold. During the spring and summer of 1897, word of a fabulous strike in the remote wilderness of the Yukon reached the outside world. Only a few hundred adventurers succeeded in hurrying north to the new goldfields that season before winter arrived to close off all access through the frozen mountain passes. But thousands more prepared to travel northward in the spring of 1898, and L.D. decided to join the stampede. He quit his job with the railway in February and came out to Victoria where he linked up with three partners – a coach driver from Philadelphia, a dentist from England, and a law clerk from Seattle – all burning with gold fever. The four prospectors returned to Vancouver to buy supplies and sailed for the Yukon aboard the CPR steamship *Tartar* in May.

The *Tartar* was a 115-metre, steel-hulled steamship recently purchased by the CPR to ply the run between Vancouver and Wrangell, Alaska, the first leg of the so-called "all-Canadian" route to the goldfields.[22] The advantage of this route, which continued up the Stikine River to Telegraph Creek, then overland to the Klondike, was supposed to be that it avoided the arduous Chilkoot and White passes and, aside from the pause at Wrangell, did not pass through American territory. Early that year, the federal government completed an agreement with railway tycoons William Mackenzie and Donald Mann to build a rail line from the Upper Stikine 240 kilometres to the head of Teslin Lake, straddling the B.C. – Yukon border. From there travellers would complete the trip down the Teslin River by boat.

By the time L.D. and his partners embarked on the *Tartar*, promoters had been touting the "Stikine Trail" for several months. When they arrived at Wrangell, they found a squalid boom town already crowded with hangers-on who made a living preying on the stampeders. Most of the forlorn wooden buildings tilted precariously on pilings above the mud; sidewalks were rotting planks stretched between tree stumps. "The streets are immense ditches," remarked one visitor, "real cesspools of dirt and street-sweepings of every kind. . . . Wrangell was an Indian village, with only three whites. Now the larger part of the population is white and very bad. It is dangerous to be out after seven o'clock at night when the days are short; they take your life there for four bits."[23] Understandably, travellers were eager to get out of town as soon as possible while they still had their grubstakes.

L.D.'s party transferred to one of the seventeen river steamers transporting prospectors inland and entered the muddy flow of the Stikine. Along the way the boat passed camps of stranded travellers tenting on the shore. These refugees had not waited for spring breakup and the beginning of steamer traffic. Instead they had set out on foot during the winter, trudging inland up the ice-covered river hauling their supplies on sleds. Now they were caught by the melt, unable to proceed any farther. Bad news awaited L.D. at Telegraph Creek, the head of navigation. The Canadian Senate had refused to pass the bill authorizing the construction of the railway to Teslin Lake. Work on the wagon road which was intended to supply the construction crews also stopped less than ten kilometres from the village. Beyond that trekkers had only a narrow Indian trail winding through the mountains. At this point, many of them turned back, sold their outfits for whatever they could get and bought steamer passage back down the river. L.D. and his friends persevered, hiking as far as the Tahltan River, a tributary of the Stikine, about forty kilometres from Telegraph Creek. There the trail deteriorated, which is perhaps why the partners decided that instead of going farther they would spend the summer looking for gold along the banks of the Tahltan.

L.D. remained in gold country for several weeks, living on salmon and berries. Confined together in the close quarters of their camp, increasingly disappointed at not making a strike, beset by rain and voracious mosquitoes, the prospectors grew bored and irritated with each other. Finally L.D. decided to pull out. He tramped back to Telegraph Creek by himself and joined the milling mob of disillusioned gold seekers

26

trying to get out of the country. "Remember, I had no money," he later recalled. "A river steamer, the *Duchesnay*, operated from Telegraph Creek to Wrangell. She was named after the CPR superintendent at Revelstoke, and I had in my possession a letter of recommendation from him. With this I tackled the captain. He told me I could sleep on deck that night and see him in the morning. Next day I saw him, he stood me a good breakfast, then showed me into a hold filled with baled hay. 'Go in there and stay there until we get to Wrangell. You won't be disturbed,' said the skipper. "So I got to Wrangell and slept out in my little tent until the *Tartar* arrived. Then I sold my tent for five dollars and went aboard. I told the purser five dollars was all I had and could I get to Vancouver. He said yes, and I had a splendid trip. When I reached Vancouver on a Saturday afternoon all the cash I had was twenty-five cents."[24]

Once again L.D. was rescued by the Bessells, who put him up on their living-room sofa until he could find his own place to live. Vancouver in the fall of 1898 was a far different place than it had been two years earlier. The Klondike gold rush was propelling the city past its rival, Victoria, in the race for economic leadership of the province. Thousands of gold seekers embarking for the Yukon bought their supplies from Vancouver outfitters. Wholesale business boomed. At the same time, immigrant farmers were flooding into the Canadian West, creating a robust market for all kinds of goods, especially wood for building farms and houses. West Coast lumbering, mining, and fishing all prospered. In this climate of optimistic expansion, L.D. had no trouble finding work as a freight handler with his old employer, the CPR. He moved into a room in a boarding house on Hastings Street, began teaching Sunday school at the Congregational Church, and settled down to make a little money.

Across the street from L.D.'s lodgings on Hastings Street were the offices of the *Daily Province*. Like L.D., the *Province* was new in town. It had begun life in Victoria as a weekly, founded by Hewitt Bostock, a Cambridge graduate, a lawyer, who had migrated to the Canadian West in search of a fresh start. A couple of years later Bostock was joined in his venture by Walter Nichol, a thirty-one-year-old, Ontario-born journalist. Together

Making
a Civic
Politician

The view looking east down Hastings Street from Cambie, circa 1900. The offices of the Province *are on the right. L.D. may have lived in an apartment in the three-storey building with the window awnings on the left* VPL 5208

they decided to make the paper a daily and move it to Vancouver. The first issue of the *Daily Province* appeared on March 26, 1898.[25]

The *Province* intruded into a market already shared by two main rivals, the *World*, owned by J.C. McLagan, and the *News-Advertiser*, edited by a local Member of the Legislature, Francis Carter-Cotton. The newcomer held its own, but it was not long before Walter Nichol complained in the paper that inadequate distribution was causing him cash-flow problems. L.D., who had gained some experience with newspaper subscriptions during his sojourn in Colorado, responded immediately to Nichol's lament, proposing an overhaul of the newspaper's system of making its collections. Impressed, Nichol offered to turn over the entire circulation department to L.D. to run. Sometime in 1899, with a $100 loan from his friend Will Tretheway, later prominent in the Cobalt mining boom in northern Ontario, L.D. made a downpayment on the entire print run of the *Province*. In other words, he bought the papers wholesale, then resold them to the public. The new system worked so well that L.D. and Nichol signed a long-term contract; later the new circulation manager joined the executive of the Vancouver Printing and Publishing Company, which owned the paper.

Over the next few years, L.D. learned the newspaper business. The more copies sold, the more money he made, so he took an active interest in making the *Province* as widely read as possible. He had only to cross Hastings Street, listening for the clanging bell of an approaching streetcar and dodging the piles of steaming manure left by the carthorses, and climb the stairs to get to the newspaper offices. "I was always in the editorial rooms," he said, "watching the news and urging publication of an extra on every possible occasion."[26] Perhaps even then, as he hung over the shoulders of the editors or made a nuisance of himself in the composing room, he had some notion that one day he would own his own paper.

Meanwhile, at the end of 1901, the budding newspaperman launched his political career.

iv

Later, L.D. was offhand about his motivation for getting involved in local politics. "I happened to walk into the *Province* office one morning and the city editor, Lou Gordon, asked me if there was any news," he told Ronald Kenvyn in 1939. "Quite casually and really without thinking, I said I was going to run for license commissioner. That evening the *Province* carried the story, so I had to run."[27] Perhaps L.D. was kidding when he made these remarks. If not, he certainly was kidding himself. In fact, his political career did not begin nearly so impulsively. On the contrary, before coming to Canada he had run for alderman at least once in his hometown in Michigan. And after settling in the city, his political ambitions found expression in the struggle to create a party which would represent the interests of its growing working-class population.

The economic boom associated with the Klondike gold rush produced a labour shortage in Vancouver. Finding themselves in a good bargaining position, workers increased their demands for better wages and working conditions and shorter hours. A flurry of strike activity welcomed in the new century as workers flexed their muscles and employers fought back with lockouts, strikebreakers, armed soldiers, and even, in one case, the murder of a labour leader. In the mining districts of the Kootenay and Slocan Valleys, miners staged prolonged work stoppages to protest attempts by owners to lower wages. Closer to Vancouver, the salmon canneries at Steveston were in turmoil over the price canners were willing to pay for fish. At one point the owners called in the militia to threaten striking fishers. And in the city proper, the CPR was at war with its mechanics, clerks, and freight handlers, a war which the railway company eventually won, destroying several unions in the process. During one demonstration, special police hired by CP shot and killed union militant Frank Rogers. No one was ever held responsible.

In this climate of intense class conflict, working people sought to create their own political parties. The more radical found a home in the Socialist Labour Party, or its less doctrinaire rival, the United Socialist Labour Party. Least radical of the "workers' parties" was the Vancouver Labour Party, formed with the support of the local Trades and Labour Council at a public meeting at the end of July 1900. L.D. claimed to have played a key role in the formation of the VLP. Newspaper accounts do not mention him prominently, but he may have been influential behind the scenes. The VLP was an alliance of workers and middle-class reformers; its objectives have been described as "liberal, reformist, and evolutionary."[28] A newspaper executive like L.D. may well have supported the party's moderate platform, which included a call for an eight-hour work day, the abolition of the federal Senate, government ownership of public services, and an end to Asiatic immigration.

The VLP was created to fight the federal election of November 1900. In September, local Liberals invited the new party to nominate a joint candidate for the election. The labourites agreed, and a veteran reform politician, Reverend George Maxwell, won the nomination. Maxwell, already the sitting member for the Burrard riding, easily won re-election. Despite this early success, the VLP did not survive for long on the highly volatile political scene. The following February, its candidate in the provincial election was unsuccessful and, after running three candidates in the 1903 election, the party disappeared, outflanked on the left by more radical alternatives.

In the Vancouver of 1901, having strong labour sympathies did not disqualify someone from being a monarchist. Despite his American background, L.D. managed to get himself appointed to the decorations committee charged with preparing the city for the visit of the Duke and Duchess of Cornwall and York, later King George V and Queen Mary, who were touring the colonies as a show of gratitude for the support given during the war in South Africa. It was customary to erect arches across the city streets to welcome visiting dignitaries or celebrate public holidays. One of these structures that survived its contemporaries was the Lumberman's Arch, erected across Pender Street in 1912 by the Lumbermen's and Shinglemen's Society to honour the visit of Canada's governor general, the Duke of Connaught, and his wife. After the festivities, the lumbermen dismantled their massive tribute, a lumber arch supported by eight thick trunks, each a different species of conifer, and floated it to Stanley Park where they reassembled it near the seawall on the site of an ancient Aboriginal village and where it stood for the next thirty-four years. But L.D. and his committee were no slouches themselves when it came to civic decoration.

When the Duke and Duchess disembarked from the train at the CPR station on September 30, they passed beneath an ornate welcome arch shaped like a turretted castle. Both the Japanese and Chinese communities built arches in their neighbourhoods, and the city fire department arranged its own arcade of ladders, beneath which the royals passed as they made their way by open carriage down Cordova Street to the old courthouse at what is now Victory Square. Every available pole and balcony streamed with flags and bunting. After touring Hastings Mill and officiating at the opening of the Beatty Street Drill Hall, the Duke and Duchess drove around Stanley Park. Photographs were taken at the hollow tree, and at Brockton Point they paused to listen to a children's choir. Back in the city they accepted a present of a headdress of eagle feathers from a group of Tsimshian who had travelled all the way down the coast from Port Simpson, then boarded a steamship to cross to Victoria. Out in the harbour, 40,000 Chinese lanterns imported from Hong Kong illuminated the gathering dusk. At a signal, a switch was thrown and the entire downtown burst into light. "The buildings were silhouetted, the doors and windows encircled and arched, the streets festooned and the arches illuminated with lines of dazzling electric fire."[29] It was generally agreed that L.D. and his committee had done a magnificent job, and this taste of public acclaim may have contributed to his decision to run for election two months later.

However strong L.D.'s labour sympathies may have been, they were not much evident in his campaign for Vancouver license commissioner. It began modestly on November 30, 1901, when the *Province* announced that "a large number of people" had requested L.D. to run and "he did not announce his refusal." The item concluded with a half-hearted endorsement: "There is no doubt that he is fit to assume the office."

The two elected license commissioners joined a board consisting of themselves, two provincially-appointed commissioners, and the mayor. They were minor officials, but issues of gambling and liquor control were at the centre of the tumultuous campaign. Sudden economic growth had caused "respectable" elements to fear that Vancouver was being taken over by prostitutes, gamblers, and saloon keepers. No question, the city had an alcoholic underside. Its very origins went back to a saloon keeper, Gassy Jack Deighton, whose Globe Saloon was the focus around which Gastown, the forerunner of Vancouver, took shape in the 1860s. "There are some shady characters in a town like Vancouver," warned Martin Grainger in his classic 1908 novel, *Woodsmen of the West*, "and persons of the underworld."[30] The city's downtown was a magnet for single men looking for work, and loggers and miners with a few days off and money in their pockets. They came to the city thirsty for strong drink and hungry for sex and found both in the brothels along Dupont Street and the watering holes of Skid Row. A town of only 27,000 people, Vancouver had forty-seven hotels, twelve saloons, seven liquor stores, and several illegal "blind pigs" which sold liquor behind closed

Chinese vegetable vendors on Dupont Street (now East Pender), Vancouver's first red light district, circa 1900. VPL 6729

doors. In B.C. generally, liquor consumption was nearly double the national average.[31] Sunday closing laws were on the books, but only fitfully observed, and most establishments remained open twenty-four hours a day.

L.D.

Police and city officials tolerated an informal "red light" district along Dupont Street (now Pender Street between Abbott and Main). By day herders drove cattle through the street on their way to Pat Burns's slaughterhouse on the water at Woodland Drive, and chain gangs of inmates from the city jail swept up the filth and carried out road repairs. By night, it was not unusual to encounter mobs of men milling about on the sidewalk waiting their turn with the prostitutes. In 1896, during one of the outbreaks of moral fervour that periodically gripped the city, the authorities condemned and burned many of the brothels, resulting in the prostitutes spreading into adjacent neighbourhoods then slowly making their way back to Dupont Street. An 1899 investigation into the civic police force found that officers were accepting protection money from the brothel keepers, selling liquor that they confiscated from illegal night spots, sharing the proceeds from fines, and, for a fee, neglecting to register criminal convictions.[32]

By the time the 1902 election rolled around, another bout of reformist zeal had gripped the city. Reformers viewed the drinking establishments, not to mention the red light district, as cesspools of moral depravity which threatened to infect the wider community. Earlier in the year a measure that would have permitted licensed music halls to operate in the city was defeated by plebiscite. Mayor Thomas Townley, who had supported the measure, was up for re-election, and his enemies accused him of turning a blind eye to the moral deterioration of the city. Along with the music hall issue, they cited the police department's inability to control gambling and the mayor's association with "the people interested in gambling." "A tide of moral revulsion is rising in this city against the present conduct of civic affairs," the Reverend E.E. Scott declared, "that will some day pour a cleansing flood on the city hall."[33]

Opposition to Mayor Townley was not confined to members of the clergy. The incumbent's most influential critics belonged to the Vancouver Electoral Union, a group of concerned business leaders who called for the stringent application of laws against vice and after-hours drinking. The Union endorsed candidates who shared their

34

concerns, among them Thomas Neelands for mayor and, for license commissioner, Louis Taylor. It is ironic that at the beginning of a political career which later would be marked by repeated charges of corruption and immorality, in his first campaign L.D. was on the side of the moral reformers. Interestingly, his own newspaper, the *Province*, was not. According to its editor, the Union was a cabal of men "whose professions are shrewdly suspected to conceal intentions which they are unwilling to acknowledge."[34] The paper labelled the contest the "hat-trick election," claiming that the Union, unable to decide which of two candidates to run for mayor, had to pick Neelands's name out of a hat. And this from a group dead-set against gambling!

Candidates and their supporters contested the campaign bitterly. Neelands, a contractor and real estate promoter, charged that the incumbent was backed by gamblers and the liquor interests. The election, he said, "was between ring rule and rule by the people." For his part, Mayor Townley called his opponent a "political minion," a puppet of the Electoral Union, a "huckster." At the largest open meeting of the campaign, held at the Public Market building on Main Street, candidates spat venom at each other while the audience became so unruly that several speakers had to give up being heard. "It was," concluded one newspaper, "the most disorderly meeting ever held in Vancouver."[35]

While all this was going on, L.D. and the other candidates for license commissioner debated the same issues. On January 6, three days before the election, they met face to face at a turbulent all-candidates meeting convened by L.D. at the Market Building, which doubled as city hall. The incumbents tried to downplay the extent of gambling and liquor infractions in the city, but they got a rough ride from an audience which clearly believed something had to be done. One candidate, Sam Gothard, presented himself as a reformed gambler who was "out for the purpose of rebuilding his character." "A dirty lacrosse player made a good referee because he had an eye for crooked work, therefore he felt that having had experience in gambling, etc., he would make a good license commissioner." L.D. spoke last and received warm applause when he observed that the present board was turning a blind eye to widespread violations of the law. He told the crowd that if elected he would oppose the granting of liquor licenses to saloons where gambling was permitted and would do his best to restrict drinking on Sunday.[36]

On election day, L.D. finished second in the polling, 120 votes behind his running mate, E.B. Morgan, and comfortably ahead of the third-place finisher. The election was a smashing victory for the Electoral Union, and L.D. and Morgan joined Thomas Neelands and thirteen other Union candidates on the victory podium. "A Turn-Down for Vancouver's Tammany," crowed the *World* newspaper, celebrating the results; "A Clean Sweep for Neelands." Voters had turned their backs on corruption and firmly declared that "laws for the safeguarding of morality, once made, must be enforced."[37] The *World* hardly noticed the victory of a lowly license commissioner. How were its editors to know that the election of 1902 marked the beginning of the most durable political career in Vancouver's history? Long after the *World* had gone out of business, L.D. Taylor would still be campaigning, and winning. There would hardly be an election in Vancouver for the next thirty-eight years that did not include this slight, bespectacled candidate.

V

The streets of Vancouver in the early years of the century were far more social than they became with the advent of the automobile. Visits from royalty were only one excuse to indulge a love of public spectacle. Elections themselves always culminated in noisy processions by the winning candidates who made their way from newspaper offices to meeting halls and theatres to celebrate with their supporters. Public holidays featured parades involving hundreds of participants. Labour Day, the first Monday in September, became the largest of these, an occasion for the city's working class to blow its own horn. L.D. would have attended the 1899 parade; he lived right along the route. The column of bands and floats stretched two kilometres and featured a group of printers working at an actual press, bricklayers building a wall, and iron workers mending a boiler, all on the back of horse-drawn wagons. There was even a $10 prize for "most comical Indian float," won by a cigar business whose wagon was driven by a "cigarstore Indian" and pulled by a donkey dressed in a bathing suit.

But Vancouverites took to the streets to celebrate more than official holidays. For several days in August 1901, a huge Street Fair and Carnival occupied a row of downtown blocks. Entertainers included Arab

Looking east down Hastings Street from Granville, the heart of the financial district, during L.D.'s term as license commissioner. CVA, R.H. TRUEMAN, CVA-2-142

tumblers, Japanese acrobats, sword fighters, sharpshooters, Spanish dancers, a contortionist named Irene, slack wire walkers, a lion tamer, and a high diver who plunged twenty metres into a tank of shallow water. All this and more for an admission price of sixty cents. L.D. hadn't seen anything like it since the World's Fair back in Chicago.

As license commissioner, L.D. bore some responsibility for ensuring that city streets did not become too unruly. During his term in office he was an inconspicuous member of the commission. Then, suddenly, early in December 1902, just a few weeks before the next municipal election, he stunned his fellow commissioners by proposing that the city shut down virtually every saloon in town. The problem, as he saw it, was the proliferation of drinking establishments unaffiliated with hotels. There were so many of these places, L.D. argued, that they were forced into violations of the liquor laws in order to compete with their rivals. If they lost their licenses, the better class of saloonkeeper would expand into the hotel business, thereby improving the quality of the buildings in the downtown core and weeding out the less desirable operators. Hotel bars, he argued, were far superior to the rundown saloons which had become nothing better than low-life gambling dens. L.D. acknowledged that in fact the city did not have the power to close all the saloons, so he suggested that it cancel every license but one and say it was merely regulating the numbers, a power it did have.[38]

L.D. received no support for his drastic measure from the other members of the commission. Perhaps he never expected to. His critics charged that he was grandstanding. Why had he waited so long, they wondered, to make such a sweeping proposal? L.D. freely admitted that he had been waiting for the election. He wanted the issue to receive a thorough public airing and let the people decide at the polls. The result was that in an otherwise boring election campaign in early January – mayor Tom Neelands was re-elected unopposed, for example – it was the race for license commissioner that attracted most of the attention. Once again the reform-minded Electoral Union endorsed candidates in the election. Two days before Christmas, the *Province* reported that the Union had offered to support L.D. if he chose to run for one of the aldermanic seats, but that he turned them down, choosing to run for re-election to one of the two positions as license commissioner. According to L.D., the Union was trying to thwart his plans to shut the saloons by getting him off the licensing board. Certainly the Union did oppose him

38

in the election, running other candidates against him. L.D. made much of this during the campaign, which peaked with a large public meeting at city hall on January 6, two days before the election.

L.D. took to the stage with what the *News-Advertiser* described as "a large scroll which resembled a map. Unrolling this, he disclosed a large poster whereon was printed a number of reasons given by the Electoral Union against his candidacy." L.D. proceeded point by point through the list, heaping scorn and ridicule on the Union, which he accused of behind-the-scenes machinations. The crowd was in a constant uproar, but it was on his side, and any opponent who tried to cut L.D. off was silenced. When he finished speaking, L.D. called for written questions from the audience. The first question asked point blank whether he was a British subject, or still an American. L.D. responded with histrionic zeal. Striding to the edge of the platform, he leaned across the footlights and demanded, "Who is this coward, that asks this question?" When no one owned up to it, some of the other candidates shouted at L.D. to answer the question. "I've got it here," he announced theatrically and, according to the *Province*, "Mr Taylor's coat was flung open with a zip-p-p-p that must have started every button. He drew forth a paper, mellowed and browned with age, and with a flourish handed it to the Mayor, who declared it to be Mr Taylor's certificate of naturalization." It was dated 1900.

Whether or not the incident was stage-managed, the support it won for L.D. in the hall that night did not carry over to voting day. He was soundly defeated, running fourth in a field of eight candidates. The *Province* claimed that given the opposition to his candidacy from so many elements of the community, "it is almost surprising that he received as many votes as he did," but this must have been small comfort to L.D. In an editorial, the *Province* explained his defeat. "There were too many forces arrayed against him. The liquor interests opposed him, and worked hard for his rejection, on business grounds. The Electoral Union cast their influence against him because he refused to act simply as their mouthpiece on the board. In other quarters he found opposition because he refused to be pliant and temporizing at the dictates of men who desired to act as his political sponsors, but whose counsel he did not regard as in the interests of the community, and which he accordingly rejected."[39]

If this analysis is accurate, then whose interests did L.D. represent

The bar at the Balmoral Hotel on East Hastings Street, one of the drinking establishments regulated by L.D. and the other members of the license commission. CVA, CVA 677-166

at this stage of his career, beyond his own? The business community, even the reformers among it, preferred other candidates. Labour had endorsed several candidates against him. And at least some members of the public found his last-minute stand against the saloons to be opportunistic rather than principled. The editor of the *World* newspaper, for instance, called his proposal "unique and somewhat hysterical" and warned that the public "does not favour the dangerous combination of radicalism and irrationality."[40] Perhaps the *World* was closer to the minds of the voters than the *Province*? At any rate, L.D.'s political career seemed to be over.

He ran twice more, for alderman in 1904 and again in 1905. At the time Vancouver had a ward system and on both occasions L.D. finished third in Ward Six behind the two winning candidates. Interestingly, electors divided their votes between a prominent member of the business elite (yachtsman William Hodson in 1904 and shipping agent C. Gardiner Johnson in 1905) and an equally prominent activist on the Vancouver Trades and Labour Council, tailor Francis Williams. Without the endorsement of either the Electoral Union or the Citizens Association, which backed a slate of reform candidates that swept into office in 1905, and sandwiched between two ends of the civic political spectrum, L.D. could not find an identity for himself that appealed to voters. His connections to labour were not as strong as Williams's, while he had no connections at all to the city's prominent social and business circles. This failure must have played a part in his decision to retire from civic politics, at least temporarily. More important, however, was that in the spring of 1905, L.D. got involved in a new business venture that would occupy all his energies and provide him with the influence and prominence in his adopted community that he so strongly desired.

L.D. of the World

2

When L.D.'s contract with the *Province* came to an end in the spring of 1905, he decided to find another way of making a living. Given that he had been working in the newspaper business for six years, it was natural for him to consider branching out on his own. Beyond that, the world of journalism allowed him to indulge his desire to take a leading role in the city he now called home. Politics had given him a modest measure of success and notoriety; owning his own daily newspaper would be a leap forward in social status and public influence. In the early years of the century, newspaper proprietors were influential opinion leaders and important entrepreneurs. People like Joseph Pulitzer and William Randolph Hearst in the United States and, in Canada, John Ross Robertson of the *Toronto Telegram* and Joseph Atkinson of the *Toronto Star* were powerful figures in the community, molders of public opinion, courted by politicians. It would have been natural for someone with L.D.'s ambition to be inspired by their example and to think he could emulate them in Vancouver. For the time being, the voters had ended his political career, but L.D. was not cut out to be a bystander. He wanted to be a "player" in the public life of the city.

L.D. approached Sara McLagan, owner of the *World*, one of Vancouver's three daily newspapers.[1] She had co-founded the paper with her husband as the city's first evening daily. Sara grew up in Matsqui in the Fraser Valley where her father, John Maclure, trained her to take over operation of the local telegraph office from him when she was just thirteen years old. When Western Union closed the Matsqui station, Sara moved to Victoria where she became assistant manager of the company's main office and where, in 1884, she met and married John McLagan, a veteran journalist from Ontario who was operating the *Times* newspaper in the capital. Four years later the couple moved to Vancouver and, partially funded by the Liberal Party, started the *World*. When John McLagan died of tuberculosis, Sara carried on, with the help of her brother Fred who was the paper's business manager. In an age when most female journalists were not allowed out of the women's department, she was the first woman to own a daily newspaper in Canada.

L.D.

By the time L.D. approached her, Sara McLagan was ready for a change. Illness had forced her brother into retirement. She was only forty-nine years old, but she had spent more than twenty years in the newspaper business and was tired of it. Her asking price for the paper was $65,000. Of this amount, $35,000 was held as a mortgage by James Sutherland, a prominent Ontario Liberal. L.D. travelled east to meet with Sutherland who agreed to continue holding the mortgage with one proviso, that under its new management the *World* continue to support the Liberal government of Wilfrid Laurier. L.D. had no objection, and the deal was done.[2] (This mortgage had an intriguing history. According to L.D., Sutherland had sent the $35,000 west in 1888 to a group of Vancouver Liberal Party supporters who were supposed to turn it over to John McLagan to allow him to establish the *World*. But McLagan only received somewhere between $26,000 and $28,000; the rest disappeared, presumably into the coffers of the local party. In 1912, railway promoters William Mackenzie and Donald Mann were negotiating purchase of land in False Creek where they intended to place the terminus for their Canadian Northern Railway. The deal had to be put to the voters for their approval in a plebiscite. L.D. opposed this particular deal, and in the pages of the *World* he urged voters to do likewise, but a few days before the vote, L.D. later claimed, a representative of the railway tycoons revealed to him that Mackenzie and Mann now held the mortgage on the newspaper and would foreclose unless L.D. stopped his campaign. He did, and the agreement passed. A few weeks later a copy of the mortgage arrived in the mail, made over to L.D., who extinguished it. His silence had been purchased for the price of his own newspaper.[3])

The mortgage only took care of part of the asking price for the *World*. The rest, $30,000, still had to be raised in Vancouver. L.D.'s partner in the enterprise was Benny Dickens, who had been advertising manager

Philip Timms took this photograph of Vancouverites enjoying a leisurely afternoon at Second Beach in Stanley Park, circa 1905. VPL 5449

at the *Province* when L.D. joined the paper. L.D. later claimed that when he bought the *World* he had less than $600 to his name. Dickens did not have much more. Needing another partner with more money, L.D. signed an agreement with Victor Odlum whereby Odlum promised to put $12,500 toward purchase of the paper in return for a share of the stock in the company and a contract guaranteeing him an editorial job for five years.[4] Odlum was the son of Professor Edward Odlum, scientist, world traveller, and sometime city alderman, whose business interests laid the basis for the venerable stock-broking house Odlum Brown. The younger Odlum, twenty-five years old in 1905, was a veteran of the Boer War, and had been editor of the *World* during McLagan's tenure. But he failed to raise the promised money. As Dickens later recalled, "Victor Odlum was the alleged secretary of the company, but he was the biggest 'false alarm' I ever met; a very much over rated man."[5] Though Odlum went to work for L.D. at the paper, the relationship between the two men quickly soured. L.D. found his young employee lazy and unreliable and asked Odlum to leave. At first Odlum refused, noting that he had a contract, but eventually he accepted a buyout and quit the *World*.[6] Odlum moved to Nelson, where he edited the *Daily News*, and then to Winnipeg. He returned to Vancouver in 1911 as western manager for an insurance company. During World War I he was one of Canada's leading generals overseas. Following the war he returned to journalism as editor, later publisher, of the *Daily Star*, then embarked on a distinguished diplomatic career which included a stint as Canada's first ambassador to China (ironically enough, given that Odlum was a virulent anti-Asian campaigner in Vancouver during the 1920s).

All this was in the future in 1905. Without Odlum's money, L.D. had to find backing elsewhere, which he was able to do. He paid Sara McLagan $10,000 down with the rest spread over the next two years. According to L.D., some of this money came from the Victoria financier, A. C. Flumerfelt.[7] The rest came from the city's postmaster, Jonathan Miller. One of the reasons Miller loaned him the money was that L.D. agreed to give two of Miller's children jobs at the *World*: his widowed daughter Alice Berry became business manager and his son F.J. Miller became secretary-treasurer.[8]

On June 1, 1905 the first issue of the *World* under L.D.'s management appeared on the streets. (Dickens soon sold his share of the paper to pursue his plans for property development at the head of Indian Arm; he later opened Vancouver's first advertising agency.⁹) A lead editorial hailed "A New World," promising that "greater mechanical facilities," by which was meant a new printing press that L.D. had just purchased from New York, would make possible an improved paper. The *World* could stand some improving. When L.D. took over it was a twelve-page daily, smaller and less attractive than its main rivals, the *Province* and the *Daily News-Advertiser*. Its pages were crammed with seven columns of small, closely-packed type, broken by headlines and subheads in a variety of lengths and sizes. More than a dozen articles were stuffed onto a single page. Advertisements were displayed prominently on the front page as well as inside. In the first issue of the new era, the front page contained advertisements for North Vancouver property, cement, tea, and stoves. There were no photographs or illustrations of any kind. There was a sports section, though it was very small, perhaps a couple of columns, a page of classified ads, a reasonable scattering of financial and international news, but no separate social pages. Along with two or three editorials, the editorial page contained letters to the editor, and more advertisements. By comparison, the *Province*, L.D.'s main rival, had a much cleaner appearance. Its front page looked less cluttered, it printed photographs, and it was four pages thicker. It also had a well-defined women's section (which on June 1, 1905 had an article entitled "Pretty Arms and How to Get Them"). No wonder it enjoyed a sizeable lead in the competition for subscribers – 8,000 to only 3,000 for the *World* – and for advertisers.

A little more than a year later, the *World* had doubled in size to twenty-four pages and was printing cartoons and photographs on the front page, which displayed fewer articles and no advertising. There were four pages of classified ads, a women's page, an extract from a serialized work of fiction, even a comics page. In other words, the *World* had taken on the look of a modern, urban newspaper. In the early years of the twentieth century, Canadian newspapers were transforming themselves from partisan voices speaking for particular political parties into more broadly focussed vehicles of news and information. Aimed at the "people" (L.D. called the *World* "the people's paper"), the newspaper became more sensational, more democratic, more innovative, less biased. Along with the usual political news, it appealed to a broader public with arts and social news, cartoons, and human interest stories. "The new journalism of profit" replaced "the old journalism of political advocacy."[10] These were commercial businesses instead of, or as well as, party organs. As such, they needed to attract advertising dollars by increasing circulation, which L.D. was able to do. Within two years he could claim that as many people were reading the *World* on a daily basis as were reading the *Province*.

L.D.

To direct these improvements, L.D. installed David Higgins as editor of his new acquisition. Higgins, a transplanted Nova Scotian who had come west in the heady gold rush days of 1858, was one of the best known journalists in British Columbia. He had once owned the Victoria *Colonist*, using it to proselytize for Confederation and making it the most influential paper in the capital. He had then gone into politics, representing Esquimalt in the provincial legislature for twelve years, eight of which he served as House Speaker. Moving to Vancouver, he served from time to time as editor of the *World* during the McLagan era. Higgins was seventy-one years old when he came out of retirement to manage the *World*'s newsroom, and if L.D. was looking for an old newshound to make up for his own relative lack of journalistic experience, he could not have made a better choice.

The period from the 1880s to the 1930s has been called "the golden age of print journalism" in Canada.[11] In the first decade of the twentieth century, the country was experiencing an economic boom. Population was growing at an impressive rate, and much of the growth was in the cities. The expansion of newspapers kept pace. In 1900, nearly 650,000 Canadians subscribed to a daily paper. By 1911, that number had more than doubled to 1.3 million subscribers.[12] In the same period, technological developments transformed the way in which newspapers were produced. Innovations such as the rotary press, the linotype machine for typesetting, and techniques for reproducing photographs made possible the high-speed production of daily papers for a mass market. As sources of information, newspapers had the field to themselves. Radio had not yet come into its own; television was the stuff of science fiction. The literate public — and by this time virtually everyone was literate — looked to newspapers to find out what was going on in the world and what to think about it.

ii

At the same time as L.D. embarked on a new business initiative with the *World*, his personal life was approaching another crisis. When he fled Chicago in 1896, one step ahead of the law, L.D. had left behind his wife Annie and their infant son, Ted. The family did not reunite for five years, during which time Louis and Annie corresponded but apparently did not think it was safe for him to visit Chicago and did not have enough money for her to come to British Columbia. Then, in the spring of 1901, Annie and Ted arrived to live in Vancouver. Two years earlier L.D. had purchased a house on Eighth Avenue near Willow Street on the Fairview Heights overlooking False Creek to the south of the urban core. This neighbourhood, stretching between Granville and Cambie streets between 12th Avenue and False Creek, was developing as a middle-class residential suburb, not as upscale as the West End or, a few years later, Shaughnessy Heights, but posher than the crowded streets adjacent to the business district and the waterfront. The area was made accessible by the construction of the first Granville Street bridge across False Creek, which opened in January 1889, followed by the opening of the Cambie Street bridge and, in 1891, a new street railway line along Broadway between Granville and Main streets. Fairview was part of the land originally granted to the CPR, and a transportation link to downtown was important to the rail company's speculative plans for the neighbourhood. The CPR encouraged the construction of the street railway line by offering the Vancouver Electric Railway and Lighting Company sixty-eight lots on the Heights which the tram company could sell to recoup its costs.[13] (Construction of the Fairview line nonetheless placed the street railway company in an awkward financial position and contributed to its collapse and eventual takeover by the B.C. Electric Railway Company.)

When L.D. moved to Fairview in 1899, the streets were dirt, the surrounding lots were filled with stumps, and his was the only house on the block. A half dozen streams spilled down the slope into False Creek. Five years later, the *Vancouver City Directory* indicated ten houses in the 700 block of Eighth, and in 1907, the *Province* called Fairview "one of the better-class suburbs of the Terminal City." "The air is said to be the purest in the neighbourhood of Vancouver; the breezes from the Gulf of Georgia sweeping gently over the district give it the natural

L.D. of the World

49

advantages of a seaside health resort."[14] L.D.'s house commanded a panoramic view of the North Shore mountains and False Creek, which at that time extended as far east as Clark Drive and north to lap at the edges of Chinatown. (The Creek did not shrink to its present size until 1916–1918 when the Great Northern Railway received permission to fill in the eastern portion to use as a station and railyard.)

L.D.

Initially the relationship between L.D. and his wife seemed to pick up where it had left off in Chicago. In July 1901, Annie's younger sister, Winnifred Pierce, paid a visit and her letters home contain no suggestion that the couple were unhappy. Louis was working for the *Province* and according to Winnifred had become an outspoken booster of his new home. "Louis says he wouldn't live 'back east', as he calls Chicago, for any money," she wrote her parents. "Judging by his talk, this is the only country on the face of the earth, climate, scenery, size, etc. He has certainly done well."[15] Annie's own letters are full of domestic detail and convey no sign of marital trouble. A second son, Kenneth, was born about a year after her arrival.

It is impossible to know why the marriage broke down. The only insight into the relationship is provided by a few letters which have survived, some of which were written more than a decade after the couple separated. They show that unlike her husband, who not only adapted to Vancouver but aspired to become one of its leading citizens, Annie did not like the city at all. The mills on False Creek and in Burrard Inlet belched clouds of smoke which hung in the air and created an almost constant fog. Much of the city was being cleared for building; it presented a desolate, lunar landscape lacking in charm. Annie complained about the incessant rain, the inability to find competent domestic help, and the fact that Louis neglected her in favour of his business affairs and political ambitions. The correspondence reveals a woman who seems to have been seriously depressed, staying up most of the night, sleeping for much of the day. Possibly she was suffering from mood disturbances associated with Kenneth's birth. A story has been handed down in the family that Annie was addicted to opium.[16] She may have started using the drug on doctor's orders as treatment for her depression. If she was dependant on opium in Vancouver, it may have contributed to the breakdown of a marriage that was already strained by money problems, especially after L.D. took over the *World,* and what appears to be a basic sexual incompatibility.

50

In letters to his father-in-law, Louis admitted that the newspaper took up most of his time and created financial pressures. Annie, he said, wanted to move to a new home, which would have to be furnished, and he could not afford it. What's more, "she is up to her old tricks of going to bed at 2 or 3 a.m. and sleeping until noon. We really have no family life on this account."[17] Two weeks later he wrote again, this time complaining in coded language that he and his wife were not having sexual relations. "I hope the day will come when Annie will appreciate the fact that an active life is happier than an inactive one and that a wife should share some of the hard knocks and housekeeping, as well as the man in business. That to be affectionate is to win the husband, to show in some way that he has her love. I thoroughly believe in affection and have a nature that craves it. I tried for many years to educate Annie that way, but she can't help her nature and probably does not realize that the wife as well as the husband should show it."[18] Pierce responded to this outpouring as reasonably as he could, observing that he had not heard Annie's side of the matter and really did not want to hear Louis's. He clearly wished that he had not been taken into Louis's confidence, and sought refuge in a few homilies about how difficult married life can sometimes be.[19]

Matters between Annie and Louis came to a head in the spring of 1906. Annie's health was poor and her behaviour was erratic. Louis arranged to send his wife, along with the two boys, to Los Angeles to stay with her parents, who now lived there. Later Annie would say that she was not consulted about this move, that she was too weak to put up any objection. Whether or not either or both of them understood that they were separating, this was in fact the case. They never lived together again.

With his family gone, L.D. moved from the house on the Fairview Slopes downtown to an address on Alberni Street between Bute and Jervis on the fringes of the West End. Then, in 1909, he moved into the Granville Mansions apartment block at the corner of Granville and Robson. This building, which was demolished in the late 1960s to make way for the Eatons Centre development, remained his home for most of the rest of his life. It put him within a twenty-minute stroll of his newspaper office and right in the middle of the burgeoning business district along Granville Street. L.D. walked to work every day. From time to time he might have hopped aboard a streetcar and paid the

This view of Granville Street looking north from Smithe shows the Granville Mansions apartment block on the northwest corner at Robson Street where L.D. lived for many years. Beyond it on the west side of the street is the Vancouver Opera House and the second Vancouver Hotel. All these buildings are gone and the site is now occupied by the former Eatons Centre. VPL 6620

nickel fair, but he was a newspaper publisher and a sometime politician and both professions required that he work the sidewalks, exchanging gossip and shaking hands. Next door to his apartment building stood the Vancouver Opera House, built by the CPR in 1891 to give the little townsite some class. When L.D. set off in the morning, the Opera House was quiet, but when he returned in the early evening he had to jostle his way through the expectant crowd waiting for the doors to open. The 2,000-seat theatre attracted an impressive roster of world-class entertainers over the years that L.D. lived next door, including Sarah Bernhardt, the Marx Brothers, and Nijinsky and the Ballet Russe. As he approached the corner of Granville and Georgia, L.D. could have checked on the progress of the new Hotel Vancouver that the CPR was building on the site of the original. When it opened on the eve of World War I, the hotel set a new standard of elegance for the city with its cavernous lobby, glass-enclosed rooftop tea garden, thirty-metre-long bar, and oak-lined ballrooms. Composed of multiple wings of different heights, the 500-room hotel, the largest in the city, had the appearance of a monstrous wedding cake. L.D. might have crossed the street to examine the display windows in the Hudson's Bay Company store, then continued on his way down the slope of Granville Street, past the grey stone bulk of the Bank of Montreal, looking very much like a Scottish castle, and past the many shops that made the street the busiest shopping district in the city. It is possible he was on the scene that October day in 1909 when the city's first motorized ambulance, out for a test drive, ran over and killed an American tourist outside Fader's grocery. If he had political business to conduct, L.D. dropped into Liberal Party headquarters in the MacKinnon Building, stopping on his way out to buy cigars at the United Cigar Store at the corner. Up ahead, at the foot of Granville, loomed the CPR station, not the modest wooden shack where he had arrived in 1896, but the red-brick baronial chateau that had replaced it. Checking his pocket watch against the street clock outside Trorey's jewellry store (known to later generations as the Birks clock), he might have swung eastward down Hastings to make his way through the banking district past Spencer's Department Store to his offices on Homer Street.

When L.D. moved into the Granville Mansions, Alice Berry, his business manager at the *World*, was also living there, in apartment 114. At some point the pair became more than business partners. Three years later, according to the *Vancouver City Directory*, in 1912, they were sharing

The CPR's second Hotel Vancouver, at the corner of Granville and Georgia. It was the city's most luxurious hotel in the inter-war period. L.D.'s apartment block is visible down Granville Street past the Opera House. CVA 677-21

an apartment. Alice Berry was a thiry-four-year-old widow when she came to work at the *World* as part of the deal that financed L.D.'s purchase. She had grown up in Gastown in a small cottage with a two-room jailhouse in the backyard that came with her father's job as police constable, and she attended the school for children of the employees at the Hastings Mill. When she was eighteen, Alice married Harry Berry, a twenty-seven-year-old widower with an infant daughter. Berry had worked on the construction of the Canadian Pacific Railway, then settled in Vancouver where he went into business. When Harry died in 1899, Alice was only twenty-nine years old, with three young sons to care for. For four years she taught piano to make ends meet, then became an office manager for an insurance company. At least one source gives her credit for organizing the deal that made L.D. the owner of the *World*.[20] Louis and Alice did not get married until 1916, about four years after they began living together, because Louis was still married to his first wife, Annie, who was living in California. When Louis eventually did divorce Annie, he and Alice were wed.

iii

Working together, Louis and Alice managed to improve the *World* until they could realistically claim that it was the equal of the *Province* in advertising revenue and circulation. (The third paper, the *News-Advertiser*, ran a distant third in the rivalry.) One of the editorial improvements was an increase in the amount of national and international news. In his later years, L.D. recalled how he was responsible for the creation of the Canadian Press, the co-operative news service that provides dispatches to its member papers. Like many of his stories, the way he told it isn't exactly accurate. During the early years of the century, Canadian newspapers received their foreign and national news over telegraph lines owned by large railway companies: the Grand Trunk Railway and, in western Canada in particular, Canadian Pacific. The telegraph companies collected the news, summarized it, and sold it to subscribing papers at a low cost. Canadian Pacific also owned the rights to the Associated Press service out of New York, by which it provided American and overseas news to its customers. In the summer of 1907, Canadian

Pacific announced that it was raising the price of its news service. The owners of Winnipeg's three daily papers, outraged at what they believed to be an act of usury, promptly organized their own news service, the Western Associated Press (WAP), using alternative sources both in Canada and the United States. This "revolt" against Canadian Pacific spread to other papers in western Canada – papers in eastern cities were less concerned because their rates were lower – and marked the beginning of co-operative news gathering in the country.[21]

L.D.

In his version of these events, L.D. and the the *World* played a leading role. According to him, he grew angry at Canadian Pacific's inefficient service and installed a wire with direct service from United Press in New York. Other papers followed suit, said L.D., and this caused Canadian Pacific to lose business and eventually abandon the news-gathering side of the business.[22] But an arrangement with UP, an American service, would not have provided L.D. with a reliable source of Canadian news. For that, he had to work out an agreement with WAP, and in these negotiations he actually played a small part. M.E. Nichols, general manager of WAP, reported that "Walter Nichol, with his *Daily Province*, was the supreme newspaper power on the coast."[23] Nichols came out to the West Coast to sign up the Vancouver dailies in 1912 and it was obvious that the *Province*, not the *World*, was his main target. "As a money-maker, it was one of three or four in all Canada that could show net earnings in six figures," he said. On the other hand, Nichols's account of his visit to the offices of the *World* has a Dickensian flavour. "A guide led me through dark passages; doors opened and closed behind us to reveal a storage room or a clerk at work in narrow quarters. This elongated labyrinth ended in a poorly-lighted office. At a desk sat an unassuming little man in his forties [actually he was fifty-five], a bright red tie relieving quiet apparel. It was L.D. Taylor, publisher of the Vancouver *World*. . . . His worried face told the story of a harrassed business life. Unlike the *Province* . . . the offices, furnishings and atmosphere of the *World* truly pictured a hungry treasury."[24] The Vancouver papers did sign on with WAP, giving them access to Eastern Canadian news, and eventually the co-operative idea evolved into Canadian Press, but L.D. played a minor role.

Nichols's account of his visit to Vancouver appeared in his memoirs, published a couple of years after L.D. died. Which was just as well, because L.D. would have been humiliated to read about himself playing second fiddle to his arch-rival, Walter Nichol. Nichol became owner of the *Province* in 1901, using money loaned to him by the CPR, and proceeded to make it the city's most successful daily and himself one of the city's wealthiest business men.[25] While L.D. struggled, ultimately unsuccessfully, to keep his paper afloat, Nichol was building one of Shaughnessy's most palatial mansions. While L.D. saw himself as a thorn in the side of the monied interests – even called himself a socialist – Nichol supported the Conservative Party, an allegiance that paid off in 1920 when he was appointed lieutenant governor of the province. But the differences were as much personal as political. Their rivalry was intense and fuelled by personal animosity that may have originated with L.D.'s decision to buy the *World*, but certainly deepened when he began running for mayor and the *Province* opposed him time after time. Veteran journalist D.A. McGregor, who worked for Nichol for several years, described his employer as being like "the small boy with a pea-shooter. Usually he hit lightly, but he hit repeatedly with a puckish persistence not untouched with malice. He flicked until he created a wound, then kept on flicking until his victim writhed and fumed."[26] On many occasions, L.D. felt the sting of Nichol's malice.

In the spring of 1905, as word started circulating that L.D. was going to purchase a paper, the *Province* published an editorial purporting to wish him well, but in fact predicting the worst. The editorial, probably written by Nichol, first belittled L.D.'s contribution during his years with the *Province*. "He was connected with this newspaper in a clerical capacity and did his work faithfully," said the editorial, but he did not make any serious contribution to its success. As for the *World*, it was a doubtful business proposition whose new owner was too inexperienced and too underfunded to make a success.[27] The editorial was mean-spirited and condescending; it rankled with L.D., who considered himself to be one of the architects of the *Province*'s recent success. As the *World* improved its appearance and expanded its circulation, it irritated him that the *Province* did not abandon its claim, printed daily on its editorial page, that its circulation, about 13,000 copies, more than doubled that of any other evening newspaper in the city. Finally, in the spring of 1907, L.D. took the unusual step of launching a libel suit in an attempt to force the *Province* to stop making this claim. He argued that he was suing because the circulation of the *World* was equal to that of its rival paper (which he delighted in calling "the junior evening paper of this city," a reference to the fact that the *World* was ten years older than the *Province*). It was a slim thread on which to hang a libel case, and in July a judge dismissed the charge, ruling that while the *Province* had indeed inflated its circulation figures, there was no proof that the *World* had suffered any damage. L.D. chose to interpret the decision as a vindication. "*World* Wins Out On The Facts," blared a front-page banner headline over a story emphasizing the inaccuracy of the *Province's* numbers. Not surprisingly, Nichol had a different interpretation. The *Province's* much smaller headline read "*World's* Action For Libel Is Dismissed," and most of its news story was spent discrediting the *World's* claim to have equal readership.[28] The whole dispute accomplished very little. It was best summed up by John McConnell, editor of the weekly *Saturday Sunset*. "There is nothing in the publishing business so futile in results and so uninteresting to the readers as a circulation dispute between rival newspapers," McConnell wrote, "and I doubt if either of the evening papers will derive any benefit from their litigation."[29] However, the dispute did indicate just how intense the competition between the two papers had become.

L.D. told another story that reveals his obsessive preoccupation with his rival. The *World* had access to stories carried by a foreign wire service that the *Province* did not and at one point L.D. became suspicious that the other paper, which came out later in the day, was reprinting foreign news that it scalped at no cost from the *World*. He concocted a story about a tidal wave overwhelming an island in the South Pacific and ran it on the front page of a few copies of the *World* which he had hand-delivered to the *Province* newsroom. Sure enough, that afternoon's *Province* carried a front-page feature about the tragic fate of the inhabitants of the fictitious island of Taut-u.[30]

Pranks like this one seem harmless enough, but there was real animosity in the rivalry. In 1913, when the *World* was having financial problems and the *Province* was gleefully reporting on them, L.D. published a full-page diatribe one day under the banner headline, "The Smallness of Walter C. Nichol." L.D. was incensed that the *Province* had published details of his financial woes on its front page. He admitted the facts of the story. What he objected to was their appearance on page one. It was all part of what L.D. claimed was a "campaign of vilification and misrepresentation" which Nichol had been waging against him for eight years. According to L.D., Nichol was "writhing with impotent jealousy" because the *World* was replacing the *Province* as the city's pre-eminent newspaper. Here he was, a "mere clerk" in the eyes of his adversary, having made a success of the *World*. How it must be "gall and wormwood" to Nichol to have to witness his success. "Nature cast him in a small mould," L.D. continued, "made him the stinging insect he is. Incapable of fair recognition of another's success, instead of prosecuting a healthy and generous rivalry with an opponent, he secretes his venom, day by day, and when circumstances permit, discharges it with loud buzzing noises."[31] This bitter attack elicited no response from the *Province* or its publisher, at least no public one. It does illustrate how sensitive L.D. remained to the condescension of the city's corporate elite, to which Nichol belonged and L.D. did not. Despite his years in public life, the "little guy from Chicago" had not grown a skin thick enough to endure the smug sense of superiority displayed by his rival.

iv

During the decade that L.D. published the *World*, he ran for mayor six times, three times successfully. As well, in March 1912, he failed in an attempt to win a seat in the provincial legislature. Which raises the question: Did he buy a newspaper in order to advance his own political ambitions? At the time L.D. owned the *World*, there was an established tradition in British Columbia of journalists turning politician. Amor de Cosmos, who was the second premier of the province and a federal Member of Parliament, established the *British Colonist* when he arrived in Victoria in 1858 and used it to attack Governor James Douglas and the colony's elite. Another premier, John Robson, got his start as editor of the *British Columbian* in New Westminster. William Templeman, who owned the Victoria *Daily Times*, became a minister in one of Wilfrid Laurier's cabinets and later a senator. Another of L.D.'s contemporaries, Francis Carter-Cotton of the *News-Advertiser*, was a prominent provincial cabinet minister. And Walter Nichol, L.D.'s arch foe, was an active Conservative. The newspapers these men published were associated in the public mind with a particular party or political faction. Objectivity in the press was not considered as desirable as it was later in the century. Readers understood that a newspaper had a point of view; for its proprietor, that was the point of owning one. When Sara McLagan owned the *World*, she used it to proselytize for women's suffrage and a variety of social reforms. It was known as a Liberal organ, and was partly financed by the party. Under L.D., the paper continued to support the Liberal Party, at least nationally, but over time he staked out a more independent position, reducing his association with the party. Finally, in 1912, after local Liberals had done poorly in the previous year's federal election, the party financed the creation of the *Morning Sun* to take over from the *World* as the official Liberal organ in the city. Not long after, the *World* started billing itself on its masthead as the "only independent newspaper in British Columbia."

If the *World* became less predictably partisan in an attempt to gain more readers, it was far from neutral in political matters. A publisher who was as politically active as L.D. could hardly be expected not to use his paper to promote his own candidacies and causes. As well, the *World* was a useful weapon for countering criticism levelled at L.D. by his political enemies, especially the *Province*.

One matter which preoccupied L.D. the publisher and the politician was race. Race had been a contentious issue in Vancouver from the city's creation. With the completion of the construction of the Canadian Pacific Railway in 1885, thousands of Chinese who had been imported to work on the mountain section of the line lost their jobs. Many of these single men drifted into Vancouver looking for work in the sawmills, stores, restaurants, and laundries and as domestic servants in the homes of the well-to-do. Anti-Chinese sentiment ran high. In July 1885, the federal government introduced its infamous "head tax," a $50 charge (later raised to $500) imposed on every Chinese immigrant entering Canada. The tax, along with other restrictions, did not go far enough for some Vancouverites, who decided to take matters into their own hands. Boycotts of businesses that gave jobs to the Chinese were organized and black xs began appearing on the sidewalk in front of them. In February 1887, a mob of 300 men attacked a camp of Chinese workers who were clearing land in the West End, beat some of them up, burned their belongings, and drove them out of town. It was "the first act of concerted physical violence against the Chinese in Canada,"[32] but certainly not the last. And Chinese were not the only targets. Japanese immigrants were denied the vote. They could not hold public office, take jobs in many professions, or own certain types of property. Similar restrictions applied to immigrants from India when they began arriving in significant numbers in the first decade of the twentieth century.[33]

60

When L.D. took over the *World* in 1905, Vancouver was experiencing a population boom, part of this boom being a sudden surge in the number of Japanese and East Indian immigrants. Despite the fact that non-Whites made up only a small fraction of the population, the Euro-American majority was sensitive to any hint that its racial hegemony might be challenged. At the end of August 1906, a large group of East Indians arrived by ship. The *World* greeted them with alarmist headlines: "Horde of Hungry Hindoos Invades Vancouver City, Starving Coolies Roam in Streets."[34] Reports claimed that the newcomers were begging for food, camping in Stanley Park, and "threatening and scaring women and children." On September 6, the paper reported that the medical health officer warned that they were a menace to the public health because of overcrowded and unsanitary housing conditions. The saga of the "Hindoos" continued to preoccupy the city for several more days until the newcomers were absorbed into the community and the number of new arrivals declined.

The "scare" of 1906 was just a prelude to the racial disturbances of 1907, the worst in the city's history. And L.D. and the *World* played a central role. This time it was an upsurge in the number of Japanese immigrants that set off alarm bells in white neighbourhoods. During the first six months of the year, more than 3,000 Japanese arrived in port, followed by 2,300 more in July alone. "Let the Jap have full fling in this country and in a few years he will soon change the complexion of the province from white to brown," wrote the editor of the weekly magazine, *Saturday Sunset*.[35] Local Liberal Member of Parliament R.G. Macpherson warned: "I can see without any difficulty the Province of British Columbia slipping into the hands of Asiatics and this part of Western Canada no longer a part and parcel of the Dominion."[36] In fact, despite the apparent increase in the number of "Asiatics," the percentage of the city's population that originated in Asia actually fell during the decade to about six percent by 1911. But the reality appeared to be something different to the vocal majority, including L.D.'s *World*. On July 20, the paper published a front-page story reporting that a pair of Japanese employment agencies were planning to import large numbers of labourers to work on railway construction. "Fears are entertained," warned the report, "that if they are not checked in time in this province this will not be a white man's country long."[37] The *World* gave prominence to Macpherson's campaign to have the federal government ban further immigration from Asia. "I regard the influx of Japanese as a menace to this country," he declared in another page-one story. "This thing has got to be stopped."[38] The *World* adopted Macpherson's cause as its own, urging the federal government in a July 25 editorial to "build up white British Columbia" by stopping "the Japanese invasion."

The labour movement, fearful that low-cost immigrants would drive down wages and take all the jobs from white workers, spearheaded anti-Asian agitation in the city. The Vancouver Trades and Labour Council helped to organize an Asiatic Exclusion League (AEL), which held its first meeting on August 12. Rhetoric at this meeting reached a fever pitch, with former Vancouver mayor James Garden imagining a future world war between whites and "all other colours" and warning that British Columbia had to prepare for the conflict by keeping people who were not white out. The League endorsed the by-now-familiar call for a ban on Asian immigration to Canada and laid plans for a huge outdoor rally to focus public indignation against the Japanese. On the evening of September 7, a long parade wound through the city's downtown toward city hall in the red-brick Market Building on Main Street just south of the Carnegie Library. Marchers waved small flags that said "A White Canada For Us" and held banners asking people to "Stand for a White Canada." A brass band played British patriotic songs. By the time this procession reached city hall, it numbered at least 10,000. After burning an effigy of Lieutenant Governor James Dunsmuir, who was unpopular because he had refused to sign provincial anti-immigration legislation, the crowd listened to a series of speeches from local politicians, clergy, and anti-Asian activists from the United States. At about nine p.m. a large mob of people left the meeting and marched around the corner into Chinatown where they began breaking store windows and smashing property. The mob moved on to Japantown on Powell Street where residents armed themselves with clubs and bottles and fought back. By the time police and fire fighters arrived to restore order, several thousand dollars' worth of damage had been done to Japanese and Chinese-owned businesses. No one was seriously injured, and of the two dozen rioters who were arrested, five were eventually found guilty and sent to jail for short terms.[39] The situation in the city remained tense for several days until things gradually returned to normal.

The *World* condemned the riot as "the mad frolic of a drunken mob" and played down its seriousness. The news columns of the paper turned the situation on its head by emphasizing the possibility of a violent reaction from Asian residents of the city. A page one report three days after the riot said that police had arrested Japanese and Chinese men armed with "long guns, knives and revolvers." Readers might logically suppose that it was "the Asiatics" who were the cause of all the trouble and the whites who were cowering in their houses.[40] In an editorial the next day the paper argued that far from a disgrace, the city deserved credit for its coolness in a time of crisis. No one had been hurt in the riot and only a few thousand dollars worth of glass had been broken. The violence was regrettable, but not serious enough to warrant some of the apologetic breast-beating that had been going on. If people were honest, the editorial went on, they would admit that the riot had succeeded in bringing attention to the matter of Asian immigration as no amount of speechifying had been able to do. If authorities in Ottawa and London had paid attention to "Vancouver's grievance" earlier, there would have been no riot. It was Ottawa's fault, not Vancouver's, that matters had been left to fester for so long. The editorial argued that the riot was a local manifestation of an international challenge: "the continued predominance of the white man in the face of the economic competition of the Asiatic."[41]

L.D. took an active role in the AEL. He was one of the featured speakers at the League's October 7 meeting, where he shared the platform at the Labour Hall on Homer Street with prominent Conservative George Cowan, prominent Liberal W.W.B. McInnes, and Reverend H.W. Fraser. "I echo the words and thoughts that have been given to you through the columns of the *World*," he told the crowd; "I am with you in this matter and will see you through the fight to the end." Then he announced that his newspaper was prepared to abandon its long-standing support for the Laurier Liberals unless the federal government took immediate steps "to stop the invasion" of Asians. "We want to preserve British Columbia for the white people," he said. L.D. closed his remarks with the familiar complaints that eastern Canadians did not understand the situation west of the Rockies, and that large corporations, by which he particularly meant the Canadian Pacific Railway, were putting their own profits ahead of the public interest by encouraging immigration.[42] The following March L.D. ran, unsuccessfully, for the presidency of the League at its general meeting.[43] On the issue of Asian immigration he shared the racist assumptions of most members of the white community, but in keeping with his left-leaning sympathies L.D. cast his opposition in economic terms, blaming employers for keeping wages low and jobs scarce by importing cheap, foreign labour.

It soon became evident that the Asiatic Exclusion League was a spent force. The federal government, responding at last to the pleas of white British Columbians, convinced the government of Japan to set its own limits on the number of emigrants to Canada, and in January 1908 passed legislation that required all immigrants to take a continuous passage to Canada from their country of birth or citizenship, thereby putting a stop to the numbers of Japanese who had been arriving via Hawaii. These measures, strongly endorsed by the *World*, took most of the steam out of the anti-Asian agitation. In 1909, only 495 Japanese arrived in Canada, along with 2,106 Chinese, and the League faded into obscurity. The following year, when Prime Minister Laurier visited the city to officiate at the opening of the first Vancouver Exhibition (later the Pacific National Exhibition), he attempted to placate local anti-Asian feeling, but refused to commit his government to a total ban on immigration. By this time L.D. and his newspaper were back onside with the Liberal Party and had only good things to say about the prime minister.

The next upsurge of anti-Asian sentiment in the city occurred in the spring of 1914. On May 23, a tramp steamer named the *Komagata Maru* arrived in Vancouver harbour carrying 376 passengers, mainly Sikhs from the Punjab who wanted to land in Canada. The voyage had originated in Hong Kong, so its passengers were in violation of the continuous passage regulations.[44] Government officials refused to allow anyone to disembark. An armed launch kept a twenty-four-hour watch on the anchored vessel while the immigration department went through the motions of deciding whether to admit the newcomers. After a month of stalling, officials convened a board of inquiry and ruled that the passengers could not land. This decision was endorsed by the provincial court of appeal in early July, but still the ship remained at anchor; the passengers would not allow the captain to depart. On July 19, in the middle of the night, a heavily-armed force of police and immigration officers made its way out to the *Komagata Maru* aboard the tug *Sea Lion*, planning to seize control of the ship and force it to put to sea. But the passengers were expecting them and began raining down lumps of coal, bricks, and pieces of scrap iron onto the deck of the much smaller tug. After almost capsizing, the boarding party was forced to retreat back to shore with the jeers of the passengers ringing in their ears. Finally the federal government called in the navy. The *HMCS Rainbow* steamed over from Esquimalt, and on the morning of July 21, thousands of Vancouverites gathered at the waterfront to watch the confrontation. But there was nothing to see. After a day of negotiations, and another day to load the ship with supplies, the *Komagata Maru* hauled anchor and left the harbour, escorted by the *Sea Lion* and the *Rainbow*. When the vessel arrived back in India, British officials attempted to hustle the passengers onto a waiting train. A riot broke out and soldiers fired on the crowd of passengers, killing eighteen. Many others were arrested and jailed. In Vancouver, the incident led to a series of shootings aimed at alleged police informants in the Sikh community, culminating in the murder of an immigration official and the trial and execution of local Sikh activist Mewa Singh, who is still honoured as a martyr by the city's Sikhs.

Through all these dramatic events, the *World* joined the chorus of voices demanding that the "Hindoos" be sent back where they came from. For L.D., who signed his own front-page editorials, it was a matter of national independence. "Canadian immigration is a subject on which Canada has the first word and the last." British Imperial policy should have no influence. East Indians were incapable of adapting to life in "the West." "East Indians cannot be made organic entities in western life," he wrote. "Those that have been admitted to British Columbia are so many artificial limbs on the body politic. The whole history, nature and spirit of the East forbids even so much as an attempt to adapt themselves to western conditions."[45] Once again it was argued by L.D. and others that the poor passengers on the *Komagata Maru* were just the thin edge of the wedge. If they were admitted, the door would open to millions of their compatriots and British Columbia would end up "degenerating into a miniature India."[46] Whereas in 1907, L.D. had emphasized the negative impact of Asian immigration on the local job market, by 1914 he seemed more preoccupied with what he argued was the inability of East Indians to assimilate. (L.D. remained antagonistic to the city's Asian population for the rest of his life. In 1937 he launched a shortlived newspaper, the *New Deal*, in which he campaigned against "the ruthlessly unfair competition" of Chinese vegetable vendors. "It will be the avowed object of this paper to protect the white store keeper," he declared in his first very issue.[47])

L.D.

L.D. never revealed why he chose the 1909 mayoralty election to restart his political career. There were already four candidates in the field in early December 1908, when he flung his hat into the ring, and all of them had more experience than he did. Charles Douglas, a wealthy, American-born realtor, had come to Vancouver from Manitoba where he had served a term as a member of the legislature. D.M. Stewart and Walter Hepburn were serving as aldermen, while Professor Edward Odlum had been on council earlier in the decade. L.D. may have believed that his chances were enhanced by the possibility that so many candidates might split the vote to his advantage. He must also have felt that his newspaper was well enough established to allow him the time for extracurricular activities. When he announced his candidacy, he stated simply that he had decided to run at the urging of "a number of progressive businessmen."[48]

As the race began, Douglas was the acknowledged frontrunner. "Mr Douglas' moderation of tone, together with his well known energy and business ability, should make him easily a favourite with the citizen who is desirous of good and sensible civic administration," declared the *Province*.[49] There was little to choose between the programs of L.D. and his leading opponent; any differences were more of emphasis than substance. Both men wanted a bridge across the Second Narrows and a drydock for the port; both wished to see improvements to False Creek; both wished to extend the boundaries of the city to absorb the Hastings Townsite and South Vancouver. But while Douglas placed issues of economic development at the top of his platform, L.D. campaigned most vigorously against waste and disorganization at city hall and in favour of the eight-hour day for civic employees. The latter was not a contentious issue, much as L.D. made himself its champion. In fact, the matter was on the ballot as a plebiscite and was endorsed overwhelmingly by the voters. L.D. characterized Douglas as a "society mayor," well-mannered and well-connected, someone who would not rock the boat. "If you merely want a society mayor, don't elect me," he told electors, presenting himself instead as an activist, a broom that would sweep city hall clean. Still, L.D. did not come across as a fire-breathing radical. As the campaign progressed, the issue on which he laid most emphasis was "the reorganization of the city hall on business principles," a platform

Until 1929, city hall was located upstairs in the Market Building, seen here circa 1910 to the left of the Carnegie Library at the corner of Hastings and Main streets. CVA, PHILIP TIMMS, CVA 677-655

promise with which his opponents could hardly disagree since he was careful never to define exactly what he meant.[50]

Civic elections in Vancouver took place under a ward system. In 1909, the city was divided into six districts. Aldermen were chosen to represent a particular ward, while the mayoralty was decided city-wide. Roughly speaking, Ward One included the West End between Stanley Park and Howe Street; Ward Two comprised the eastern business district between Howe and Abbott streets, False Creek, and Burrard Inlet; Ward Three was a narrow strip between Hastings Street and the harbourfront from Abbott to the eastern boundary of the city; Ward Four, with the most voters, encompassed Chinatown and the eastern part of the city between Hastings and Sixth Avenue; Ward Five was in the southeast, and Ward Six in the southwest, bearing in mind that Point Grey, the Hastings Townsite, and South Vancouver were at the time separate municipalities. To qualify for the franchise, an individual had to own a certain amount of property and be resident in the city for at least six months. Single women who owned property had the vote, but not married women and not aboriginals, Chinese-, Japanese-, or Indo-Canadians. In the 1909 election there were 16,825 eligible voters, of which only thirty-one percent cast their ballots, meaning that in a city of close to 100,000 people, only about 5,300 chose the government.

As expected, L.D. lost the election to Douglas. Nevertheless, he had reason to feel pleased with the result. It was his first attempt to win the mayoralty and in a crowded field he finished a respectable second. Though he was trounced by Douglas in the two downtown westside wards by about three votes to one, he captured two of the other four wards (Four and Six) and won more votes overall than the other three losing candidates combined. He had campaigned aggressively and, judging by the newspaper coverage, had managed to put his opponents on the defensive. There was every reason to think that if he ran again he would do better.

Before 1927, mayors served one-year terms, so eleven months later L.D. was back on the hustings. The difference this time was that it was a head-to-head contest with Douglas; there were no other candidates. Campaigns were pressed into a short, two-week period between close of nominations and election night. L.D. set a furious pace, addressing at least one meeting every night, often bustling between three or four. One night it was the basement of All Saint's Church on Victoria Drive, the

L.D.

68

next the Oddfellows' Hall in Mount Pleasant, then a drafty auditorium in Fairview. The campaign climaxed with a noisy assembly at city hall on the eve of the vote. L.D. always opened his meetings to any candidate who wished to attend, relishing the opportunity to tackle his opponents face to face. Douglas had not managed to accomplish a great deal during his term – making his appeal to voters, he promised little more than a continuation of "the safe and conservative manner in which civic business has been conducted" – and once the campaign got underway L.D. was able to focus debate on his issues. These were, first of all, the failure of the Douglas administration to introduce the eight-hour day for civic employees, in spite of the fact that the proposal had been approved by plebiscite the previous year. Douglas claimed that voters had not understood that the issue was eight hours of work for nine hours of pay, which would cost the city an extra $100,000 per year, so he had favoured putting the matter to another plebiscite. L.D. ridiculed what he called "a passion for plebiscites." Voters had already approved the eight-hour day and council members, including Douglas, had shown their contempt for "the declared will of the people" by ducking the issue. "Even if this eight hour day is carried again," L.D. asked from the platform, "how do you know that the same influences in the council will not be at work to undermine it?" Linked to the eight-hour question was the city's practice of contracting out construction work instead of hiring its own "day labour." Again, Douglas argued that his policy saved thousands of dollars. For L.D., it was an excuse to pay lower wages. "What did it matter if the work cost a little more," he challenged, "as long as the money was spent in the city? Didn't it all go to make for the welfare of the community at large?"[51]

The second major issue in the election was the future of False Creek, a large tidal basin approximately five times the size it has since become. The Squamish people, based at their village of Snauq at the entrance to the basin on the east side of Kitsilano Point, had hunted and fished along its marshy shores. At high tide the waters of the Creek almost reached across the narrow neck of land at the east end of the downtown peninsula to join with Burrard Inlet. Small boats could be paddled across, though for larger vessels it was a dead end, hence its name. When the Canadian Pacific Railway arrived in 1886, the civic government offered the company thirty tax-free years on its property on the north side of the Creek in return for locating its yards and roundhouse there. W.C.

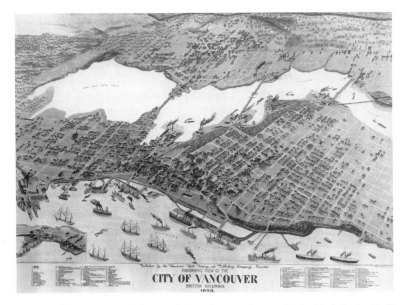

This view of the city in 1898, looking south, shows the original extent of False Creek. During World War I the eastern section of the creek was filled in to about Main Street, the easternmost of the bridges shown on the map. The other bridges, left to right, are the Cambie and Granville bridges, and the Kitsilano Trestle. CVA, MAP.P.38, N.68

Van Horne, the CPR's general manager, hoped that eventually the Creek would be filled in.[52] Instead it developed as an industrial neighbourhood. Sawmills, machine shops, brickyards, wood-product factories, shipyards, a gas works, wharves, and booming grounds all proliferated around its shores. East of the Main Street bridge, the inner creek consisted mainly of mudflats that were too shallow even at high tide to allow navigation and consequently did not attract significant industry. This section of the Creek posed a challenge for the city. In 1902, council convinced the provincial government to turn over all the eastern creek bed. Then, in 1905, engineers drew up plans to dredge the bottom to create a navigable lagoon surrounded by docks.[53] This ambitious scheme was abandoned when, in 1909, the Great Northern Railway (GNR) got involved. The GNR, an American line, had extended its mainline into Vancouver in 1905 via a subsidiary, the Vancouver, Westminster, and Yukon Railway. Its original terminal building was on Pender Street in Chinatown, but the company already owned property along the False Creek shoreline east of Main Street, and wanted to extend its property out into the mudflats below the highwater line with the intention of filling it in and building a new terminal. In 1910, voters were asked to endorse by plebiscite a deal with the GNR giving the company what it needed. Douglas favoured the deal, the value of which would be settled by arbitration, because it meant that development in False Creek would go ahead quickly. L.D. agreed, but argued that the mayor had been dragging his heels on the matter.

A third major issue which divided the candidates was a new city hall. Everyone agreed that the bureaucracy had outgrown its offices in the Old Market, but there was no agreement on where to locate a new building. This matter was also before the public in a plebiscite proposing that the city exchange the site of its old hospital at Pender and Cambie streets for the provincial courthouse site down the block on Hastings Street between Hamilton and Cambie (now Victory Square) where it was proposed to build a new civic hall. L.D. opposed this move. He favoured building a new city hall next door to the existing one, at the corner of Pender and Main, on the grounds that it was more centrally located.[54] Under the influence of the CPR, the centre of gravity of the city was shifting westward toward the Granville Street corridor. L.D. hoped to slow this trend by keeping the civic government anchored on the east side.

Perhaps because both sides understood that the outcome would be close, the rhetoric of the 1910 campaign was more bitter and personal than it had been a year earlier. Douglas and his supporters suggested that L.D. was a dangerous radical whose election would jeopardize good relations with "the financial leaders of the Dominion." The *Province* went much further, accusing L.D. of "megalomania" and claiming that he was pitching his appeal to a single class, the city's workers. "The attempt by any demagogue to set class against class, and cause distrust and disturbance in a peaceful and prosperous community should be discouraged." L.D. hit back defiantly at the accusation that he was a socialist. "If a Socialist is a man who stands by what he thinks right and does not fear to express his opinions irrespective of monopolies, corporations, and other similar influences, who dares to speak on behalf of the masses of the people, then I am a Socialist."[55]

L.D. could not contain his frustration at the manner in which the other newspapers, particularly the *Province,* covered his campaign, which is to say hardly at all. There was, he charged, a conspiracy of silence to ignore all criticism of city council. He knew that the other papers would not support him. "They had always been against the masses of the people and in favour of corporations and they always would be." But he had a right to expect fair play. The *Province* happily admitted that its coverage was one-sided. There was no need to report what L.D. said, argued one of its editorials, because he said nothing new. One did not have to be a fan of L.D. to recognize that many of the *Province's* criticisms of him were either untrue or irrelevant. L.D. was from the United States, charged the paper, and had little familiarity with "our system of government." But Douglas was born in Madison, Wisconsin, and the *Province* didn't seem to mind. (Interestingly, they remain the only two American-born mayors in the city's history.) L.D. had no experience in city government, continued the editor. But he had served a term as license commissioner, and as a newspaper publisher was a close observer of the local scene. Besides, only a year earlier Douglas had been a newcomer to civic politics and that had not stopped the *Province* from backing his candidacy. L.D. "has nothing of value to propose to the public," concluded the paper.[56] But wasn't that for the public to decide, based partly on what they read in the newspaper?

In the end the voters did not agree that L.D. was the dangerous class warrior the opposition made him out to be, and they elected him. Once again Douglas won Wards One and Two, but L.D. carried the other four wards by a substantial majority. "People Showed Wish for New Blood at City Hall in No Unmistakable Manner," declared the *World*. For its part, the *Province* concluded that L.D. won by virtue of "the solid Socialist vote," which it somehow calculated to be 1,500.[57] While this is an exaggeration, it was true that L.D. had the official backing of organized labour during the campaign and, by his strong support of the eight-hour work day, had positioned himself as the voice of the ordinary working person. The 1910 election established L.D. as an "anti-establishment" politician who would always draw more of his support from the eastern and southern portions of the city than from the enclaves of the wealthy and prominent in the west.

At its first meeting, the new council voted to introduce the eight-hour work day for civic employees with no reduction in pay, a measure which had been solidly endorsed by voters.[58] Another measure which had passed by plebiscite, the land swap with the province to make possible the construction of a new city hall, ran into a roadblock when the province decided not to make the exchange. Instead, council voted to go ahead with the more conservative scheme that L.D. had favoured all along and for which he argued vehemently, the expansion of the old city hall on its present site.[59] Of the main election issues, that left the most intractable, the future of False Creek.

By a margin of three to one, voters had endorsed plans to make a deal with the Great Northern Railway that would allow the company to take over and fill in the north side of the head of the Creek for use as a terminal. However, the details remained to be ironed out. City council passed a bylaw granting sixty-one acres (nearly twenty-five hectares) of False Creek foreshore to the Great Northern in return for clear title to the centre of the Creek as well as a commitment from the company to spend $2.5 million on improvements, including the erection of a terminal. In June, when the bylaw went to a plebiscite, the matter blew up into the most controversial issue of L.D.'s first term as mayor. Opponents of the plan argued that the railway was getting a valuable piece of property for almost nothing, and that the city had not received adequate guarantees that other railways would be allowed access to the head of the Creek.[60] L.D. denied these claims. Based on legal advice, he said, the city had made the best deal possible. Many residents of Grandview, the neighbourhood centred on Commercial Drive just up the slope from the east end of the Creek, wanted False

Creek kept open to provide access to their neighbourhood for small cargo vessels. Their spokesperson was former alderman Edward Odlum, who lived in Grandview, where he had significant real estate holdings. When L.D. travelled to Ottawa at the end of April to obtain federal government approval of the reclamation scheme, Odlum went along as a representative of the Grandview Property Owners' Association to present the case against the city's plans. But federal officials agreed to allow the city to go ahead.

L.D.

In 1963, American historian Richard Hofstadter coined the phrase "the paranoid style" to describe a recurring tendency in American public life to blame sinister conspiracies for everything that is wrong in the world. He cited the strident anti-communism of Senator Joe McCarthy and the John Birch Society as examples. Long before either of these, Louis Taylor was a practitioner of the paranoid style. When his opinions and policies were challenged, he often saw conspirators instead of opponents, malevolent forces who wielded power behind the scenes, shaping events to their own purposes. The debate over False Creek was a case in point. The day before the plebiscite, L.D. charged that "somebody" was waging a $10,000 campaign to defeat the bylaw. "Who is Putting Up the Money?" asked the *World*. Who was printing circulars opposing the plan? Who was hiring cars to take ratepayers to the polls? "Is he acting in his own interest or in the interest of some corporation?" asked the mayor, calling for the anonymous wire-puller to "come out into the open and show themselves."[61] This was not the first time that L.D. conjured up a mysterious conspiracy, nor would it be the last. It was one of his favourite techniques for rallying support behind his causes, to paint himself as the defender of the public against powerful, unnamed interests.

The plebiscite drew a heavy turnout of voters, surprising one reporter, who wrote that "usually a money bylaw in Vancouver is about as animated as a country funeral in a snowstorm on the day before Christmas."[62] If dark forces were at work in the background, they did not have much influence on the result. Ratepayers endorsed the bylaw by much more than the three-fifths majority required – the Ward which actually contained the Creek voted seven to one in favour – and the way was clear for the reclamation of the east end of False Creek and the transformation of this part of the city into a major railway terminus. The job was not completed until the end of the War, and there were many modifications and disputes still to come, but in terms of its impact on the city, the deal with the Great Northern which led to the filling-in of the head of False Creek was the most significant accomplishment of L.D.'s first terms as mayor.

vi

In 1910, arrangements were made to absorb into the city the neighbouring areas of Hastings Townsite and District Lot 301. The Townsite was a 1,195-hectare block of land east of the city limits running all the way to Boundary Road between Burrard Inlet and 29th Avenue. District Lot 301 was a smaller piece, only 142 hectares, a predominantly blue-collar suburb lying south of Sixteenth Avenue east of Main. When they were annexed on January 1, 1911, the size of the city increased by almost one-half, while its population jumped to 93,700. But this was just the first step in the Greater Vancouver movement. South Vancouver had been incorporated as a municipality in 1892, encompassing the area west of Boundary Road and south of Sixteenth all the way to the Fraser River. (In 1908, Point Grey was carved out as a separate municipality.) Most of this large tract had been logged and was rural in character, with small communities at Cedar Cottage, Eburne (Marpole), and Collingwood. After about 1905, the pace of residential development picked up, and South Vancouver became home to a growing number of working-class homeowners. By 1911, its population of 16,126 made it the third largest municipality in B.C. With growth came an increased need for services: streets, sidewalks, parks, water and sewage, public transit. As the size of the municipal debt rose to pay for these amenities, union with Vancouver looked ever more attractive and in January 1911, residents voted 1,194 to 200 in favour of annexation. L.D. made annexation one of his priorities, but ultimately it was up to the province to decide, and Premier Richard McBride's government applied the brakes. There were problems involving the franchises granted the B.C. Electric Railway Company, which operated the streetcars in both municipalities, as well as uncertainty about the provision of basic services. It would be another eighteen years before amalgamation took place.

True to his restless personality, L.D. turned out to be an activist mayor. Later he recalled this period of his career with special fondness. "The people were all working harmoniously and there was an absence of cliques."[63] It was also a period of rapid economic growth and a boom in construction. The city's infrastructure was expanding, and as a result council handled an unprecedented amount of business. At one meeting in December, for example, aldermen sat until 1:45 in the morning passing nineteen money bylaws worth close to $3.5 million for everything from street paving to new firehalls to the construction of the Burrard Street Bridge. All of these bylaws were put to the voters the following month and sixteen of them passed, amounting to $2.5 million worth of new projects.[64] (The Burrard Street Bridge was not among them; it was defeated.) L.D. did not always get everything he wanted; his impulse to get things done was reined in by council's more cautious temper. On the issue of a new city hall, for example, council decided, against his objections, to put the project on hold. But he managed to make at least some progress on major issues that had been in discussion for years, notably the future of False Creek, the eight-hour work day, and the expansion of the city's boundaries. So it was with confidence that he carried his record into the re-election campaign.

The mayor's opponent in the 1911 election was Alexander Morrison, an affable, portly engineer who was partner in the bridge-building firm of Armstrong and Morrison. Morrison had achieved local notoriety a decade earlier when he purchased the city's first automobile, a steam-powered Locomobile, but his political career was destined to be brief. Once again L.D.'s critics portrayed him as a class warrior who "played up the labour vote." L.D. made no apology for his support of labour. "I have stood for labour every time," he declared as the campaign got underway. But he also promised that he would work for the city "without regard to class." L.D. made much of Morrison's lack of originality, claiming that he had no policies of his own to offer and mocking him on the campaign trail as "Me Too" Morrison. It was an uninspired campaign. The two candidates spent much of their time sparring about which of them provided better working conditions for their own employees. Even the *Province*, which as usual came out against L.D., could find little for which to criticise him except the condition of city streets.[65] Then, a few days before the vote, Alderman T.J. Whiteside dropped a bombshell by charging that L.D. was using his influence as mayor to extort financial support for his new newspaper building, and the campaign veered

A piece of sheet music, featuring a photograph of L.D., written for the 1911 election campaign.
COURTESY ALICE GAVIN

away from policy issues altogether to concentrate on accusations of corruption.

When L.D. purchased the *World* from Sara McLagan in 1905, it was located in a building on Homer Street near Pender. During 1909, he had decided that his operation needed roomier premises and he set out to erect a new building farther east along Pender at Beatty Street. For this purpose he created the World Building Limited, a separate company from the newspaper, which issued 6,000 shares at $50 each. In order to attract investors, L.D. promised that the paper would lease part of the finished building. The World Building put L.D. in a vulnerable position, financially and politically. Alderman Whiteside claimed that L.D. had pressured certain business owners to invest in the building in return for favours at city hall. In particular, Whiteside cited the case of a city hotel, the Vandecar, whose owner had purchased stock in the World Building and, Whiteside claimed, had then had his liquor license renewed by the city's license commission with L.D., who was a member of the commission, casting the deciding vote. "We should not for the sake of our city's good name allow men to occupy public office whose design is to employ their position for personal ends," huffed the *Province*'s editorial page. "The public representative who will use any power, entrusted to him, for his own advantage is unfit for political life."[66] L.D. responded on the front pages of the *World*. He denied involvement in the sale of stock in the building company and denied offering favours to prospective investors. In the specific case of the Vandecar's license, he presented convincing evidence that Alderman Whiteside had his facts confused and that he, L.D., had not had to cast a vote on the matter because a majority of the other commissioners approved the renewal. The incident had little impact on the voters, who returned L.D. to office with an increased majority a few days later, and the story quickly dropped out of the newspapers.

L.D. defeated Morrison by a hefty majority. He won every ward except, as usual, Ward One on the downtown west side, and even there he received almost double the votes that he had won the previous year. Once again his opponents attributed the outcome of the election to L.D.'s "socialist" support, but it is doubtful there were enough "socialists" in the city to elect anyone. L.D. enjoyed the support of organized labour, but his success at the polls had more to do with his record, the lack of a strong opponent, and Morrison's failure to articulate any issues during the campaign. Begrudgingly, the *Province* added its congratulations. "It must be frankly recognized . . . that Mr Taylor has won his spurs as a public man. Whether his critics agree with certain courses of conduct that have marked his career or not, it is obvious that the people want him. . . ."[67] The paper predicted that L.D. would soon be a candidate for the provincial legislature, even the federal parliament.

vii

Among the non-participants in the election were most of the women who lived in the city. Along with Aboriginals and Asians, women possessed neither the provincial nor the federal franchise. Vancouver had its own civic charter which did grant female suffrage, but only to widows and single women who owned property. Married women could not vote in municipal elections, except for school board, and they could not stand for office themselves. The fight for women's suffrage had been simmering for several years, but it reached a boil in December 1910 with the creation of the Political Equality League in Victoria. The next month the Vancouver branch of the League held its founding meeting, and in May 1911 the city hosted the province's first suffrage convention. In the pre-World War I era, married women more or less belonged to their husbands. Few of them worked outside the home. When couples separated, it was the fathers who took custody of the children. A bereaved widow had no legal claim on her husband's estate; adultery on the part of a husband was not grounds for divorce, but an adulterous woman could not only be divorced but could also lose all access to her children. In this context, a husband was considered to express the political will of his wife, and many people believed that granting the franchise to married women was simply granting a man two votes. "Legislators of today are afflicted with a mania for experiment and certainly the extension of the suffrage to women is an experiment," warned the *Province*. "It may look harmless enough, but history teaches that changes lightly made have from a ripple of apparent harmlessness spread with far reaching consequences."[68]

L.D., on the other hand, was a strong supporter of women's suffrage. During his first term as mayor, city council had approved extending the municipal vote to married women, and during 1911 he had seen that this change was put into effect. He served as chairperson of the May suffrage meeting at the O'Brien Hall and in his opening remarks told the delegates that support for their cause had been instilled in him by his mother. He had watched her raise a family and pay taxes, he said, yet "she had no right or voice in civic affairs." L.D. believed that it "would raise the standard of political life" to give women the same political rights as men. For him it was a question of basic democracy. "After all, what was the government? Essentially, the government was the people, but at present the people were not the government because only a small proportion of the people voted for the election of the government." L.D. ended by pledging to do anything he could to support the cause of women's suffrage, including opening the pages of the *World* "to help on the propaganda work."[69] Despite his support, it took another six years, and a province-wide referendum on the question before women achieved the provincial franchise, and it was 1937 before the first woman, Helena Gutteridge, was elected to Vancouver's city council.

L.D.

. . .

viii

When L.D. went to Ottawa in the spring of 1910 to seek federal support for changes to False Creek, he continued on to Toronto to research another issue that was beginning to gain support among councillors, the board of control form of government. Toronto had such a system, and L.D. wanted to see firsthand how it worked. Three years earlier the province had amended the city charter to allow for a board of control, pending voter approval in a plebiscite. Such a plebiscite took place during the 1908 civic election and a proposal calling for the creation of a three-person board was approved. The issue had little support on council and it languished. It was raised again by the 1910 council, which voted unanimously in favour of a board of control. But when the matter was put to a plebiscite in November, it failed to get the required majority and the *News-Advertiser* concluded that "there were no signs that the citizens generally were seriously interested in the matter."[70] Still, there was a feeling in some quarters that the city was outgrowing its system of government, that it needed new, more efficient, means of civic administration. Councillors complained that they were overwhelmed by the amount of work that their job required. The board of control was conceived as a form of executive committee that would relieve council of some of its responsibilities. Its members, three or four controllers plus the mayor, would be elected city-wide, not by ward. The matter was put to another plebiscite during the 1911 election when voters were asked to choose between the status quo, a board of control, or a third option, a commission form of government. L.D. himself had been converted to commission government, but it was not at the top of his list of priorities; at the final meeting of the campaign he did not even include it among the things he hoped to accomplish with a renewed mandate. At any rate, about twice as many voters registered a preference for commission government than for either of the other options. But once again, as in the case of the annexation of South Vancouver, the provincial government preferred to go slow. It decided not to amend the civic charter, instead appointing a royal commission to investigate the broad question of municipal government. The Royal Commission was not convinced that any change was necessary and, with the outbreak of war, the urgency of reform dissipated. Vancouver kept the ward system and the form of government it had always known.

L.D. had more success with another of his reform projects, the "single tax." Among the welter of radical ideas that circulated through progressive political circles in the pre-war era – social gospel, Marxism, impossibilism, physical culturism, theosophy and other brands of spiritualism, pacifism, evolutionism – the single tax was one of the most widespread. It originated with the American social reformer Henry George. George was born in Philadelphia in 1839. When he was not yet twenty years old he felt the lure of the Fraser River gold rush and spent a few months in Victoria working in his cousin's general store. Moving on to San Francisco, he became a journalist and a familiar figure in reform circles, writing articles condemning land speculation and social inequality. In 1879, George published *Progress and Poverty*, one of the best-selling books of the 19th century. In it, he made the case that private ownership of land was the root cause of economic inequality. George believed that wealth was created by the partnership of capital and labour working together. The problem was the landlord, who was taking unearned profits from escalating property values and draining away the economic surplus that should be going to create wealth, instead creating poverty and misery. The solution? A tax on land intended to control speculation and confiscate excess rents for the good of the community. Among George's followers, this became known as the "single tax." Taxes on improvements and incomes were ultimately taxes on labour, the argument went; they stifled initiative and economic development. A tax on unimproved land value and unimproved land value alone, a single tax, removed wealth from the speculator and reapplied it for the benefit of the community.

L.D.

During the 1880s, the influence of *Progress and Poverty* spread among a wide variety of political activists, including Irish nationalists, English socialists, and American progressives. In 1886, the "prophet of San Francisco," as George came to be called, ran for mayor of New York City on the labour ticket, finishing second to the Democrat but outpolling his Republican opponent, Teddy Roosevelt.[71] In Canada, the single tax movement flourished as well. In Ontario, the influential Toronto *Globe* endorsed the single tax, while radical journalist Phillips Thompson and popular cartoonist J.W. Bengough, editor of the satirical Toronto magazine *Grip,* both adopted the cause.[72] Out West, the Manitoba Labour Party added the single tax to its platform, at least temporarily, and the idea also appealed to elements in the farmers' movement.[73] But it was in Vancouver that the single tax achieved mainstream respectability by becoming a cornerstone of municipal tax policy. And its main proponent was Louis Taylor, who became so associated with the idea that he was known across North America as "Single Tax Taylor" and Vancouver as "The Single Tax City."

It was during his second term as mayor that L.D. hopped aboard the "single tax" bandwagon. Though he became its most insistent advocate, he was by no means the "father" of the single tax in Vancouver. As early as 1895, city council had reduced the tax on property improvements by fifty percent in order to stimulate construction. In 1906, the improvement tax was reduced by another twenty-five percent. There is no record of the single tax being an issue during L.D.'s first term. In June 1910, he claimed in a magazine article that Vancouver was "the only City of metropolitan size on the continent to elect a municipal government on a Single Tax platform," but the issue had been mentioned hardly at all during the election campaign earlier that year. Nonetheless, in the spring of 1910, council approved the complete abolition of the tax on improvements, and L.D. came to credit this step for the incredible economic growth being experienced by the city. "Under the Single Tax," he declared, "as it is operated in Vancouver, a new sky line is being built up for the city, a sky line of tall, substantial buildings of stone and granite, and under the Single Tax, not only is the man who builds benefited, but also the land owner, the tenant and the man who works with his hands in the city's factories and saves his money to build his family a place they can call home." According to L.D.'s version of events, the flame of support for the single tax was dying out everywhere in North America until "a casting vote given by the mayor [i.e., himself] in the council chamber of Vancouver suddenly fed it with new fuel." Instantly, with Vancouver's example before them, "the single-tax associations of the continent renewed their activity." "As Macaulay said of Byron," he boasted, "the city awoke one morning and found itself famous." Newspapers and magazines all over the United States were discussing the issue; city hall was flooded with inquiries for information. The city "had been set as a beacon upon a hill," L.D. told the readers of the *World*. And it was largely down to himself.[74]

During 1911, the provincial government appointed a royal commission into taxation and when the commission came to Vancouver to hold hearings, L.D. presented his views. The single tax was a matter of simple justice, he explained. Land values were created by the community so the community, not the individual property owner, should share in the profits. Not only did L.D. wish to exempt property improvements from taxation, he saw no need for a poll tax or an income tax either. Instead he suggested that all provincial revenues should come from taxes on natural resources. "They are not placed there for the special interests," he argued, "they are placed there for all the people who live on the face of the earth, to be shared equitably among them. The natural resources of the province, the mines, fisheries, timber and land, should bear the whole expense of the government."[75]

Early supporters of the single tax thought that it would be the first step in the abolition of poverty and a thorough transformation of society. By the time L.D. took it up, however, the tax was less an instrument of social justice than a tool for economic development; its success was measured by the number of new buildings it encouraged. L.D. argued that the tax was completely responsible for the pre-war boom in construction in the city. Since he was the chief proponent of the idea, he was more or less taking credit for the economic good times. But this was claiming too much. All of western Canada enjoyed unprecedented levels of economic prosperity during the period, and nowhere else except Edmonton was the single tax implemented. It is not possible to calculate what role the abolition of the tax on property improvements played in encouraging pre-war prosperity. It is interesting, however, that once the war ended and the post-war recession set in, the city re-introduced the improvement tax and the single tax was quickly forgotten. (Years later, when L.D. published his reminiscences with journalist Ronald Kenvyn, he did not even mention the single tax among his many accomplishments.)

L.D.

In 1911, though, the single tax was a live issue, and as the annual civic election approached, the debate heated up. At the end of November, the *Province* published an editorial warning that L.D. and his council planned to increase the tax on land to its full market value. The effect of such a policy, warned the editorial, would be to drive capital away from the city and "render valueless and non-producing every mortgage held on every foot of land in Vancouver." The city would end up owning all the land and that, said the *Province*, amounted to "the reign of socialism."

> Surely the affairs of Vancouver can be conducted without giving way to every form of Socialistic fad and scatter-brained folly. The mayor and the aldermen – or a majority of them – seem to be going about with open arms to pick up every extreme radical notion that is a-wing, and have it incorporated in the city charter. We are building for ourselves a mausoleum of misery and poverty, and it is time to call a halt.

City lawyer and author F.C. Wade, a prominent Liberal, wrote a letter to the editor in which he dismissed the claims being made for the benefits of the single tax as "humbug." All Vancouver did, Wade pointed out, was abolish the tax on property improvements. This was a far cry from what Henry George meant by the single tax, said Wade, and it was a far cry from being responsible for the city's prosperity. Wade wondered why land owners should be saddled with taxes while "the quick rich apartment houses, business blocks, and hotels are to go free?" In his view, this placed an unfair tax burden on property owners both large and small. Unsurprisingly, L.D. dismissed these claims as the scare tactics of the moneyed interests. To the charge of socialism, he answered: "I am not a Socialist, but there is no disgrace in being one. A Socialist is a man who has advanced many years ahead of the time. He is a man who is fighting for what will eventually come. I am not ashamed to stand up and say that I respect any man who is trying to alleviate the sufferings of his fellow man." He answered Wade's argument with a blizzard of statistics purporting to show that everyone was better off under the single tax regime.[76]

ix

The 1912 civic election was about much more than the single tax. L.D.'s opponent in the mayoralty campaign was James Findlay, a retired mine superintendent who previously had served three terms as a city license commissioner. Findlay entered the race as a result of a bargain struck in the backrooms of the local Conservative Party. In the summer of 1911, some high-level provincial Conservatives tried to install Findlay, a friend of Premier Richard McBride, as the party's nominee for the Vancouver seat in the upcoming federal election. The problem was that city alderman Harry Stevens had already been promised the nomination and he refused to step aside, not even when he was offered the party's support if he chose to run for mayor instead. Stevens, a rabid anti-Asian activist, got the nomination, and subsequently won the seat for the Tories in that September's election; he represented Vancouver in Parliament for the next nineteen years. Meanwhile, Findlay got the consolation prize, a run at the Vancouver mayoralty.[77] During the civic campaign, Findlay showed little interest in debating the fine points of tax policy. His platform was more concerned with nuts and bolts issues: sewers, harbour improvements, railways, public transit, and so on. One issue which he did manage to make his own was urban crime. Findlay argued that Vancouver was experiencing a crime wave and advocated more police and better street lighting to combat it. Further, he proposed taking a hard line with transients, whom he blamed for much of the crime. As the *Province* reported: "One of the best forms of punishment, in Mr Findlay's opinion, was the whipping post. This was an old-time method of punishing criminals, he said, but was one which was very effective. There were many transients here and some of them were of a very dangerous character. They should be made to understand that they cannot come over here and practice lawlessness without being detected, captured and punished, he declared."[78]

By transients, Findlay was referring to unemployed workers whom the radical members of the Industrial Workers of the World, the Wobblies, were trying to organize at street meetings. Founded in Chicago in 1905, the IWW had spread quickly into B.C. where it alarmed employers with its call for general strikes and worker control. The Wobblies found a sympathetic audience among the unskilled and seasonal labourers who congregated in Vancouver during the off-season or when jobs were in short supply. This floating population of transients and immigrants was a constant source of anxiety for city authorities, who didn't want to bear the cost of extending relief to the unemployed and feared the potential for civic unrest and even criminal activity. What authorities definitely did not want was IWW "agitators" and socialist militants using city streets to recruit members and stir up the disaffected. Matters had come to a head initially on April 4, 1909, when speakers from the IWW and the Socialist Party of Canada, whose headquarters were in Vancouver, were addressing a crowd at the corner of Hastings and Carrall.[79] Acting on instructions from civic officials, police broke up the meeting and charged six of the orators who refused to move along. Ostensibly the police were clearing the streets for pedestrians, but the labour movement believed its freedom of speech was being suppressed and responded with a series of rallies and protest meetings. One of the men charged in the April 4 incident was found guilty and went to jail for ten days rather than pay a five dollar fine. Another speaker was arrested in a separate incident and fined $100. But after several weeks of street protests, the police backed off, and the first round of the "free-speech fight" went to the militants.

The second round began in January 1912. Unemployment was running high that winter. In order to discourage migrant workers from coming to the city, authorities took a hard stand against vagrancy. In response, the IWW organized street protests, and Findlay promised that he would not countenance the presence of layabouts and agitators. For his part, L.D. relied for re-election on his record and many of the same, fairly non-controversial, policies that he had been promoting during the previous two years: the single tax, commission government, development of False Creek, annexation of South Vancouver, and a new city hall. Six days before the election the *World* published a special 148-page "Progress and Building Edition," with a front-page picture of the mayor hard at work at his desk. The economic boom was at its height and L.D.'s *World* was one of the city's most enthusiastic boosters. "Vancouver is growing as no other city today is growing," it boasted. "Vancouver's destiny is a theme for the dreamer."[80] In this special edition, nicely timed to coincide with the election, L.D. wanted to remind voters how much progress had been made during his two terms in office; or, to put it another way, how much he had done for them. It was a rude shock, therefore, when the voters did not see it the same way. On election day they ended L.D.'s two-year tenure, electing Findlay by a 1,314 vote majority.

Why did he lose? L.D. himself blamed "the vested interests" and the campaign of "unparallelled abuse" carried on against him by, among others, the *Province*. The editor of his longtime rival blamed L.D.'s "manifest incompetency," charging that "the present condition of the city, its streets, its sewerage system, all its public works and its various departments have been left in such a state of muddle that it will require devoted labour and time from his successor to bring them into some kind of order."[81] Findlay was a strong candidate with experience in civic government and an effective campaign organization based in the local Conservative Party. His tough talk about vagrants and radicals may have played a role in his success. A general strike among building trades workers in mid-1911, followed by a recurrence of the "free speech" issue early in 1912, heightened class tensions in the city and might have made some voters wary of supporting L.D. because of his reputation as a "socialist" who was closely allied with labour. The *Province's* post-election advice to the new mayor — "The gang of thugs and thieves who have made life a burden here for weeks should be run out of town without delay" — must have been widely endorsed in the city. Immediately, the new city council passed a bylaw banning outdoor meetings. The IWW took this as a provocation and began holding meetings in defiance of the ban, some of which attracted as many as 10,000 people. Police responded by making arrests, which only galvanized support for the protests, at least among the labour movement. At a large meeting at the Powell Street Grounds (now Oppenheimer Park) on January 28, a phalanx of police on foot and horseback attacked the crowd with clubs and whips and arrested more than two dozen people. Undeterred, the Wobblies and members of the Socialist Party continued to stage meetings, on one occasion taking to boats off Stanley Park from where they spoke to the crowd using a megaphone. And the police continued to make their arrests.[82] Eventually labour leaders and politicians, both local and provincial, brokered an end to the cycle of protests and arrests, and by mid-February street meetings took place without police interference.

L.D.'s attitude to the "free speech" struggle changed with his political circumstances. During the initial episode in 1909, he had just lost his first attempt to win election as mayor and, with plans to run again, he did not want to seem to be too sympathetic to radical elements. His appeal as a politician was as a friend of labour, but not of "anarchists and socialists." As a result, the World's coverage of the arrests and subsequent trials was muted. L.D. took no stand in support of free speech or the right of assembly, for example. He merely objected that the size of the fines seemed excessive. In 1912, however, L.D. and his paper took a stronger stand. With the election lost, L.D. saw a way to make political capital on Findlay's handling of the protests. In its news and editorial columns, the World blamed the new mayor for giving the police free rein to brutalize innocent demonstrators. The paper referred to "Findlay's cossacks" and described mounted police "riding down" peaceful protestors who were simply "endeavouring to exercise the right of British free speech."[83] The World criticized Findlay's "tactless prohibition of all out-door public meetings" and characterized the events at the Powell Street Grounds as an assault by the police on an orderly crowd legally assembled. The problem was not with the crowd, continued the World editorial, but with the mayor's determination to run the city with an "iron hand." "This is not Russia and the sooner the authorities remember that fact the better."[84] The issue was no longer the alleged radicalism of the speakers, but rather their right to be heard and the repressive attempts by Mayor Findlay to muzzle them. On this issue, L.D. positioned his paper on the side of free speech.

Whatever role the street disturbances had played in L.D.'s defeat at the polls, they were probably not the deciding factor. Civic politics were extremely volatile in the early years of the century. The last three-term mayor was James Garden, who served from 1898 through 1900. Half of the six mayors since the turn of the century had served just a single term. The city was growing quickly, which meant that the electorate changed significantly between elections. It was difficult for a local politician to consolidate consistent support. In the end, L.D.'s ability to win two terms was probably more notable than his failure to win a third.

The Pre-War City

3

With his civic political career on hold, L.D. looked around for another election in which to run, and found one almost immediately when Premier Richard McBride announced that provincial voters would go to the polls on March 28, 1912. It is difficult to say what drove L.D. back onto the hustings. He had a business to run in Vancouver. He had no chance of winning. He was unknown in the Kootenay, where he chose to run, and McBride's Conservatives clearly were headed for victory. He had wanted to run in Vancouver, but by now he was no friend of the local Liberals, who made sure he was denied a nomination. Instead, he obtained the party's nomination for the Rossland riding and travelled to the interior by train to campaign. Rossland was a gold mining centre and a bedroom community for Trail where Cominco had its huge smelter. Residents liked their politics raw. "Talk about your frontier meetings," L.D. later recalled. "We had everything except guns." On one occasion tempers flared and the meeting erupted into a series of fist fights. Chairs were thrown, windows broken, and a few noses bloodied before order was restored. "It was the most lively meeting I have been in," said L.D. He must have thought that his labour sympathies, and his stories of his own days as a gold prospector, would win him support from the miners. If so, he was wrong. Back in Vancouver, the *World* kept up a drumbeat of support for its proprietor, bravely predicting that the former mayor was a sure thing, but in the end he was trounced by the Conservative candidate, the general manager of the local power company. L.D. might have taken solace from the fact that every other Liberal candidate in the province

L.D.'s pride and joy, the World Building, completed in 1912 at the corner of Pender and Beatty Streets. At seventeen storeys, it was for two years the tallest building in the British Empire, until it was eclipsed by a Toronto bank tower. When this photograph was taken it had become the Bekins Building; later it was occupied by the Vancouver Sun *newspaper.* VPL 4658

went down to defeat as well; the Conservatives captured sixty percent of the popular vote and all but two of the seats in the legislature, those two being won by Socialist candidates.

With no other elections in the offing, L.D. had to content himself for the time being with running his newspaper. There was a lot to keep him busy. Shortly after the 1912 civic campaign the paper moved to its new home in the World Building. At seventeen storeys, it surpassed the Dominion Building just around the corner to become the tallest building in the British Empire (remaining so until a twenty-storey bank went up in Toronto in 1914). It was designed in the Beaux-Arts style by the architect William Tuff Whiteway. Whiteway had established a practice in Vancouver in 1900 and was responsible for many of the city's pre-World-War-1 landmark buildings, including the Kelly Building (now the Landing at the western entrance to Gastown), the Holden Building, the original firehall on East Cordova Street, and Lord Roberts School. Built of brick from the Maclure brickyards at Clayburn, the World Building (more commonly called the Sun Tower) is a warehouse-like, eight-storey structure topped by a nine-storey tower which soars to a copper dome that glints green in the sunlight. A row of nine semi-draped female figures, sculpted by Charles Marega, supports a cornice about halfway up the building; the bare breasts and sensuous poses scandalized the city's bluenoses.

The World Building has been called a first-rate building on a second-rate site, a reference to its location away from Hastings Street, the city's main business thoroughfare at the time it was built. It was conventional wisdom, then and later, that the building's financial troubles were the result of it being situated in a bit of a backeddy as far as potential tenants were concerned. But this is overstating the case. Perched on a rise near the entrance to Chinatown, the World Building was a brief walk from Woodward's Department Store, the main streetcar depot, and the bustling shops and restaurants on Hastings. Until it moved to the head of False Creek during World War 1, the depot for the Great Northern Railway was on Pender Street just three blocks away. Far from being off the beaten track, L.D.'s building was in fact close to the centre of the action. If he was hoping to leave a permanent mark on the city, he chose his location wisely. Not only has the building survived, it remains a highly visible landmark, from many vantage points still not obscured by the steel and glass towers that surround it.

Because of its status as the city's tallest structure, the World Building attracted a fair share of attention over the years, but nothing equalled the much-publicized attempt by Harry Gardiner, "The Human Fly," to scale the outside of the building at noon on Hallowe'en in 1918. By this time L.D. had lost control of his newspaper, but he would have been in the crowd that day – who wasn't? It was the largest gathering the city had ever seen. Pender and Beatty Streets were a moving sea of people for several blocks. As well as standing in the street, onlookers crammed the windows of neighbouring buildings and sat on the edge of every available rooftop. A great roar went up when, at the appointed hour, the Fly emerged from the front door of the building. He was dressed in a white canvas suit so as to be visible from a distance as he made his climb. The newspapers remarked on his "long, powerful hands" and his jaunty manner. The ascent took an hour and a half, during which the people below alternately held their breath and cheered him on. There was a fire truck parked in the street with its ladder extended straight up into the air about three storeys high, and at one point a young woman named Lottie Fletcher climbed to the top of it and unfurled a banner displaying the total amount of money that had been collected in Vancouver for Victory Bonds. The war was still two weeks from being over and the purpose of the Fly's stunt was to raise support for the bond drive. Then all attention reverted to the Fly as he continued his assault on the walls, "a speck of white on the face of the building." Finally he scrambled up the slippery copper dome to the summit. "Then, crowned by the brilliant sunlight, he waved once again to the crowd, now scarcely able to see him, and vanished into the interior of the building."[1]

i

During 1912, Vancouver experienced another of its periodic moral panics about the rising tide of vice, in particular prostitution. The city was especially susceptible to the "social evil." As a port and an economic metropolis for a natural resource hinterland, it experienced a regular inflow of seasonal labourers, merchant seamen, and unemployed transients, all of whom provided business for the city's brothels. At the same time, opportunities for women in the work force were limited; the sex trade offered an alternative to low-paying, menial jobs, or no jobs at all. Toleration of prostitution went up and down like a see-saw. At one end sat the church-based moral reformers, temperance advocates, and social workers who wished to see the "social evil" eradicated. They raised the alarm about "white slavery," warning that black and Chinese pimps were luring white women into the sex trade by force or with drugs, and they did not believe that police were doing enough to enforce moral standards. At the other end sat police and most civic politicians, who despaired of ever suppressing prostitution completely and wanted simply to regulate it. As James Findlay concluded after almost a year in office, "a segregated district, under absolute control, was probably the best means of handling the matter."[2]

L.D. belonged in the camp of the regulators. Prior to his election as mayor, the city's "red light" or "restricted" area was located on Dupont Street, later East Pender Street, just down the hill from where he would eventually erect the World Building. During 1907, responding to a public outcry, authorities closed the Dupont Street bawdy houses and arrested many of the prostitutes. But the brothels simply relocated around the corner in Canton Alley and Shanghai Alley, then the centre of Chinatown, and later a couple of blocks south to Shore Street, a short lane of ramshackle buildings running off Main Street. In 1910, a resident of Shore Street reported that "there are seven houses of prostitution all showing red lights" and "every night hundreds of men may be seen going to and from these houses."[3] As long as the madames who kept the houses observed certain informal rules, authorities were prepared to tolerate their operation in this so-called "restricted district." Answering an inquiry from Winnipeg, Mayor Taylor's secretary described how the regulatory policy had evolved:

> About three years ago [i.e., 1906] – to give you a brief history
> of the experience with the Social Evil in this city – it
> was decided to clear out the undesirable women from a
> certain quarter, close to Chinatown, in fact almost in the
> Oriental section, also from a number of cribs. Accordingly,
> a number of the habitués were deported under the
> Immigration regulations and the others were given notice
> to leave town.
> Following this, several of the keepers of houses of ill fame

purchased property and built themselves houses on the end of a street terminating in False Creek [Shore Street], where they established themselves with a small percentage of the demi-monde. They have since then been allowed to reside in the section where they congregated but they have strict instructions not to appear in public places or theatres, not to parade the streets, or dress conspicuously. . . .

Judging from other cities on the Pacific Coast and their efforts to cope with the evil, His Worship thinks this city has the condition well in hand under the present system. . . .[4]

However, this *modus vivendi* did not last for long. Businesses along Main Street did not welcome the proximity of the brothels, and in mid-1911 the board of police commissioners, of which L.D., as mayor, was a member, asked the police to clean up Shore Street. As a result, a new "restricted district" developed on Alexander Street, closer to the waterfront north of Powell, where once again prostitution was allowed to flourish more or less openly. L.D. and the police were attempting to find some place in the downtown core where brothels could operate without detracting from other businesses or outraging public opinion. As long as the houses did not advertise themselves too blatantly, conformed to liquor regulations, and the women did not solicit too aggressively, authorities were willing to tolerate them. Recognizing that they could not stop the sex trade altogether, they preferred to confine it to a single area, believing that otherwise it would spread to other locations throughout the city.

This pragmatic response to the "social evil" was not acceptable to the moral reformers. In March 1912, a delegation of about forty representatives from the city's churches and women's organizations, the Good Government League, the YWCA, and the Social and Moral Reform League visited city hall to demand that the police commission close the Alexander Street brothels. Reverend D.C. Pidgeon, speaking for the group, suggested that not only was the red light district flourishing, it was doing so with the tacit approval of the police. Toleration of vice merely encouraged it, said Reverend Pidgeon; "a policy of suppression is the only way of reducing the evil to the irreducible minimum." Other speakers warned of the influence a "restricted district" had on the young men and women of the city. George Gibson declared that his organization, the Good Government League, was "absolutely against

L.D. in 1911, age 54, during his second term as mayor. COURTESY ALICE GAVIN

the recognition of the social evil in any shape or form and would fight it to the last breath." Reverend Kaburagi said that the location of the brothels so close to the Japanese residential district was a disgrace. In response Mayor Findlay and the other commissioners denied that they in any way condoned "the social evil" or approved of what was happening on Alexander Street. That said, they urged a "go slow"

policy. They pointed out the difficulty of building a legal case against the brothels and the likelihood that the brothel keepers, if evicted from one neighbourhood, would spread to others. And what about the women, asked Mayor Findlay? In the event that the houses were suddenly closed, where would they go? "He thought that to clean up the city step by step would be better than trying to carry out any drastic policy that might scatter these women all over the city again."[5] For once, Findlay and the labour movement found themselves on the same side of an issue. In an article in the *British Columbia Federationist*, J.W. Wilkinson, president of the Vancouver Trades and Labour Council, endorsed the designation of a red light district. He ridiculed the "smug self-righteousness" of the "Goody Government League type." The issue for Wilkinson was economic, not moral. Young single men were going to want sex, he said. As long as wages were low and the cost of living was high, they were not going to be able to marry and so would have to resort to casual encounters. For their part, the prostitutes were girls "who cannot support themselves on the low wages paid to them by their employers." Wilkinson was contemptuous of the moral hypocrites who condemned prostitution, but would not do anything to improve the economic conditions which he argued promoted it.[6]

Adding to the concerns of the moral reformers was the ominous presence of Chinatown. Pressed into a couple of blocks along Pender Street, it was a swampy district of boarding houses, warehouses, shops, and businesses that was regularly inundated at high tide by the waters of False Creek. Residents were overwhelmingly single men, most of whom could not afford to pay the head tax required to bring families from China. The Chinese congregated together for their own protection; the riot of 1907 illustrated how hostile the wider society could be. They also appreciated the proximity to services and the company of relatives and friends. But Chinatown was also a creation of the outside world, which discriminated against the Chinese by not allowing them to own property or operate businesses in other parts of the city, or to take jobs in most professions. Segregation was not a choice; it was enforced by law.

Chinatown (or "Celestialland" as it was sometimes called) was mythologized by the white majority as a place of filth, vice, and moral depravity.[7] The Chinese were believed to live in squalor, many people to a room, without moral standards or healthy pursuits. Their quarter was seen as a place of opium factories (which were legal until 1909), whorehouses, and gambling parlours. Chinatown was represented as depraved and exotic, a dark underworld where innocent young women fell prey to the clutches of the white slave trader and innocent young men consorted with prostitutes and drug addicts. Writer and police magistrate Emily Murphy described it in *The Black Candle*, her classic anti-drug exposé, as "that queer district where men seem to glide from nowhere to nothing."[8] In February 1912, one of L.D.'s reporters took readers of the *World* on a tour of this "plague spot." "Whether you believe it or not, the vice is there, and if you will go there some day you may see with your own eyes what I saw with mine. . . ."[9] The article was a compendium of the stereotypes about the Chinese rampant in white Vancouver at the time. Venturing into one of the "opium joints" in the company of a guide, the reporter described entering a small apartment, dimly lit by a single light, crowded with thirteen "Chinamen" lying on couches "engaged in the several occupations of smoking opium tobacco." Proceeding through the room, which was littered with dirty dishes and the remains of food, he emerged into a passage lined by tiny compartments occupied by individual smokers. "I beheld stretched out in a space barely large enough to accommodate his length a man completely under the influence of the drug. He twisted this way and that in his visions, while the caricature of a smile graced his lips, and he mumbled soft gutterals to himself as the hallucinations became more and more vivid." The reporter and his guide moved on to a series of gambling rooms, "run in a wide-open fashion after the style of the early wild west mining camp days," where they witnessed Chinese and non-Chinese playing games of "chuckaluck" and fan-tan. Everywhere they saw signs of the Chinese lottery, "which is patronized by practically nine-tenths of the Chinese population," the yellow paper tickets "with their scrawling hieroglyphics" littering the sidewalk. "But the lottery is the lesser by a large margin of the other gambling, and it is no exaggeration to say that of the 200 or more stores and places of business in Vancouver's Chinatown, at least 100 are conducted solely for the purpose of gaming, opium smoking and other unlawful and nefarious uses." But the worst was yet to come. In the company of a health official, the reporter made his way late in the afternoon into "the most vile opium joint in the city." Passing through "a sinister doorway" on Pender Street, they descended a staircase to a basement apartment where about fifty smokers, including two white women, lay on couches wrapped in filthy blankets and *L.D.* stupefied by drugs. One man, the reporter was told, was a woodcutter who worked for part of the year to make enough money to spend the rest of his time "in one long debauch," not even bothering to leave the apartment until his money had run out. The reporter asked who was to blame for the sordid situation. "As long as there are Chinese in Vancouver, it is said, there will be gambling and opium smoking. The needed reform lies in the necessity for immediately segregating the whites from contact with the yellow men. . . . Will prevailing conditions in Chinatown be allowed to continue indefinitely? What is Vancouver going to do about it?"

This kind of reporting fuelled the sense of moral panic that bubbled to the surface of political life in the city during 1912. Elected officials, church leaders, police, and social reformers debated the best way to deal with the enforcement of moral standards. In November, with the civic election approaching, the debate was joined in earnest, led principally by the newly-launched *Sun* newspaper, whose editors saw an opportunity to embarrass the provincial Conservative government and particularly William Bowser, the attorney general and Premier McBride's right-hand man. Early in the month, several prostitutes who had been arrested at Alexander Street brothels were released when the warden at the provincial penitentiary refused to accept them, apparently on Bowser's orders. At a public meeting at the Savoy Theatre, Reverend Spencer decried the moral state of the city, and particularly the attorney general's interference in the judicial process. "We have liquor dens and gambling dens. I cannot tell how many, and alongside of these there are the disorderly houses. Excuses are made for these things, but I tell you there is no excuse that can be made before Almighty God for the house of ill fame." Spencer urged his listeners to vote in the next civic election for candidates who would "ensure a cleansing of the city." Bowser was unapologetic, making it plain that he did not want the jails filling up with prostitutes, a position which outraged the *Sun*'s editor, who claimed that the attorney general had become the "champion" of a class of criminals "that spreads its pollution through the whole social fabric, that allures and attracts to every community which it infests many other classes of criminals and constitutes a permanent menace to the safety as well as the morality of the public." Soon the city would be swarming with criminals from all across North America who had been issued a veritable free pass by the government and Vancouver would be "engulfed in immorality." The paper went on to call for a provincial royal commission into the issue of prostitution.[10] Meanwhile, L.D. and the *World* went easier on Bowser, instead blaming the police commission for the increase in prostitution in the city. Against all evidence, the *World* made the preposterous claim that "the social evil was little heard of in Vancouver" when L.D. was mayor and that only during 1912 was it "permitted to assume proportions hitherto unknown in the city."[11] L.D. seemed less interested in debating the issue than he was in defending his record as mayor.

ii

Prostitution and the wisdom of tolerating a restricted district might have been the focus of a spirited campaign for mayor. But on January 2, Vancouver voters were surprised to learn that there would be no campaign. Alderman Truman Baxter had been declared the new mayor by acclamation. L.D. had intended to run, but for some reason he had waited until the last moment to file his nomination papers. In fact, he waited too long. It was ruled that he had missed the deadline by a few minutes, and anyway, his papers were missing a crucial signature. Such carelessness by a candidate as experienced as L.D. is inexplicable, but it left Truman Baxter mayor of Vancouver for 1913.

Voters were not to be denied a Baxter-Taylor showdown, however, and in terms of political theatre it was worth the wait. When the next election rolled around, L.D. threw his hat into the ring yet again, with sensational results. His opponents, learning of his intentions, picked this exact moment to press a legal suit that had been hanging fire for some time. Apparently, three years earlier L.D., among others, had pledged some money to a mining syndicate. Since no mine was developed and no money was paid, the matter seemed to be dormant until suddenly the principals in the syndicate demanded $1,000 from investors; or more accurately, from one investor, Louis Taylor. L.D. saw no reason why he alone should be required to pay the full amount and he ignored the claim, with the result that he was cited for contempt of court and arrested by a sheriff's officer who intended hauling him off to the county jail. Last minute negotiations resolved the matter and L.D. agreed to pay $60 in court costs.[12] It was a rousing beginning to what turned out to be a very nasty election campaign.

L.D.

L.D. began by running on his past record of achievements as mayor. He reminded his audiences that he had championed the single tax, the vote for married women, the eight-hour work day, and various civic improvements, and he compared these to Baxter's allegedly meagre accomplishments during the past year. Once again L.D. ran as a friend of the working man, emphasizing fair wage issues for civic employees. But times had changed in the two years since he had occupied the mayor's office. Principally, the province, Vancouver along with it, had plunged into a recession. The building boom was over; revenues were down. In this new, more stringent economic climate, Baxter painted L.D. as a free-spending profligate whom the city could no longer afford.[13] As the new year began, however, these political differences took a back seat to the question of whether L.D. was legally qualified to run for mayor. Election officials accepted his nomination papers, but Baxter and the *Province* continued to raise doubts about whether L.D. met the property requirement. Candidates were required to own $1,000 worth of property in the city, which L.D. did, a piece of land on Trinity Street in the former Hastings Townsite. Beyond that, candidates were required to show that their property had been unencumbered by debts for at least thirty days prior to nomination day. This last condition was newly imposed, L.D. charged, at the insistence of Mayor Baxter. It had never been a condition before and he announced that he would not acknowledge it. "I leave it to you," L.D. told a meeting of supporters, "whether a man who will resort to the tactics that my opponent has done is a fit and proper man to represent the city of Vancouver." Baxter announced that he would not challenge L.D.'s qualifications, even though he knew that his opponent had only cleared his property of debt within the thirty-day period, but at the same time the incumbent pointed out that any other citizen was free to make the challenge in court. While L.D.'s critics tried to make a meal of it, the controversy likely cost Baxter as much support as it won him.

In an editorial pronouncing itself lukewarm about both candidates, the *Sun* summed up public opinion when it disparaged Baxter's "ferret-like watch of an opponent's standing." "It looks too much like espionage, like sharp detective work."[14]

The final week of the campaign was bogged down in charges and counter-charges. While it did not take seriously the controversy over L.D.'s qualifications, the *Sun* did express qualms about his competence and honesty. In an editorial three days before the election, the paper argued that the financial situation of the *World*, which was perilous, had left L.D. with "a reputation for irresponsibility, lack of foresight and imprudence which should utterly disqualify him for any public position. . . ." The editorial revealed that during his last term as mayor L.D. had accepted a loan to erect the World Building from railway tycoon James J. Hill at the same time that Hill's Great Northern Railway was negotiating the False Creek agreement with the city. "A graver breech of public 'etiquette' could scarcely be charged against a mayor," charged the *Sun*. "We know the use he made of the position during his last incumbency. In his present desparate condition what other more sinister uses may he not make of it?" L.D. denied any impropriety in the building loan, though it was at the very least careless of him to have mixed personal and public business. With so many charges being flung in his direction, it was no surprise that Baxter outpolled him on election day.[15] Since the annexation of the Hastings Townsite and District Lot 301 the city had eight electoral wards, and L.D. managed to win just one of them.

Post-election, L.D. accused the usual conspiracy of vested interests of plotting against him. More probably, his own financial problems at the *World*, and his critics' claims of impropriety were enough to deny him a victory. By the election of 1914, an interesting pattern had emerged in the campaigns that L.D. had run since he began his political career. His opponents and critics consistently cast him as an outsider with a questionable right to hold public office. The pattern can be traced all the way back to his second campaign for license commissioner in 1903. It will be recalled that in that campaign L.D. was erroneously accused of being an American citizen and therefore ineligible to run. His American background was raised again during his first mayoralty campaign against Charles Douglas, even though Douglas, too, was an American by birth. It was also during these campaigns that L.D. was portrayed as a socialist demagogue promoting class warfare in Vancouver. His opponents denounced him as a representative of the working class, as if someone who spoke for that class was unqualified to be mayor. During the 1910 contest, the *Province* went so far as to refuse to publish reports of L.D.'s public meetings, as if he did not exist. Two days after he was elected, the paper carried a report that L.D.'s legal right to hold office was being questioned by "eminent legal authorities" because his newspaper, the

L.D. *World*, carried civic advertising and he might be in a conflict of interest.[16] Nothing came of this insinuation, just as nothing came of the sudden accusation, during the 1911 campaign, that L.D. had used his position as mayor to do favours for businesses investing in the new World Building. In 1912, two days before that election, the *Province* again came out with a sensational story that in return for a payment of $10,000 L.D. had promised to deliver the "labour vote" in British Columbia to the Liberal Party in the previous federal election (as if that were possible). And then, in 1914, came the attempt to disqualify him on a technicality from running for mayor. Some of this was the rough-and-tumble of civic politics, and L.D. gave as good as he got. But there is something in the persistent attempts to disqualify him that suggests that powerful circles in the city thought he was not just an unfortunate choice for mayor, but completely beyond the pale even as a candidate. Why? No one knew about his questionable past as a fugitive from American justice. While he was a self-proclaimed advocate for ordinary wage earners, his ideas were not radical. Despite claims to the opposite, he was not a socialist. He was an entrepreneur and a civic booster, very much in the style of the middle-class self-made man of the era. Obviously, voters who had twice elected him mayor did not find him frightening. Yet he had become by this point in his career a pariah to the elites. His advocacy of labour issues, such as the eight-hour day and fair wages for civic employees, and his outspokenness about the influence of large corporations in public life, had made him a force not just to oppose but to silence.

iii

In spite of his support for organized labour and his antagonism to large corporations, L.D., as both newspaper publisher and mayor, shared the booster mentality that pervaded pre-war Vancouver. He liked nothing better than to sing the praises of his adopted city and province. The decade leading up to the war were "the golden years," as Alan Morley called them in his history of the city.[17] The population was growing by leaps and bounds; the 1911 census showed that Vancouver had become Canada's fourth-largest city, not far behind Winnipeg. Construction was booming; in 1912, at the height of the good times, the value of building permits in the city approached $20 million. The street railway, always an indicator of urban growth, doubled in trackage in the five years leading up to the war. The Great Northern Railway reached the city from the U.S. in 1904, while the first Canadian Northern passenger train from eastern Canada arrived in August 1915. A new fire station, courthouse (now the art gallery), post office (now part of the Sinclair Centre), the Birks Building, Woodward's Department Store, a new Canadian Pacific rail station, and a scattering of hotels, banks, and warehouses are some of the landmark buildings that date back to this period. The steady rise in property values prompted almost everyone to invest in real estate. The city was in the grip of a speculative mania. "It would almost seem as if the inhabitants must be a race of financiers," the British historian J.A. Hobson reported after a visit, "concerned purely with money and stocks and shares."[18] The most lavish development was the subdivision for the super-rich laid out at a cost of $2 million by the CPR on its holdings south of 16th Avenue. Shaughnessy Heights, named for company president Thomas Shaughnessy, featured curving, tree-lined streets (mostly named after CPR bigwigs, their wives and children), leafy estates, and mansions designed by the city's leading architects. A golf course, lawn bowling club, and tennis courts were built close by. Work began in 1909 and by the outbreak of war there were more than 200 homes in "CPR Heaven," Vancouver's newest most fashionable address.

L.D. could not afford a home in Shaughnessy, but he, too, was swept up in the prevailing enthusiasm for growth and expansion. British Columbia, he told a journalist, was a place of immense potential. "She is Opportunity," he said during an interview for a 1910 magazine profile, "knocking every day on the door of every man who is alert enough to hear her call and energetic enough to answer it." He continued: "We are just beginning. The constantly widening activities in the Province are opening up more and more paths to prosperity."[19] As the article made clear, L.D. subscribed fully to the myth of the self-made man that underlay the era's economic expansion.[20] After all, he was one himself.

"It would take me a good while to mention all the men who came here at about the same time I did, and in the same condition, with nothing, and who have since risen to affluence and prominence." These were men with no other advantages but "steam in their mental boilers" and the flexibility to adapt to new circumstances. Back home, such men may not have accomplished much, held back by a lack of money, status, or family connections. But in B.C., said L.D., a person needed only "ambition, energy, and intelligence" to make a success. This rags-to-riches scenario was a key element not just in the pitch L.D. made to sell his city, but also in the narrative of his own life that he presented to the voters.

L.D.

Unhappily for L.D., and for British Columbia generally, opportunity stopped knocking in 1913 when the provincial economy, which had been riding a decade-long boom, slid into recession. Worried about the looming possibility of war in Europe, British investors, who had financed much of the boom, began withdrawing their money. In Vancouver, construction came to a standstill. The value of local real estate plumetted. Business of all types fell, throwing thousands of people out of work. By October 1914, the number of unemployed in the city reached 15,000. The population dropped for the first time as, first, the jobless left in search of work elsewhere and then, with the outbreak of war, men began enlisting in the army.

Emblematic of the economic downturn was the demise of the Dominion Trust Company. Since it was founded in 1903, Dominion Trust had become one of the largest investors in the local real estate market and had opened offices in other parts of the country. In 1909, it built a new, thirteen-storey headquarters across Hastings Street from the present site of Victory Square. The city's first skyscraper, the Dominion Building, enjoyed the distinction of being the tallest building in the British Empire (until the World Building eclipsed it). With its soaring mansard roof and multi-coloured terracotta exterior, the building, and the company that occupied it, were considered symbolic of Vancouver's energy and prosperity. But as property values tumbled, loans made against real estate had to be written off and investments that looked like sure things in boomtime turned out to be busts. As well, the thirty-two-year-old general manager of Dominion Trust, William Arnold, had been making unauthorized loans that became worthless. On October 12, 1914, in the garage at his Shaughnessy home, Arnold shot and killed himself. In a front page editorial, L.D. called Arnold "one of the most vigorous

The Dominion Trust Building on Hastings Street, completed in 1909, was a symbol of the pre-war economic boom, and the bust that followed it. CVA, STUART THOMSON, CVA 99-232

and capable members of the commercial community." He did not mention that the death was a suicide.[21] L.D., like the rest of the business community, hoped that the company would rescue itself, but less than two weeks later, Dominion Trust went bankrupt.

L.D.

L.D. watched the Dominion Trust drama with particular anxiety since his own business was teetering on the brink. Newspapers all across the country were hit hard by the recession. The price of newsprint rose at the same time as advertising revenues fell. Between 1914 and 1922, forty Canadian daily newspapers failed; many others changed hands.[22] The *World* no longer enjoyed the patronage of the Liberal Party. Veteran journalist D.A. McGregor recounted what happened. "In the Dominion election of 1911 the Liberal Party received a terrible beating in British Columbia, every candidate in the Province being defeated. In the post-mortem it was decided that the reason for this disaster was lack of adequate newspaper support. So it was resolved that Liberalism must have a daily paper on which it could depend."[23] Apparently, local Liberals no longer had confidence in L.D. to carry the party banner. At first, organizers tried to buy one of the existing Vancouver papers. Finding this to be too expensive, they instead struck a deal with John McConnell and Richard Ford, owners of the weekly *B.C. Saturday Sunset* magazine. Together they founded the Burrard Publishing Company, which on February 12, 1912 began publishing the *Sun* newspaper. McConnell and Ford were directors of the company, whose president was F.C. Wade, L.D.'s old opponent in the single tax debate. The launch of the *Sun* brought the number of daily newspapers in the city to four: two in the evening, the *World* and the *Province*, and two in the morning, the *Sun* and the *News-Advertiser*. The addition of another paper to an already crowded field must have contributed to the financial difficulties L.D. was experiencing with his *World*. The situation was exacerbated by the collapse of the real estate market, upon which the papers depended for much of their advertising revenue. What's more, L.D. was in over his head with the financing of his new office tower. In his ambition to build the city's tallest, most impressive skyscraper, he had overreached himself. The *World* only occupied part of the building; the rest of the office and loft space was supposed to be rented out. With the recession, much of this space lay vacant, and the building company could not make its mortgage payments. L.D.'s financial situation was perilous.

iv

On August 4, 1914, the World War began. Two days later, Prime Minister Borden pledged to send Canadian troops overseas. In British Columbia, young men responded to the call to arms with enthusiasm. Eager recruits began leaving the city by the trainload, heading for Valcartier, Quebec, where an expeditionary force was assembling. When the first contingent sailed for England early in October, it included 3,411 men from the West Coast. Per capita, Vancouver would send more soldiers to fight in Europe than any other city in Canada. Province-wide, 55,570 British Columbians would sign up during the next four years, and 6,225 would die in the conflict. Around the city, trainees drilled in the parks while their wives, mothers, and sisters stood on street corners collecting money for the war. "Vancouver today is an armed camp," reported the *World* on August 10, following the call up of the militia. "This morning street cars and automobiles bore the hundreds of officers and soldiers to headquarters in preparation for a war that may last twenty years or as many months." Anxiety, even panic, accompanied the elation. Anyone who spoke with an accent was suspected of being a spy or a saboteur. "Enemy aliens" were required to register with the authorities. People began hoarding food against an imminent attack. Germany had war ships in the Pacific and these were rumoured to be steaming toward the West Coast. "How will this defenceless province protect herself from raids by hostile cruisers?" asked the *Province*.[24] Defensive gun batteries were placed in Stanley Park and at the tip of Point Grey, but it was not until the end of the year, when the Germans were defeated by British ships off the Falkland Islands, that the fear of a naval attack on the coast subsided.

Excited enthusiasm for the war did not last long. Euphoria gave way to gloom. The economic recession continued to hold the city in its grip. Unemployment was on the rise, along with the cost of relief payments for the jobless. The civic government had to cut back on public works. Business in the port declined as most shipping moved to the Atlantic coast to take part in the war effort. In the hinterland, mining and logging were both in the doldrums. By the time the 1915 civic election rolled around, the city had lost the spirit of buoyant optimism which marked L.D.'s first terms in office. Instead, the candidates faced a sombre and unsettled electorate.

When nominations closed on January 2, 1915, L.D. found himself in a four-cornered race for the mayoralty. The incumbent, Truman Baxter, was running for a third term. He had been a conscientious mayor, but he suffered from being in office during the worst of the recession. Charles Douglas, L.D.'s sparring partner from the 1909 and 1910 elections, was dismissed by one opponent as too "good-natured and easy-going" for the job, and the voters seemed to agree. The wild-card candidate was former B.C. premier Joseph Martin. Martin was a transplanted Manitoban who had taken root in Vancouver in 1897 and made a fortune developing real estate in the Hastings Townsite. A lawyer by profession, he was a politician by avocation (he had been a cabinet minister in Manitoba and a Member of Parliament in Ottawa before moving to Vancouver) and a contrarian by nature. No one made enemies as easily as Martin. Loud, brash, and a champion talker, he was known as "Fighting Joe," perhaps for the occasion when he and Richard McBride came to blows on the floor of the legislative assembly over who had the right to occupy the leader of the opposition's chair. He was elected to the legislature for the first time in 1898, served as attorney general in the government of Charles Semlin, and, improbably, became premier early in 1900 when the lieutenant governor couldn't find anyone else to appoint. The choice was improbable because Martin enjoyed no support whatsoever: the day after he took office, a motion of non-confidence in his government passed in the legislature by a vote of thirty to one, the single vote being his own. Nonetheless, Martin managed to cling to power for 106 days before he finally had to resign. He later moved to England where he got himself elected to the British House of Commons. He began dividing his time between London and Vancouver and he was still a British MP when he joined the race for mayor in 1915.

As ornery and erratic as he was, Martin could nonetheless be expected to drain away some of L.D.'s support since both men were maverick Liberals who represented themselves as friends of labour and enemies of the vested interests. Recognizing this, L.D. trained his biggest guns at the former premier, who promised to reduce "extravagant and reckless" civic expenditures and increase revenues by repealing the single tax. It was the very success of the single tax in encouraging building in the city that Martin argued was its chief fault. "The strongest condemnation is that the single tax has induced people to build houses for which no occupants can be found and banks to build skyscrapers for which there are no tenants," he told an audience at the Labour Temple.[25] L.D. jumped to the defense of the policy with which he was so closely connected. He argued that Martin, by opposing the single tax, showed himself to be in favour of land speculation and higher taxes for working people. He reminded his audiences that Martin owned a great deal of land in the east end of the city and stood to profit from the reduction in the property tax that he, Martin, was proposing.

Aside from defending the single tax, L.D. reiterated his familiar support for a bridge across the Second Narrows, the construction of a municipal market, and fair wages for civic employees. His one new idea was a proposal to establish a municipal savings bank. It was not extravagant civic spending, or the war, that was causing the recession, L.D. said. It was the banks. "These institutions had reduced the note circulation, thereby contracting the currency and destroying the purchasing power of the community, the result being dull times for all." The banks were controlled by "eight men," he declared, the same eight men who controlled the railways and the life insurance companies and used their power to deny credit to local businesses in favour of "eastern interests." A municipal bank would issue its own scrip that would be accepted as legal tender by businesses in the city, and it would support the development of local industry. "I have worked consistently for the masses and don't care a hang for the bankers and the classes," L.D. cried at one meeting. "I'd rather have a starving man on the street for my friend than any banker in the city of Vancouver."[26] L.D.'s municipal bank idea, dismissed by one critic as "a moonshine plant to make paper money," was unlikely to receive the support required from the provincial government to amend the city's charter, and as the campaign progressed he placed more emphasis on the bread-and-butter issues summed up in his slogans: "a full dinner pail" and "a fair day's wages for a fair day's work."

The result of what the *World* called "the most exciting mayoralty contest in years" was a victory for L.D. Polling thirty-three percent of the total vote, he defeated his nearest opponent, incumbent Mayor Baxter, by 686 votes. It was not an overwhelming endorsement. Still, it was a gratifying win, marking as it did the first time in Vancouver's history that a candidate had reclaimed the mayoralty after a period out of office. As was customary on election night, the mayor-elect made a slow tour of the city in an automobile, visiting theatres and newspaper offices.

A festive atmosphere took over the downtown, including a military marching band parading down Hastings Street. Stopping outside city hall to receive the applause of his supporters, L.D. told them: "I have no strings on me, because I was not elected by any particular organization, but by my friends and those who believe that I can administer the affairs of the city better than the others. . . . From tonight, Vancouver is going to take on the spirit which it had five years ago. There is going to be progress. We are not going to retrench in every direction in order that we may save a few dollars for a few taxpayers who think they are being pinched, and we are going to pay a fair day's wage for a fair day's work."[27] L.D. had offered a clear choice to the voters and they had taken it. In a phrase that would become popular later in the century, he intended to spend his way out of the recession.

v

On January 15, 1915, the day after L.D. was elected mayor, his financial house came tumbling down. A judge ruled that L.D. had to sell his newspaper to pay off his creditors. In March, a group led by John Nelson, formerly manager of the *News-Advertiser*, paid $25,000 for the *World*. As one of the unsecured creditors and owners of common stock, L.D. received nothing from the sale. He had opposed the deal in court, pleading for more time, but the judge had ruled against him.[28] On March 17, L.D. published a front-page farewell letter "To the Public" in which he charged that a conspiracy of special interests had deprived him of his paper. In L.D.'s view, the *World* under his ownership was "the only city paper to advocate reforms that would benefit the masses." As a result, "the large bondholders had made up their minds to eliminate me from the newspaper life of the city and put me down and out once and for all." He blamed in particular the owners of the Powell River Paper Company, the largest creditor who, he claimed, overworked their employees for "a small minimum wage" and fired anyone who objected. In other words, it was exactly the sort of rapacious, foreign-owned enterprise that L.D. claimed was out to silence him and render the *World* just another "mouthpiece of the special interests — advocating reductions of wages and the enslavement of the masses."[29] Undoubtedly it was true that members of the business elite were happy to see L.D. deprived of his journalistic voice. But his real problem was a lack of access to patronage of any kind, either cash or credit. The *World* had been launched with the help of the Liberal Party, but with the creation of the *Sun* early in 1912, that source of support had dried up. A friendly provincial government might have sent advertising and printing contracts in the *World*'s direction, but L.D. was no friend of the Conservative administration. Most of that money went to the *News-Advertiser*. Martin Robin has argued that the McBride government was successful in buying off most of the newspapers in B.C. The *World* was one of the few Liberal papers to survive what Robin called "the seduction of the press" by McBride.[30] It was a crucial blow to the paper, therefore, when it also lost the backing of the Liberal Party. Along with government, banks and large corporations were also vital sources of credit for daily newspapers.[31] The CPR, for example, supported the *Province.* The *World* had no such patron. Without friends in high places, or deep pockets himself, and with increased competition in a worsening economic climate, L.D. and his paper could not survive.

Fearful that the building company would retain the paper's physical plant until the back rent was paid, John Nelson moved out of the World Building in the middle of the night and relocated the *World* to new offices on Hastings Street. (The building, which still stands near the western entrance to Chinatown, was home to the *Sun* between 1937 and 1964; it was among the first buildings given heritage designation by the city. The *World* remained in business until it was purchased by the *Sun* early in 1924 and closed down.)

No sooner had L.D. lost his paper than he and his companion/business manager, Alice Berry, were planning to launch another. The *Vancouver City Directory* for 1915 carried an advertisement announcing a new newspaper, the *Daily Globe*, "under the management and control of the former owners of the *Daily World*" and listing L.D. as editor and Berry as managing director. Like the *World* before it, the *Globe* billed itself as "the People's Paper" and promised to be "The Only Paper in Vancouver that is free from corporate influence." The advertisement went on: "If you desire to read unbiased Editorials by writers who are not afraid of the System then you must have the *Globe*." As always, L.D. painted himself as a critic of established interests and a friend of the "little guy." Early in April he began publishing *L.D.'s Bulletin*, a four-page dispatch he intended to issue twice a week until he got the money together to start up the

Globe.[32] But in the end he failed to find financing. The *Bulletin* folded and the *Daily Globe* never appeared.

L.D.

Meanwhile, L.D. had a city to run, if only his opponents would let him. But they were more interested in refighting the recent election, and they found a pretext in the legal requirement that a candidate had to own a piece of property within city limits valued at $1,000 or more and the property had to be free and clear of all "charges, liens and encumbrances." Five ratepayers petitioned the provincial Supreme Court to unseat L.D., arguing that he did not meet the qualification. The property in question was the same lot on Trinity Street in the East Hastings neighbourhood that had been challenged the previous year. This time L.D. had not been as careful about clearing any debts against the property; apparently a mortgage had not been paid off until after the full thirty days required before the election. On February 17, Mr Justice Clements nullified the outcome of the recent vote, ruling that L.D. had not met the qualifications to run for office and ordering a new election. On the day of the judicial decision L.D. staged a dramatic return from Victoria, where he had been on business. Arriving by steamer at the CPR terminal, he was met by a crowd of well-wishers who had been mustered for the occasion, along with a brass band playing "For He's A Jolly Good Fellow" and a limousine to drive him to his apartment. Before disappearing into the back seat of the car, L.D. announced that he would be in the running to succeed himself. When none of the other candidates from the January election declared themselves, Alderman Walter Hepburn resigned his seat on council and entered the race. L.D. suspected a trap. He believed that his opponents had agreed among themselves to run a single candidate so that if L.D. won and was disqualified again, as he possibly would be, the other candidate would be declared the victor. To foil this tactic, L.D. convinced William Tuff Whiteway, a friend and the architect of the World Building, to join the race, guaranteeing that if the second election did not stand up in court, there would be yet another.[33]

Although he was not a candidate, "Fighting Joe" Martin made the most remarkable speech of the campaign. Appearing at one of Walter Hepburn's meetings at the Dominion Hall, Martin let loose a vituperative attack on L.D., charging him with personal dishonesty and corruption. "Here's a man of no substance, owing everyone round town," Martin began, making a reference to L.D.'s financial troubles with the *World*. "Yet he's masquerading as a fit and proper man for mayor and doesn't own one quarter of an inch of property he wants to qualify with. He's broke, he pays nobody, yet he has all the money he wants. Where does it come from? It's volunteered and paid by the trust of Chinese gamblers in the town and by the people who want to re-open Alexander Street [i.e., the red-light district]. L.D. can go to the courts of law about these statements and I'll prove them." Actually, Martin couldn't prove anything, and four days later he retracted his remarks, which he agreed were libellous and unsubstantiated, and apologized for making them.[34]

If Martin supplied most of the campaign's vitriol, Whiteway supplied its humour. He was not a complete political neophyte, having run for alderman in the January election in Ward 2, where he finished far behind the other four candidates with only 400 votes. In the March campaign, voters recognized that the architect was not a serious candidate. At meetings, whenever he predicted his own victory, he did so with a broad smile on his face and his audience, sharing the joke, responded with knowing laughter. Walter Hepburn, meanwhile, seemed almost irrelevant to the campaign. L.D. paid far less attention to his actual opponent than to Joe Martin and the "ring of interests" who, he said, had used a "miserable little technicality" to overturn the expressed will of the voters. It was a successful tactic, and the second campaign ended the same way the first had, with a comfortable margin of victory for L.D. (Whiteway received eighty-five votes.)[35] After three unsuccessful attempts, and barring another challenge to his qualifications, it looked as if L.D. had successfully fought his way back into city hall.

vii

At age fifty-eight, L.D. was going through the best of times and the worst of times. Politically, he appeared to be at the peak of his popularity and influence. The day after the March election, fellow newspaperman, John

P. McConnell, co-owner of the *Saturday Sunset* magazine and editor of the *Sun* newspaper, called him "the most strongly entrenched political factor in Vancouver." McConnell, who had backed L.D. in the campaign, was an independent and influential voice in the city; his remarks are an accurate reflection of L.D.'s standing at this stage of his career. L.D.'s strength, observed McConnell, was based on the east side, among "the working men and women of this city. They regard him, and I think justly so, as their champion, and they endorse his democratic principles and ideas." Opposed in the election by both Conservatives and Liberals, L.D. nevertheless prevailed, a sign, thought McConnell, that he was "the strongest personal factor in a political sense in the city."[36] Despite attempts to impugn his honesty and ability, and despite the lack of support from either of the major political parties, L.D. had held on to his core vote and even expanded it somewhat.

At the same time, his personal life was in turmoil. He had lost the *World* to creditors, he was no longer involved with the World Building, and his attempts to drum up financing for another newspaper had failed. As if that were not enough, he decided that the time had come to regularize his domestic life. He had been living with Alice Berry for about four years, but he was still married to his first wife, Annie. In mid-April he wrote to her proposing a divorce. Over the years L.D. had been in irregular contact with Annie and his sons. Judging by correspondence that has survived, he paid just one visit to California to see them, in December 1909, though he apparently helped Annie financially whenever he could. "It is now almost eight years since you have lived in California," he began his letter. "We did not live together as man and wife for two years previous to that. To me it is clear that we never will again. There is no use going over the old arguments pro and con the cause of this position. It is sufficient that we do not live together and I am frank enough to admit that for me I never can assume that relationship. I have hesitated for years about asking you to relieve this situation, waiting till such time as Theodore [who was now fourteen] had grown up so that he can in a measure understand the situation." L.D. assured his wife that he had "no desire to get away from my responsibility to the family" and offered to make support payments of $100 per month for the first year, increasing to $125 per month thereafter. "In return I am asking you to get a divorce. This I understand can be done without undue publicity in Los Angeles, providing both parties are willing – I to pay all legal fees."

There was no mention in the letter of Alice Berry.[37]

Annie was thunderstruck. She sought advice from her cousin, Clarence Chapman, a lawyer. "I have never wished for divorce – but always hoped for a harmonious outcome," she wrote him. "That we have not lived together is wholly his decision, adopted without consulting me or giving me any reason." She referred to her "broken health" and complained that "the continual sense of insecurity and suspense and uncertainty" created by her separation had kept her from getting better.[38] Chapman wrote back, counselling her to think the matter over while he obtained more information about the terms L.D. was offering. "When a man feels as he does," wrote Chapman, "perhaps there is little to be gained by opposing him, providing a reasonable settlement can be obtained."[39] Annie received similar advice from her sister-in-law, Kate, who thought that Annie should accept the offer and get on with her life. In fact, Kate suggested that Annie owed L.D. a divorce "to recompense him for the lonely years," by which she seems to have meant the years in Vancouver before they separated when Annie was more or less incapacitated by depression.[40] Also adding pressure to Annie's decision was the arbitrary nature of L.D.'s offer of support payments. In a letter to his mother-in-law, harsher in tone than the one he had written to his wife, he clearly laid out his position: if Annie agreed to a divorce, he promised to make monthly payments, but if she did not, "I am not going to put myself in a position of slaving in order that she may have a good income."[41] Since support was voluntary, L.D. held all the cards and Annie came to realize it. In August she wrote to her cousin Clarence, "I am anxious that the divorce should go through, if I can be assured of enough to live on decently."[42] She knew that L.D. had been living with another woman "for years," but she agreed with Clarence, who was also her legal advisor, that there was no point in making trouble with this information. "I do not see that you have much to lose in divorcing him," advised Clarence, "as you have no way of changing him or holding him. From the fact that he has kept up remittances in the past for so long a time, and under such circumstances, I think it likely he will try to keep them up in the future. . . . If it is true that he has been going with another woman all these years, it has not caused him to forget his duty to you and the boys, which at least shows that he has a strong sense of duty."[43]

On May 10, 1916, the Superior Court of California in the County of

Los Angeles issued a final decree of divorce. As usual with such decrees, the divorce only became final after a year had passed. Therefore, L.D. remained married to Annie until May 1917. Nonetheless, on June 8, 1916, he married Alice Berry. In other words, for eleven months he was a bigamist. Whether he failed to read the fine print, or whether he just did not care, it seems like an astonishing thing to do. After all the years he and Alice had already lived together, what was the hurry? He must have calculated that no one in Vancouver would know of his situation. And apparently no one did. The divorce decree had been issued in California, and the newspaper item in the *Province* announcing the marriage (there was no mention in the *World*) made no reference to the existence of a former wife.

viii

While divorce negotiations with his wife went ahead, L.D. served his abbreviated third term as mayor. It had gotten off to an exciting start just two weeks after the election when the Vancouver Millionaires hockey club brought the Stanley Cup to the West Coast for the first time. The Millionaires belonged to the Pacific Coast Hockey Association, a league of western teams organized at the end of 1911 by the Patrick brothers, Lester and Frank. Using money provided by the sale of their father's Nelson lumber business, the Patricks launched the new league with franchises in Victoria and New Westminster as well as Vancouver, where Frank built a roomy new artificial ice rink. Denman Arena, at the corner of Georgia and Denman Streets near the entrance to Stanley Park, held 10,500 hockey fans, making it the second largest indoor sports facility in the world after New York's Madison Square Garden. Its construction put Vancouver in the big leagues in the world of sport. Frank stocked his team with some of the best players from the rival eastern National Hockey Association, including the legendary Fred "Cyclone" Taylor. In those days the winners of each league played off for the Stanley Cup. In 1915, the Ottawa Senators travelled out to the coast to take on the Millionaires in a three-game final. It was no contest. On a ten-man roster, the home team had seven players who eventually would end up in the Hockey Hall of Fame. One, Barney Stanley, scored five goals in one of the games. But it was Cyclone Taylor who was the acknowledged leader of the Millionaires as they swept all three games, outscoring Ottawa by a total of twenty-six to eight. The victory earned each player a bonus of $300. It also prompted the editorial writer at the *World* to pull out all the stops. "The victory last night of the Vancouver hockey team in annexing the world's title is historic in the annals of that whirlwind winter pastime as it means that for the first time since the trophy was donated by Lord Stanley, Governor General of Canada, 22 years ago, this vice-regal emblem of mundane superiority in the Canadian national winter sport will sojourn in the sunset doorway of the Dominion for a year at least."[44] (The Millionaires, renamed the Maroons, left Vancouver when the Pacific Coast Hockey Association folded in 1926. The barn-like Denman Arena remained a city landmark until it burned to the ground in 1936.)

Many of the hockey fans who cheered for the Millionaires made their way to the Arena using the city's newest form of transportation, the jitney. In 1915, only the wealthy few could afford to own their own automobiles. Urban travel was still predominantly by horse-drawn vehicle and the electric streetcar. Jitneys represented the first attempt to make automobile travel available to the wider public. Basically, they were an early form of taxicab that flourished during the war years. Any car owner who wished to go into business simply stuck a sign on the windshield offering rides to all parts of the city for a five-cent fare (the nickel coin was also known as a jitney), then toured the streets picking up passengers. As many as 200 of these transit entrepreneurs appeared during the daily rush hour, stealing business from the streetcar company. With its ridership falling, B.C. Electric fought back by improving service on downtown routes and lowering fares to eight tickets for twenty-five cents. It also used its considerable political influence to lobby the provincial and civic governments to ban the jitneys as unfair competition. L.D. was unsympathetic to the street railway company, not least because it had refused to assist him when he was looking for a way out of his financial difficulties with the *World*. However, he and his council did strike a special committee to investigate the issue of "Motor Vehicles plying for hire." Before the year was out, council passed a bylaw setting limits on the number of passengers a jitney could carry, restricting their routes, and requiring operators to obtain insurance. Eventually, the B.C. Electric Company was able to convince the province to take more drastic action. In 1917, a provincial commission came out against the "jits" and the government passed legislation allowing the City of Vancouver to ban them, which it did in August 1918.[45]

Vancouver at the time of the World War was a community dominated by railways. The "Terminal City" owed its very existence to the arrival of the Canadian Pacific in 1886, but CP was far from being the only railway in town. By 1904, the Great Northern had arrived at its modest station on Pender Street in Chinatown. Between 1910 and 1916, the province as a whole experienced a mania for railway building as 4,000 kilometres of new rail were laid down. The two transcontinental lines already serving the city were joined by the Canadian Northern, with its depot and related maintenance yards on the reclaimed False Creek lands near Main Street. (The Great Northern moved there as well.) In 1914, Canadian Pacific opened its third, most lavish, station on the waterfront at the foot of Seymour, next door to the previous station, which it demolished. For most Vancouverites, this beautiful building came to symbolize the importance of the railway in everyday life and of the CPR in the life of the city. Arriving to catch the transcontinental, travellers passed beneath the ten-pillared classical colonnade fronting the Cordova Street entrance. Inside the cavernous booking hall, tickets were purchased and relatives given a last embrace. High up at ceiling level, the walls of the concourse displayed a series of murals showing the mountain landscapes through which the train would soon be passing. But you didn't have to be going anywhere to feel the presence of the railway in the city. For years all traffic through the east side would stop several times a day as CP shunted freight cars from its roundhouse and sprawling yards on False Creek across downtown to the harbour. This street-level right-of-way ran right behind L.D.'s World Building, across Pender and Hastings streets, and through today's Pigeon Park on its way to the waterfront. L.D.'s days at his newspaper office were punctuated by the puffing of steam locomotives and the sounds of freight cars bumping and clanking below his window. (This disruption to the flow of downtown traffic got to be such a nuisance that in the 1930s CP built the Dunsmuir Tunnel under downtown to get the trains off the streets.) And the giant transcontinental lines were only part of the story. The city's fleet of streetcars had grown to 230. People travelled everywhere by tram: downtown from Fairview, Mount Pleasant, and Kitsilano, to Stanley Park and the Exhibition Grounds at Hastings Park, and all the

L.D.

way to Marpole on the Oak Street line. Special "owl cars" operated until three o'clock in the morning. A favourite outing was to climb aboard the open-air observation car for a tour of the downtown. Conductor Teddy Lyons kept up a steady patter of one-liners as he drove his "rubberneck wagon" through the streets. Along the way a photographer snapped a picture from the window of his upstairs studio and quickly developed several prints. His young assistant pedalled up beside the observation car as it completed its tour and dropped the photographs into a special box where, with a flourish, Lyons would recover them to sell to the tourists for a dollar each. Down at the corner of Hastings and Carrall, the B.C. Electric Railway had its own terminus where larger, interurban trains from Richmond, New Westminster, and the Fraser Valley came and went daily. For a three dollar return fare, passengers could travel 100 kilometres to Chilliwack and back, stopping at any one of the sixty-five stations along the way. On a single day in 1910, the Vancouver streetcar system recorded 122,455 paying customers, in a city whose population (including South Vancouver and Point Grey) had just reached 120,000.

ix

One of L.D.'s favourite anecdotes involved the train. In July 1915, former American president Theodore Roosevelt paid a visit to British Columbia. Roosevelt was on his way to San Francisco to attend the Panama-Pacific International Exposition and was going to be in Vancouver for less than an hour before catching a boat to Seattle. The Board of Trade had laid on a welcoming committee to greet the former president who was arriving aboard the CPR. The civic VIPs included a variety of business, political, and military leaders, but notably, not Mayor Taylor, whose name had been left off the guest list. L.D. got wind of the Board's plans and arranged to have a car ready outside the new CPR station on the Sunday of Roosevelt's arrival. Early that morning he intercepted the train when it paused at the Westminster Junction, boarded and went in to see Roosevelt, whom he had met a few years earlier in New York. When the transcontinental arrived at the Vancouver station, which was thronged with people who had turned out to see the president, who should step out onto the platform but L.D. The mayor made a show of introducing

L.D. leads former U.S. president Teddy Roosevelt through a throng of well-wishers to a waiting limousine outside the CPR station in July 1915. CVA, STUART THOMSON, LP 158

Roosevelt and his wife to the local bigwigs, then hustled them into the waiting car. Roosevelt at the time was a controversial figure in the U.S. where he loudly advocated an American entry into the war against Germany. Speaking from the back of the car, he told the cheering crowd: "Every Canadian will walk with his head higher for thinking of the manner in which the sons of his country have responded to this great rallying call of Empire." Then it was off for a quick tour around Stanley Park before L.D. delivered the couple to their steamer just as it was about to sail. Years later he was still gloating over it.[46]

There were more pressing problems facing L.D. than a cold shoulder from the city's business leaders, however, principally the recession, and the desperate state of the city's finances. L.D. had campaigned against retrenchment, but the local economy was in a shambles. Unemployment was running at double the national rate. There were as many as 15,000 jobless men in the city.[47] Half the lumber mills in town had shut down. To preserve their jobs, many workers accepted wage cuts. The construction industry was as depressed as it had been since the beginning of the century. The value of building permits in 1915 ($1.6 million) was less than ten percent of what it had been three years earlier.[48] The city, which was spending $16,000 a month on relief, was hard pressed to help the jobless. Some were put to work at a dollar a day cutting firewood or tending roads, parks, and grounds around public buildings. Others received a simple meal and a bed for the night.[49] As meagre as this assistance was, city council early in April suspended it for "workless single men from outside the city," sparking an outburst of violent protest. On April 6, an estimated 2,000 men who had been denied relief, "mostly Austrians and Russians" according to the *Province*, marched down Hastings Street smashing windows, demanding free food in restaurants, and pelting the police with pieces of fruit and tobacco tins. The next day at a public meeting at McLean Park in Strathcona, speakers threatened more violence unless city council did something to restore relief. Meanwhile, police were arresting protestors who ordered meals in restaurants and refused to pay for them. That afternoon council met in special session. It stood by its earlier decision to restrict relief to residents, but also appointed a delegation, led by L.D., to go immediately to Victoria to ask the provincial government for help. By the end of the week the province had agreed to forward $10,000 to the city and once again meal tickets were issued to single men.[50]

For the time being the crisis had passed. But by the end of June the treasury was near empty once again. In a city-wide vote, ratepayers defeated a series of bylaws proposed by L.D. which would have given council approval to borrow $750,000 for a variety of public works. The defeat was widely interpreted as a message that the public wanted council to stop "promiscuous spending" and get its financial house in order. Council appointed a special subcommittee on finance which recommended "the immediate necessity of retrenchment." L.D. and the aldermen had already taken a pay cut themselves. Acting on the subcommittee's recommendations, council reduced the hours of all civic workers by a quarter and began laying off employees.[51] Projects such as the Second Narrows Bridge and a new city hall, both of which dated back to L.D.'s first term as mayor, were put on hold. With the defeat of the money bylaws, there was barely enough cash to fix the potholed streets and install the occasional sewer line.

The city's finances continued to preoccupy L.D. and his council for the rest of their term. Not until 1916 did the local economy begin to rally and with it the city's revenues. This was not why L.D. had wanted to be mayor. He had campaigned against the very policies of restraint that circumstances forced him into adopting. L.D. had never been a politician who favoured retrenchment and economy. He preferred the good times when money was available for spending. Quite probably this was one of the reasons why, in the fall, he decided not to seek re-election to a fourth term. There were other reasons. He may simply have been tired. Over the previous seven years, he had fought seven elections while running a newspaper full-time. It would be understandable if he had lost some of his enthusiasm for the campaign trail. With divorce proceedings underway, it would not be long before he and Alice were free to marry, and she may have preferred that he give up politics. The timing of his "retirement" suggests that this was the case. The loss of the *World* meant that he was broke and needed to find another source of income. The mayor's job paid a reasonable sum, but not as much as he might make doing something else. As well, the loss of his newspaper, and his failure to find financing for a new one, meant that L.D. lacked the most useful tool he had had for promoting his candidacy. Without the *World*, he would have had to rely on other papers to get his message out, papers which had opposed him in the past. Despite his success at the polls just a few months earlier, re-election was far from a sure thing.

Making his farewell address to the final meeting of the outgoing city council, L.D. congratulated the aldermen on what they had accomplished during a year made difficult by straitened financial conditions. He admitted that he left office with regret. "He had always felt it a great honour to be elected mayor and doubly so to serve the city three years in that capacity. He had been elected four times in order to serve three years, and this was a record anyone could be proud of. . . . During the past year he realized he had made some enemies but he had also made some friends and he felt that his standing in the community was just as high as it was a year ago."[52]

And with that, L.D. retired into private life.

The Middle Act: L.D. in the Twenties

4

With his withdrawal from politics, L.D. more or less disappears from the view of the historian. City directories reveal that he and Alice lived in rooms at the Granville Mansions apartment building. Failing to raise the money to start a daily newspaper, Louis instead published a magazine called *The Critic*. Its contents may be imagined, given the title and L.D.'s known opinions, but no copies have survived. The directories also reveal that in 1917 he was working as the editor of the *B.C. Mining News*, an industry journal, and three years later he was editor of the *Oil and Mining Record*, perhaps the same publication under a different name. During 1919, he was preoccupied by Alice's poor health. In the spring, she took sick with what her death notice identified as pernicious anaemia, a blood disorder. In mid-October, she had to be hospitalized, and she died on November 23. She was only forty-eight years old. She and Louis had been business partners since they took over the *World* in the spring of 1905. Many people believed that it was Alice's managerial acumen that kept the paper afloat. They had lived together for seven years, three of them as man and wife. Her death must have been a terrible blow. L.D., who was sixty-two years old at the time, did not marry again.

If Alice had influenced L.D. to retire from politics, her death may have released him for a return to public life. To put it differently, without any domestic life to divert his attention, someone of L.D.'s temperament would naturally consider a return to the busyness of politics. He may also have established the necessary financial security to allow him to indulge his main interest. Or perhaps the opposite was the case and the salary attached to the mayor's job appealed to him. Certainly, later in his life he admitted that it was the need for a steady income that kept him in pursuit of public office. For whatever reason, in the fall of 1922 he announced his intention to run once again for the mayoralty.

L.D.

i

While L.D. had been taking a holiday from public life, his adopted city was struggling to emerge from the economic recession that had set in prior to the war. The war itself brought some relief, principally in the form of a surge in the shipbuilding industry. Shipyards in False Creek and Burrard Inlet produced wooden and steel vessels of various types for the war effort. In 1915, the first grain elevator opened in the harbour. At first so little grain moved through the port that the structure was known as "Steven's Folly" after H.H. Stevens, the local Member of Parliament who had lobbied for its construction. By the mid-1920s, however, there were five more elevators and Vancouver was trans-shipping a growing percentage of the Canadian prairie grain harvest. To handle increased traffic, the Harbour Commission built Ballantyne Pier and the CPR followed suit with its own Piers B and C. The Panama Canal had opened during the war. Again, its significance to the economy did not materialize immediately, but by the twenties the value of the canal was apparent as it significantly reduced shipping costs for goods – timber and grain, for example – bound for the east coast of North America and Europe. Exports boomed and deep-sea shipping became one of the city's major industries.

Along with the rest of the world, Vancouver was hit hard by the epidemic of Spanish influenza that accompanied the end of the war. The so-called "Spanish Lady" killed an estimated twenty-one million people worldwide, 50,000 in Canada. The first case appeared in the city in early October 1918. The disease was characterized by fever, headache, sore throat, cough, and general achiness and lassitude, often followed by pneumonia. Schools shut, churches, pool halls, and theatres emptied, shops closed early, and authorities imposed a ban on all public

126

The mayor at his desk, 1925, a portrait by photographer Leonard Frank. VPL 12602

meetings. The medical community was powerless. There was no drug or vaccine; patients could only stay in bed waiting it out. Hospitals filled to overflowing. On the advice of public health officials, people wore cheesecloth masks over their mouths, doused themselves in camphor, and avoided low necklines and wet feet, but it was all to little effect. By the time the sickness faded away at the end of March 1919, one-third of the population had come down with it. The final death toll in the city reached 900. There were so many funerals that winter that it was hard to find fresh flowers to bury a relative.[1]

Terrible as it was, the flu epidemic did not interrupt the financial recovery or the mood of optimism which followed the long years of war. Reflective of a renewed confidence in the local economy, the twenties saw the construction of many of the buildings which since have become emblematic of the city. After years of delay, work began at the Point Grey site of the new campus of the University of B.C.; the first classes were held in 1925. The Marine Building (1929), the Georgia Hotel (1927), the Commodore Ballroom (1929), a new Orpheum Theatre (1927), at the time the largest theatre in Canada, all date from this period. So do the New Year's Day Polar Bear Swim in English Bay, inaugurated in 1920 by Peter Pantages, the owner of the Peter Pan Café on Granville Street, and the first incarnations of both the city's symphony orchestra and its art school (now the Emily Carr Institute). Nat Bailey launched his chain of White Spot drive-in restaurants. A granite war memorial was erected on the site of the city's first courthouse, renamed Victory Square. B.C. Electric supplemented its fleet of streetcars with the first motor buses. Automobiles were crowding horse-drawn vehicles off the streets. On the first day of 1922, the city broke with one reminder of its British past by switching traffic flow from the left to the righthand side of the road. ("With the customary adaptability of the West and its attitude of studied calm in the presence of an approved reform or of anything which it does not understand," reported the *Province*, "the City of Vancouver kept to the right at 6 a.m. on Sunday and has kept there ever since, just as if it had been doing it for centuries. It was supposed and prophesied by croakers that there would be a scene of wild confusion at all the great nerve centres of the traffic system, that there would be innumerable accidents, that people would be killed every ten minutes and the gods of all old customs would rise up and demand a continuous stream of human sacrifices. But there were no sacrifices and no confusion."[2]) The first traffic light was installed at the corner of Carrall and Hastings in 1928, the same year that the first motion picture with sound to screen in Vancouver, *Mother Knows Best*, premiered at the Capitol Theatre. And every New Year's Eve, Colonel A.D. McRae and his wife Blaunche hosted a masquerade ball for the hoi polloi at Hycroft, their thirty-room Shaughnessy mansion. It was for many people an era of exuberant expansion and unprecedented personal mobility.

On the other side of the social and ethnic divide, life in the city was as much of a struggle as it always had been. While statisticians recorded that British Columbians enjoyed rising per capita incomes (about $1,100 for a male worker in 1921 and $675 for a female), they also recorded that the rising post-war cost of living more than ate up the wage gains. And then there were the unemployed, who had no wages at all. With the end of the war, soldiers returned home to flood the job market at the same time as the munitions and shipbuilding industries were laying off workers. Every autumn, conditions were made worse by the arrival of loggers, cannery hands, and other seasonal workers who were laid off for the winter. Unemployment in B.C. consistently ran above the national average from the end of the war until 1924.[3] Thousands of jobless men idled away their days in parks and streets, creating an awkward problem for civic officials who feared the influence that sidewalk Bolsheviks and other political agitators might have on these men. Recognizing that the situation was desperate and unprecedented, both the federal and provincial governments agreed to contribute to the cost of unemployment relief in the city. Men were put to work clearing land, breaking rock, or building roads. In December 1921, more than 600 jobless were installed in a military-style relief camp at Hastings Park where they cut firewood and landscaped a new, nine-hole golf course. They received twenty cents an hour, out of which they had to pay for meals and a bed for the night.[4]

A city divided by class was also divided by race. In 1921, the *Vancouver Sun* published Hilda Howard's apocalyptic novel, *The Writing on the Wall*, in which the author, a freelance journalist writing under the pseudonym Hilda Glynn-Ward, imagined a British Columbia where plague spread by the Chinese was killing off all whites while Asians competed for political mastery. At the same time, the Children's Protective Association wanted to remove all Chinese students from the city's classrooms because they were said to slow the progress of Caucasian students. The Board of Trade and farmers' groups lobbied for an end to "Oriental" ownership of land. George Nitta, who was of Japanese heritage and lived in Vancouver between the wars, recalled that "discrimination was floating in the air. For example, they wouldn't allow anyone of Oriental descent into the White Lunch Restaurant. And it was the same thing in the public swimming pool. In the movie theatres, upstairs was for coloured people, including us."[5] The senior law officer in the province, Attorney General Alex Manson, campaigned for the exclusion of "Asiatics" from the workplace: "The man who is not patriotic enough to employ white men in his industry is not a good citizen and I am not hesitating to tell him so."[6] There was even a brief revival of the Asiatic Exclusion League. This activism bore fruit on July 1, 1923, when the new Chinese Immigration Act came into effect banning almost all immigration of Chinese people into Canada.

The extent to which racism pervaded Vancouver society was revealed by the sensational Janet Smith murder case. Smith was a twenty-two-year-old nanny from Scotland working for a prominent Shaughnessy family when she was shot and killed while ironing clothes on the morning of July 26, 1924. Initially, police incompetence led to the conclusion that Smith had killed herself, and crucial evidence was destroyed. When it became clear that the nanny had been murdered, suspicion focussed on the family's houseboy, Wong Foon Sing, who had discovered the body and was the only person known to be in the house at the time of the crime. Lacking any evidence, the police could not hold Wong, despite intense pressure from the local Scots community. Lurid rumours of drug trafficking, white slavery, and Jazz Age orgies swept the city, but no arrest was made. Eight months after the murder, Wong was kidnapped by a group of private detectives, civic police, and members of the United Council of Scottish Societies. For six weeks, his kidnappers imprisoned Wong in a Dunbar house where they tried to beat a confession out of him, at one point stringing him up by the neck from the rafters in the attic. All of this occurred with the knowledge of the Point Grey municipal council, which had voted funds for the kidnapping, and Attorney General Manson. Finally, when Wong wouldn't confess, he was released, then formally arrested for Smith's murder. That fall a jury ruled there was insufficient evidence to try him. Wong eventually returned to China. Meanwhile, the men who were behind his abduction, including a Point Grey police commissioner and its chief of police, were tried for kidnapping, and acquitted. No one was ever convicted for the murder of Janet Smith.[7]

ii

This was the city that L.D. aspired to lead when he emerged from his political sabbatical in 1922. His first attempt at recapturing the mayoralty was the election that took place that January. For someone as experienced on the hustings as he was, he put together a very lacklustre campaign. Apparently his years on the sidelines had atrophied his campaign skills. His issues — "a full dinner pail," construction of a crossing at the Second Narrows, annexation of South Vancouver — were the same ones he had been trumpeting a decade earlier. L.D. had never been the most dynamic speaker on the platform, but at least he had been able to force his opponents to respond to his agenda. This time out, they more or less ignored the sixty-five-year-old "Ex- and Next- Mayor," as he billed himself. So did the press. The frontrunner and eventual winner, Charles Tisdall, was a fifty-six-year-old sporting goods merchant, a pillar of the business establishment, who had served in Richard McBride's cabinet in Victoria and was a well-respected city alderman. It was a surprise, therefore, that despite running such a poor campaign, L.D. received nineteen percent of the vote, enough to finish a respectable third in a field of five candidates. Defeat never seemed to discourage him — he had already lost more elections than he had won — and the result gave L.D. reason to think that with a little time, and some new issues, he would regain his winning form.

The 1922 election was the second civic campaign featuring the preferential ballot. Under this system, voters marked their choices for mayor and aldermen in order of preference. As well, the at-large system replaced the wards for aldermanic races. When ballots were counted the candidate receiving the fewest votes was eliminated and his or her second preferences were distributed among the remaining candidates. This process was repeated until a winner emerged. The system was confusing for the voter and a headache for officials who had to count, and recount, the ballots. And the results were disappointing. In the overwhelming majority of cases the candidate who led on the first count ended up winning the election. In 1922, for example, Tisdall led his chief opponent by 428 votes after the first ballot and almost the same number after the last. The same was true for all but one of the aldermanic contests. In other words, the preferential system had hardly any impact, which is why, after three elections, the city returned to the single-choice ballot.

Over the next three years, L.D. managed to increase his vote total by almost 2,000 votes in each of the annual elections. In the 1923 contest (which took place in December 1922), he was up against Tisdall and former alderman J.J. McRae, the two candidates who had bested him the previous year. This time he passed McRae and finished a strong second, losing to the incumbent Tisdall by less than 300 votes in what L.D. dubbed the "woodpecker election." As he told the story, there was a heavy snowfall on election day and late in the afternoon electricity went off, shutting down the street railway and stranding many of his working-class supporters, leaving them unable to get to the polls. "That cost me the election," he claimed to a reporter. The B.C. Electric company blamed a bird which had flown into high-tension wires on the outskirts of the city and shorted out the system. A picture of the blackened bird duly appeared in the newspaper. (L.D. said it was a woodpecker; the *Province* reported that it was a crane.) But L.D. blamed the outage on dirty tricks. "My information is that some opponent of mine threw a chain over positive and negative wires, and caused the damage."[8] The 1924 election (which took place in December 1923) also had its humourous moments. Tisdall having retired, L.D. was matched against William Owen, a realtor and veteran alderman who promised "necessities before fads and frills," and the well-known socialist, Parm Pettipiece. L.D. took such a commanding early lead in the polling that the *World* in its early edition declared him elected. He even gave a speech thanking his supporters, only to learn before the evening was over that he had lost to Owen by fifty-three votes. Pettipiece received half as many votes as L.D., indicating that L.D.'s appeal to the working-class voter held firm, even when a strong labour candidate was in the field. This was the first campaign following the abolition of the preferential ballot, and most observers agreed that had the preferential system still been in use, L.D. would have carried most of Pettipiece's support on the second ballot and probably would have won the election.[9] Both these campaigns focussed on nuts and bolts issues of civic government – water supply, garbage removal, sewers, road improvements, and the like – and took place against a background of a generally improving economic climate in the city.

After three unsuccessful attempts, L.D. finally completed the long road back from retirement on December 10, 1924. Without a third candidate to drain away votes, he defeated Owen in a head-to-head rematch and reclaimed the mayoralty. The campaign featured a nasty personal attack by Owen, who took out a large advertisement in the newspapers drawing attention in coded language to L.D.'s precarious financial position. "Common courtesy does not permit us to publicly analyze Mr Taylor's record, or to make capital from his mistakes," the notice read. "His position in life is not an enviable one.

> Yet Mr Taylor has the effrontery to attempt to belittle
> a man like Mayor Owen and actually ask the citizens to
> accord him (Taylor) the highest honour it is within their
> power to bestow.
> It would be more to Mr Taylor's credit if he were to first
> endeavor to re-establish himself as a good and useful
> citizen.

This jibe suggests that L.D.'s personal finances continued to be undependable, and that the public knew it. Nonetheless, L.D. refused to be drawn out on the matter, instead countering with his own advertisements in which he set out an extensive platform of improvements. "People want work, not charity. Citizens will vote for money by-laws if they see that it is being spent wisely. The spending of money by the city encourages private enterprise, and creates industry – the enemy of charity." His opponents argued that L.D.'s past record showed that he was a reckless free-spender, the last thing the city needed now that it was reducing its debt load and stabilizing its tax rate. "A vote for Owen is a vote for quiet, slow progress and sanity," the *Province* told its readers. "A vote for Taylor is a reckless plunge into the dark." It turned out the majority of voters were feeling a little reckless. On election day, they returned L.D. with a 647 vote majority. He won five of the eight wards, retaining his solid east side support. As well, voters approved bylaws authorizing expenditures of a million dollars on a variety of projects. The election was a resounding victory for L.D.'s activist approach to civic government.[10]

The cartoonist Fitzmaurice has a little fun at L.D.'s expense in the Province *newspaper in 1925.*

VPL 12611

L.D. now began an uninterrupted four years in the mayor's office. Once again he was the dominant force in civic politics. If his public career is a three-act drama, this was the middle act, and it featured most of his major accomplishments. Civic finances were healthy, the mood was buoyant; it was just the kind of atmosphere in which he thrived. He was ten years older than the last time he had been in office and he found the job more tiring than he had remembered. He wrote to his son Ted: "Being Mayor is not what it once was, it is strenuous. Never a moment to myself. The city is growing rapidly and is the mecca for tourists and conventions and I must take an official part in all functions large and small." Still, he did not mean to complain. "It is a meal ticket and work I enjoy," he told Ted. "I hope to hold the job next year, but one can never tell. Our people seem to be satisfied with my administration up to date, the general opinion is that no man can defeat me. . . ."[11] L.D. read the public mood accurately. He won the next two elections with overwhelming majorities. Even the *Province* had to admit that "Vancouver has been through prosperous times during the last two years and citizens today have increased confidence in Mayor Taylor and the City Hall generally."[12]

iii

The most important accomplishment of this middle period of L.D.'s career was the amalgamation of Vancouver with South Vancouver and Point Grey. With amalgamation, the city grew to fill the entire peninsula between the North Shore mountains and the Fraser River, completing the transition from its origins as a tiny lumber village on Burrard Inlet to its modern contours as the third largest city in Canada. The new, enlarged Vancouver had a population of 228,193, an area of 114 square kilometres and pretensions to being, in L.D.'s words, "an entirely different city." The progression was a natural one. Long before they merged, the three municipalities shared services such as transit, sewers, and water, and most people had assumed that union would arrive some day, in some form. But as inevitable as it seemed, the project still required some deft political stickhandling. South Vancouver and Point Grey were dissimilar municipalities with dissimilar interests. The former, bounded on the west by Cambie Street and on the east by Boundary Road, was a predominantly working-class suburb of modest homes. It was hit hard by the 1913-15 economic slump. Tax revenues fell and the municipality verged on insolvency. In 1918, the province had to step in, pay off a huge loan that had come due, and take over administration of the municipality through an appointed commissioner. For five years, until April 1923, the issue of amalgamation sat on the backburner while South Vancouver regained its financial health, and its own government. Perhaps it was because they had come so close to bankruptcy that residents voted overwhelmingly in favour of joining Vancouver when the issue was presented to them in a plebiscite early in 1924. On the other hand, Point Grey, which included the neighbourhoods of Shaughnessy, Kitsilano, Dunbar, Marpole, and Kerrisdale, was much more well-to-do. The CPR owned one-third of the land and had no trouble paying its taxes, recession or not.[13] As a result, Point Grey took a more stand-offish approach to the unity question.

L.D. was a champion of amalgamation and had been ever since he entered public life. Quite simply, it seemed to him that a Greater Vancouver would mean a greater Vancouver. But he was willing to compromise and negotiate to achieve the end result. Residents of Vancouver proper did not see why they should pay for South Vancouver to upgrade its inferior infrastructure, so the initial merger plan called for each municipality to retain its own budgetary process. As the *Province* explained: "Under this plan, the city and municipality, though united, will operate for a time under separate budgets, and the revenues necessary to cover the expenditure of each will be raised within its own boundaries. . . . After a few years of separate budgets, it is assumed, reassessment and financial readjustments will make a single budget possible."[14] In 1925, when merger was put to the voters, the proposal did not include separate budgets. As a result, Vancouver residents voted against it, thinking that they would be paying for all sorts of salary increases and infrastructure upgrades in the southern suburb. L.D. maintained his support for amalgamation, however, and before long the proposal was back on the table. In the winter of 1926-27, voters again went to the polls in their separate municipalities, this time to choose between three options: amalgamation, a county council or borough system, or the status quo. The county council idea enjoyed favour with at least some Point Grey politicians who wished to retain a measure of autonomy. It called for two levels of government: one, city-wide

L.D.

136

administration responsible for common services and a second, borough council responsible for local services. Voters in all three municipalities endorsed amalgamation, rejecting the county council idea decisively. That left the details of a merger to be worked out, including redrawing of the ward boundaries, plans for a single budget, combining of police and fire services, hiring of civic employees, and dozens of other housekeeping matters. Once more the plan was put to ratepayers in all three municipalities, who voted strongly in favour. The provincial legislature passed the necessary statute early in 1928, and on January 1, 1929, the new Vancouver was born.[15]

iv

Another item high on L.D.'s agenda during the 1920s was the creation of a Town Planning Commission. The origins of planning in Vancouver can be traced back to the City Beautiful movement, a pre-war, continent-wide enthusiasm for the planning of improved urban spaces. The idea was to replace the disfigured urban jungle of haphazard streets and buildings with cities that were beautiful, diverse, and integrated; in a word, planned. The key to this transformation was the "civic centre," an open space surrounded by monumental public buildings that would act as a focal point for the city. In 1912, the Vancouver Beautification Association was working on plans for just such a civic centre in the downtown. The Association welcomed a visit by the prominent British landscape architect Thomas Mawson that spring. The Park Board had hired Mawson to advise it about the "beautification" of Coal Harbour and Stanley Park. In a speech to the local Canadian Club, Mawson laid out a grandiose vision for the development of the Georgia Street corridor leading down to Coal Harbour and the entrance to the park. "I propose to regard Georgia Street as the Champs de Elysees of Vancouver," he told his audience. This wide boulevard, closed to traffic, would slope down to a large square ("a Place de la Concorde"), then run into a man-made lake where Lost Lagoon is now located, encircled by another broad pedestrian boulevard. A monument would rise from the centre of the lake, "one of the most magnificent that Art could dream of." Beyond it all lay the park itself, which Mawson thought of as a wild version of the gardens

L.D. hurls the first ball of a cricket match in Stanley Park on May 1, 1926. VPL 12608

of the Tuileries. This was heady stuff for a city just twenty-five years removed from the forest; no wonder the audience rose to give him a sustained ovation.[16] But Mawson's timing was bad. His vision foundered with the recession that set in the following year, and Vancouver never did become the Paris of the Pacific Northwest.

Following the war the planning movement turned away from monumental beautification projects to advocate more practical solutions to urban improvement: adequate housing, zoning, public transit, traffic flow, and so on. In Vancouver, the Board of Trade and the real estate industry began lobbying for provincial town planning legislation. City Council added its support. It established a town planning committee early in 1925, and once the province passed a Town Planning Act at the end of the year, council appointed the first Town Planning Commission, consisting of fourteen members, one of whom was the mayor, L.D. Almost immediately the new commission touched off a noisy debate when it attempted to introduce zoning regulations that would have prohibited the construction of apartment buildings in the West End near Stanley Park. Once home to the city's elite, this neighbourhood was moving down market and many property owners wanted to build apartments and convert existing houses into multi-residential blocks. If they were not allowed to, they complained, the value of their property would plunge. Powerful economic interests were involved in this dispute, and when an interim zoning bylaw was enacted early in 1927, the West End was designated an apartment district.[17]

The planning commission also hired the St Louis consultant Harland Bartholomew to put together a comprehensive plan for the city. By the time Bartholomew submitted his report in 1929, L.D. had left office, but the plan was another of the major legacies of his middle years as mayor.[18] Bartholomew's proposals were designed to meet the needs of the city until it reached a population of a million. His report covered everything from the width of the streets to the placement of parks, from the cleanup of False Creek to the landscaping of residential gardens. One of the more ambitious proposals was for a six-square-block civic centre overlooking English Bay west of Burrard Street. This development would include a new city hall and other government and cultural facilities. Along with many other recommendations in the Bartholomew report, the civic centre never came about. The Depression intervened to frustrate such grandiose plans. Still, several of the proposals were followed in the end,

During Babe Ruth's visit to the city in 1926, Mayor Taylor backstops the Yankee slugger on stage at the Pantages Theatre. Police chief H. W. Long plays umpire. VPL 22436

including the layout of major streets, the construction of the Burrard Street Bridge, and the distribution of city parks.

v

As significant as amalgamation and the Town Planning Commission were, they did not top L.D.'s own list of his most important accomplishments. That precedence belonged to the creation of the Greater Vancouver Water District Board. Vancouver had been receiving its drinking water from the flanks of the North Shore mountains since 1889. That was when the privately-owned Vancouver Water Works Company harnessed the flow of the Capilano River at a small wooden dam ten kilometres upstream from its mouth and began delivering water to the city via pipes laid under the First Narrows and through Stanley Park. Early in 1892 the city purchased the water works and a few years later the Seymour River was similarly tapped. As the surrounding communities of Burnaby, South Vancouver, and Point Grey grew, they purchased their water from Vancouver. Following World War 1, the Capilano Logging Company was active in the watershed, hauling logs by rail down along the river to a mill and booming ground on Burrard Inlet. Loggers, hikers, anglers, and prospectors freely visited the watershed, and public health officials began to be concerned that human activity might contaminate the water supply. Their concern peaked in 1922 when the provincial Comptroller of Water Rights, the engineer Ernest Cleveland, submitted a report to the government warning that the water supply was at risk from logging and recommending the creation of a water board. Powerful interests both inside the government and from industry lobbied against protection and in the fall of 1924 the province, which obtained royalties from logging activity, considered leasing even more land in the watershed to be logged. This prompted a public outcry, and a threatened mutiny from within the ranks of the Liberal government. In response, the province created the Greater Vancouver Water District and named Ernest Cleveland the first Chief Commissioner. The GVWD became active in February 1926. Initially it included Vancouver, South Vancouver, and Point Grey, but over the years other municipalities joined until by 1931 it covered most of the Lower Mainland. The GVWD became owner of the water works and sold water to each participant municipality, which then sold and distributed it to consumers.[19] Under Cleveland's stewardship, the GVWD expanded public ownership of land in the watershed and protected it from industrial activity. L.D. was not directly involved in the creation of the GVWD, but he recognized the crucial importance of the preservation of a pure water source to the public health of the city and always considered the water district to be one of the high points of his years in office.

vi

In the fall of 1927, L.D. visited Seattle as a guest of the mayor to attend a banquet in honour of the American aviator, Charles Lindbergh. At the time, just six months after his solo flight across the Atlantic, Lindbergh was the most celebrated person in the world. For millions of people he embodied the courage, humility, and altruism that made up a true hero. As one of his biographers wrote, "People behaved as if Lindbergh had walked on water, not flown over it."[20] He was in Seattle with his plane, the *Spirit of St Louis*, as part of a promotional tour of all forty-eight American states. "Lindbergh has landed" was already one of the catchphrases of the twentieth century. But Lindbergh would not land in Vancouver. According to his version of their meeting, L.D. invited him, but the aviator responded, "I could only fly over the city. You have no landing field, and I would have to return to Seattle." Lindbergh advised L.D. that Vancouver would fail to capitalize on the development of commercial aviation if it did not build an airport.[21]

Aircraft had been buzzing around Vancouver since a visiting stunt pilot made the first flight in British Columbia at Richmond's Minoru Park race track on March 25, 1910. Following World War I, the development of aviation picked up speed. In 1920, the federal government had established a seaplane base at Jericho Beach, but for wheeled aircraft there was still only the rough landing strip at Minoru Park, the field that Lindbergh refused to use. L.D. returned home from their meeting determined to do something about it. With the support of city council, he appointed a special committee to plan an airport. In the meantime, council agreed to lease a field near Lansdowne race track, also on Lulu Island, to be the

The original Vancouver airport on Lulu Island, in 1929, created on L.D.'s initiative. It was replaced by a new facility at its present location on Sea Island in 1931. VPL 70491

city's interim landing field. This facility had two runways, a hangar, and a basic waiting room. Eventually council approved construction of a proper airport on Sea Island, which began receiving flights in 1931.[22]

L.D.'s enthusiasm for aviation almost cost him his life. On July 23, 1928, the day after his seventy-first birthday, he was aboard a B.C. Airways flight inaugurating passenger service between Victoria, Vancouver, and Seattle. When the Ford Trimotor in which he'd made the flight taxied to a stop at the interim airstrip, L.D. bounded out of the plane and straight into the path of one of the propellors, which was still slowly rotating. His skull was fractured and doctors had to operate to remove pieces of bone embedded in his brain. For a few hours his life hung in the balance, but by morning he was out of danger. (Late that summer the Trimotor crashed into the sea, killing all seven people on board, and B.C. Airways folded.) According to one of the surgeons, if the mayor had been half an inch taller he would have been killed. A less kindly observer was supposed to have remarked that if he'd had an ounce more brains he'd be dead. L.D. made a complete recovery and by the end of August he was back chairing city council meetings. When the next election rolled around, he was able to make good use of the incident. Thinking he was going to die, the daily papers had prepared obituaries for L.D. which included some flattering remarks about his career. He obtained these notices and delighted in reading them to his campaign audiences, especially since the papers all opposed his re-election. "Here is what they said of me when they thought I was about to die," he crowed.

Another transportation project that L.D. had supported far longer than the airport was the Second Narrows Bridge. When it opened on November 7, 1925, it was the fulfillment of one of his campaign pledges dating back to the 1909 election. The bridge had turned out to be a particularly difficult project to bring to completion, not just for L.D., but for several other mayors who had made it a priority. While private developers and all three levels of government had negotiated back and forth, the only way to travel across the harbour to the North Shore was by passenger ferry. The boats ran from the foot of Lonsdale Avenue in North Vancouver and from Ambleside and Dundarave in West Vancouver to a wharf at the foot of Carrall Street on the Vancouver waterfront, disgorging thousands of passengers into the busy downtown east side every day. But with the growth of automobile traffic, the need for a bridge became pressing. Finally, the City of Vancouver formed a consortium with North and West Vancouver and together the three municipalities built the span. Actually L.D. had had little to do with planning the final project, he just happened to be mayor when construction finished. Which was just as well for him since the bridge turned out to be a disaster. It was a wooden and iron structure with two lanes for motor vehicle traffic divided by a centre rail line. One of the spans lifted to allow ships to pass through. In order to save money, builders had installed this moveable span at the south end of the bridge instead of in the middle where the water was deeper. As a result, ships routinely struck the piers, causing expensive damages and extensive closures. The worst incident occurred in September 1930 when a huge log barge got wedged under the centre span. As the tide rose it forced the barge up against the underside of the bridge, dislodging the span and dropping it into the water. "The Bridge of Sighs," as it had become known, was out of commission for nearly four years before it was rebuilt with a new, improved lift span.

Of all the civic projects that L.D. saw to conclusion during the 1920s, the one which gave him the greatest pleasure was the agreement with the Canadian National Railway to build a new downtown hotel. He was especially proud of this deal because it showed him getting the better of one of the country's leading captains of industry. Back in 1912, when the city was making its deal with the Canadian Northern (later Canadian National) to fill in the eastern end of False Creek, the rail company agreed to build a tunnel beneath Grandview to carry track to its Main Street station. CN also agreed as part of the deal to build a 500-room hotel. During the war, the railway converted the False Creek mudflats into a main depot and railyard – the first CN train from eastern Canada arrived in Vancouver in August 1915 – but it reneged on the other promises. During L.D.'s tenure, city council authorized him to press the railway, which by then was owned by the federal government, to make good on the agreement. Initially, it refused, and the city prepared to sue. According to L.D., it was at this point that he met CN president Sir Henry Thornton and pointed out to him how many customers his railway was losing by not having a local hotel. CN spent a lot of money convincing travellers to come to Vancouver, argued L.D., but when they got to the city they stayed at the Canadian Pacific-owned Hotel Vancouver (then at the corner of Granville and Georgia streets) where CP ticket agents convinced them to travel home using the rival rail line. Whether it was

L.D. poses on the beach in 1928 with a motorcyclist who had just crossed Canada from coast to coast as a promotional stunt for an oil company. CVA, STUART THOMSON, CVA 99-1862

the force of L.D.'s argument, or the threat of a lawsuit, CN sat down to negotiate. The city offered to waive the promise of a Grandview tunnel in return for the construction of the hotel, and late in 1928, L.D. took part in the sod-turning that marked the beginning of work on a new, CN-owned, British Columbia Hotel at the corner of Burrard and Georgia.[23]

vii

L.D. always supported the expansion of the city, but he remained strongly identified with the east side. The east side was the source of his political support and, despite the fact that he lived over on Granville Street for most of his life, the east side was where he spent most of his time. His milieu was around the corner from city hall along Hastings Street where he went every day to eat lunch or conduct civic business. During the interwar period, Hastings Street between Main and Victory Square was the beating heart of the city. Of course it had its seamy side, being close to the flophouses, bars, and brothels that catered to the shifting flow of seasonal workers for whom the Downtown Eastside was a temporary home. But it also attracted a steady influx of suburbanites who came downtown on business or for shopping, or to take in a show and get a bite to eat. In their guidebook to the city, John Atkin and Michael Kluckner estimate that at this time 10,000 people arrived in this neighbourhood each day through the B.C. Electric tram station and the North Shore ferry terminal. The main attraction was Charles Woodward's giant department store, where shoppers could find all manner of goods for sale under one roof, including groceries on the legendary self-serve food floor. Speaking of the roof, that is where, in 1927, Woodward erected a twenty-five-metre replica of the Eiffel Tower as an attention-grabbing gimmick. For years the tower was topped by a revolving searchlight so powerful that it was visible from Vancouver Island. (When the light proved confusing to airplane traffic, it was replaced in 1944 by the red neon w that became such a familiar part of the cityscape that it has been designated an historic structure.)

When they got hungry, shoppers had an array of neighbourhood cafés and restaurants from which to choose. Some of these offered

The B.C. Electric Company's main terminal at the corner of Hastings and Carrall Streets during the 1920s. Interurban cars from the suburbs pulled right into the building to allow their passengers to disembark. VPL 22735

elegant surroundings of a type no longer seen in the city. Across the street from Woodward's, for example, the Bismarck Café featured an indoor fountain and music performed by a full orchestra. Down the street, the White Lunch was a less pretentious, cafeteria-style eatery whose name referred to its Whites-only service policy. The Vancouver Oyster Saloon dished up some of the best seafood in town; in 1924 it became the Only Seafood Café and is still in business. Other Hastings Street cafés from this era had names like the Wonder, the Star, the Horseshoe, and the English Kitchen. At night, East Hastings was transformed into Vancouver's "Great White Way." Neon arrived in the city during the twenties. One of the first businesses to put up a sign was Con Jones's "Don't Argue" Smoke Shop ("Don't Argue, Con Jones sells fresh tobacco"), a few doors away from the Only. Hastings Street was the original theatre district, boasting eight theatres in a four-block stretch, their marquees sparkling with "liquid light." It was the age of live vaudeville, presented courtesy of Alexander Pantages, the American impresario, who opened his first Vancouver theatre on East Hastings in 1907. By the twenties, he had sold out to Charles Royal and moved down the street opposite Woodward's to operate the Beacon. There was also the Rex, the Princess, and the Crystal, and just around the corner, the Savoy Music Hall, where Al Jolson once performed. Following World War II, the shopping and entertainment focus of the city shifted westward to the Granville Street corridor, but during the twenties and thirties, the Downtown Eastside was where the action was.

viii

By any standard, L.D.'s accomplishments during his middle terms make an impressive list. Yet they were overshadowed by another issue that preoccupied the city during the final months of his tenure. In April 1928, Alderman T.W. Fletcher, a member of the police commission, charged that members of the police force were receiving bribes from underworld figures. Fletcher suggested that criminal influence reached all the way to city hall and asked for a provincial royal commission to investigate. Instead, city council appointed local lawyer R.S. Lennie to look into the charges. Between April 30 and July 6, Lennie heard 180 hours of public testimony from ninety-eight witnesses, including police officers and civic officials, L.D. among them. Day after day the city was rivetted by sensational stories in the press speculating on ties between local mobsters, police, and city hall. Fletcher hired his own lawyer, the fiery former Liberal MLA Gerry McGeer. McGeer quickly made himself the centre of attention at the inquiry, lashing out at Commissioner Lennie, proclaiming that "organized lawlessness has taken charge of the town," and demanding that L.D. be removed from office.[24] McGeer was out for L.D.'s head, and though he failed to get it, he landed enough punches to leave the mayor bloodied and a little dazed.

The Lennie hearings focussed public attention on the police force, but they did not reveal anything that Vancouverites had not suspected for years. It was widely assumed that criminal elements were operating with the knowledge of police, and L.D. made no secret of his own lenient attitude toward certain types of crime. As he said on more than one occasion, he did not believe that he was elected to make Vancouver a "Sunday school town."[25] His opponents claimed that L.D.'s so-called "open city" approach was an invitation to criminals to set up shop. But L.D. explained to the Lennie inquiry that he was just facing facts. Vancouver was a port city with an understaffed police force. A certain amount of gambling and prostitution was going to occur. He was not as concerned about it as he was about "major crimes"; that is, murder and property crimes. His approach, which he stated openly, was to regulate vice crimes while at the same time committing the city's limited police resources to protecting citizens from violent crimes and tracking down serious criminals. The city's religious leaders and middle-class moral reformers could not accept L.D.'s approach. What they wanted was an all out war on vice. On the other hand, one person's vice was another's harmless recreation. Years later Nora Hendrix, a black woman (grandmother of legendary rock musician Jimi Hendrix) who lived in the Downtown Eastside, recalled that "everybody liked Mayor Taylor 'cause he was one of those kind of plain men, he looked like he was for everybody."

> And he had the town fixed so that the sporting people
> lived in one part of the town and the other class of people
> lived in another. He had them all separated. And they had
> a red-light district, you see? That was what a lot of people

liked about Taylor, having this red-light district, because
it did help to keep the people, you know, the what-you-
m'a-call women was all in this one category. And when the
boats come in, when those fellows want to go somewhere
for a good time, well they knew where to go. See, they'd go
to this street in this neighbourhood 'cause it was all set for
them. And the women had these houses and they had these
girls in there and they had doctors that looked after them
and all that, you see. All that was when Taylor was in.[26]

Mrs Hendrix may have given L.D. too much credit for "fixing" the
segregation of "vice" in certain neighbourhoods, but there is no question
that he saw no need to impose middle-class morality on all sections of
the city. And for this he paid a heavy political price.

As the Lennie inquiry made clear, white, middle-class Vancouver
associated crimes of vice with Chinatown and, not far away, Hogan's
Alley. Little had changed in the outside world's attitude toward
Chinatown. As before the war, it was still viewed as a centre of gambling
and prostitution, a place of immorality where drug use flourished and
white women were corrupted. At the same time, Chinese residents
were discouraged from living or doing business elsewhere in the city.
They were compared to a spreading contagion that had to be confined
so as not to infect the entire body. In 1922, Emily Murphy, an Alberta
magistrate and well-known writer under the pseudonym "Janey
Canuck," published her alarmist exposé of the drug trade, *The Black
Candle*, in which she claimed that Vancouver's Chinatown was the
headquarters for "the most powerful and wealthy criminal organization
on the American continent." Murphy argued that the drug trade was
part of a conspiracy by "the yellow race" to engineer "the downfall of
the white race" and to take control of the world.[27]

A few blocks to the south, Hogan's Alley was a dirt lane running
between Union and Prior just east of Main Street. It disappeared with the
construction of the new Georgia Viaduct, but in the 1920s and 1930s, to
outsiders at least, Hogan's Alley was synonymous with gambling joints,
blind pigs, and brothels. It was apparently named for Harry Hogan, an
Irishman who lived in the alley and hosted some of its wildest parties.
The area's criminal reputation had been confirmed in 1917 by the murder
of police chief Malcolm MacLennan just around the corner on East

The notorious Hogan's Alley in 1958. During the 1920s and 1930s this was the centre of Vancouver's after-hours nightlife. CVA, BU.P.508-53, N623-53

Georgia Street. A black, heavily-armed drug addict named Robert Tait barricaded himself in an apartment with his girlfriend. He wounded two police officers who came to the door, then shot and killed a young boy in the street. MacLennan decided to lead an assault on the apartment and he died during the gun battle. The standoff ended when Tait committed suicide. This sensational incident, featuring drugs, prostitution, race, and murder, shocked and titillated the city, and Hogan's Alley and its environs were fixed in the public imagination as the centre of Vancouver lowlife. Police went there in their off-hours to gamble and drink, and it was widely believed that bribes were paid so that they would tolerate the illegal nightlife.

As is so often the case, the people who actually lived in the neighbourhood knew a different Hogan's Alley. Former B.C. Supreme Court judge Angelo Branca grew up nearby. "One or two murders took place in Hogan's Alley," he recalled, "but you could go down through there alone at night and no one would ever touch you." Peter Battistoni, whose father ran a bakery in the neighbourhood, thought that most of the trouble was caused by outsiders who came "slumming." "There was every kind of people there, Hindus and Negroes and white people. And, funny you know, they're all good in a way. They wouldn't steal from you, and if they could give you something, they would. Most of the evil would come from the outside, actually, into this alley looking for something different."[28]

In the mid to late 1920s, Vancouver had about 500 female prostitutes employed on the streets or in brothels in hotels and bawdy houses or in rooms above legitimate businesses. Police carried out periodic raids on the "disorderly houses" and tried to confine them within certain areas. On occasion they leaned on troublesome pimps to leave town. Fines were treated by operators more or less as a business tax, as was the protection money paid to police. A typical operation was one run by Kiyoko Tanaka-Gota out of upstairs rooms in a hotel on West Hastings. She was a picture bride who came to B.C. for an arranged marriage. After working as a farmhand and laundress in the Gulf Islands for a few years, she moved into Vancouver and invested in a blind pig (an illegal drinking joint) on Powell Street. In 1927, she leased the hotel and installed a dozen prostitutes in the rooms, keeping thirty percent of the proceeds. "Those days you could get a white woman for $2 and a Japanese woman for anywhere from $3 to $5," she recalled.

The Japanese women cost more because they were more in demand. At first I hired someone to look after the business because I didn't know anything about it, but after a year I knew how to run it myself. My job was mainly being friendly with customers and with the police. If a policeman wanted a woman I arranged it for him. And of course they didn't pay, I paid the girls, but it's cheaper than getting arrested. And then I had to check our customers to make sure they didn't have a disease the women could get.

L.D.

Tanaka-Goto remained in business until she was interned with other Japanese at the start of World War II.[29]

There were many small-time bootleggers, pimps, and gamblers known to police, but public attention focussed on Joe Celona, dubbed both the "King of the Bootleggers" and the "King of the Bawdy Houses" in the local press. Celona, who was born in Italy in 1898, arrived in Vancouver shortly after the war and began to establish himself as "the mayor of East Hastings," as one newspaper columnist called him.[30] Testimony at the Lennie inquiry identified Celona as the owner of a brothel on Keefer Street "where several young white girls received Chinamen." According to one police detective, Celona had boasted about his friendship with L.D., to whose campaigns he allegedly contributed, and warned the detective that he would be fired if he interfered with Celona's business. This may well have been bluster; certainly it was never proved. L.D. claimed that he bought cigars from Celona's shop, a block from city hall, but did not know about his other businesses, a claim that stretches credulity. If L.D. was ignorant of Celona's reputation, he must have been the only person in the city who was.

Though hearsay linking L.D. to underworld characters was rife during the Lennie inquiry, it remained just that, hearsay. At no time did Lennie find that L.D. ever accepted a bribe himself, and nowhere was there evidence that the mayor had interfered on behalf of a specific felon. There was no question of him being charged with influence peddling or some other crime, or even resigning. Still, the Lennie inquiry was a disaster for L.D. In his final report, the commissioner identified the mayor's "so-called open policy" as one of the root causes of "demoralization and inefficiency" in the police force. Testimony had made it clear that officers believed there were instructions from the

154

mayor's office not to be overly concerned with vice crimes. As a result, concluded Lennie, the force was confused about its role. There were other problems as well. Evidence was clear that officers were taking bribes, that the force did not have enough members, and that salaries were low compared to other jurisdictions, all factors contributing to low morale. Lennie also found that the Police Commission was doing a poor job of supervising the force. The Lennie report can only be seen as an indictment of L.D.'s lax administration of police affairs. It didn't matter that one RCMP inspector told the inquiry that as far as he was concerned, Vancouver "is one of the cleanest seaports that I have ever been in, so far as crime, serious crime, is concerned." The overall impact of the inquiry was to reveal a police force that appeared to be incompetent and corrupt and a civic administration that was soft on crime.

ix

In the fall of 1928, L.D. was up for re-election. Not surprisingly, his opponent, the grocery tycoon William Malkin, focussed his campaign on the Lennie report and the issue of police corruption generally. The problem, said Malkin, was not with the individual police officer. The problem was L.D., his lax attitude toward vice and his interference with the operations of the force.

> You all read the report of the police enquiry. You know
> what awful things are going on. We as parents want the
> streets of this city to be safe for our children. We know this
> is a seaport, and that certain things do go on in seaports;
> but the kind of thing which was going on here was a
> disgrace to us, and the chief disgrace was the disintegration
> of the police force. . . .
> Conditions of this kind came to pass because Mr Taylor had
> lost his vision, lost his idea of what law and order should be
> in a seaport town.[31]

L.D. had little to say in his own defence. The 1928 election was not his finest hour. Sensing he was in trouble, he resorted to personal abuse.

Enjoying one of the perks of the job, Mayor Taylor judges contestants at the 1928 Jantzen Knitting Mills Bathing Beauty Contest at English Bay. He can be seen in the back row in front of the flag standing beside a woman holding aloft a trident. VPL 9463

He accused Malkin of receiving support from the Ku Klux Klan, which attempted to establish itself in the city during the twenties. It was a hypocritical charge, coming from somone who early in his career had courted the extreme anti-Asiatic vote, and completely untrue. L.D. also claimed that he had been offered a bribe by Malkin supporters to withdraw from the election. He said Malkin was an elitist because he drove a Packard, that he was a tool of eastern capitalists, that his grocery business sold produce grown in the United States. In other words, he stayed as far away as he could from the issues.

Age may also have been a factor in the election. At seventy-one, L.D. was eleven years older than Malkin. As voters watched their veteran mayor slowly recover from the head injury he sustained at the airport, they may have decided that he was getting too frail for the job. Furthermore, Malkin was a pillar of the local establishment, a patron of the arts, owner of a successful business. Amalgamation was set to take effect at the beginning of 1929. If voters were looking for someone to run a vastly expanded civic administration with all the complexities that it would bring, they might naturally have opted for the prosperous merchant rather than the failed publisher. Another factor was the revised electoral arrangements that came with amalgamation. The new city was divided into twelve wards. L.D. did not like the ward system, believing that aldermen who were elected locally did not always keep the good of the entire city in mind. Nonetheless, the system was retained, at least for the time being. The three downtown wards and the Hastings neighbourhood remained more or less the same. Otherwise, the city was divided longitudinally into eight strips running across the peninsula to the Fraser. Results of the 1928 election showed that L.D. and Malkin ran neck and neck in the old city, that L.D. outpolled his opponent in the predominantly working-class South Vancouver wards, but that Malkin, who lived in Point Grey, trounced L.D. in the new western districts.

The most important issue, however, the one that more than any other caused L.D.'s defeat, was police corruption. It was the first plank in Malkin's platform and the constant headline in the daily press. The election, said Malkin, who was supported by an anti-vice group called the Christian Vigilance League, was a fight for "clean government." His first act as mayor would be to "purify" the police force. The mayor's office was under the influence of "a vicious professional vice ring," charged the *Sun*. L.D.'s administration of the police was "a scandal and a shame," proclaimed the *Province*. Everyone seemed to agree that hoodlums ruled the streets while venal politicians looked the other way. In the end, the surprise is not that L.D. lost but that he came as close as he did to winning.

L.D.

X

In 1924, L.D. had gotten back in touch with his elder son Ted. He had not seen or heard from either of his boys for several years. Kenneth lived with his mother, Annie, in Hollywood and worked as an editor at the *Los Angeles Times*. Ted, who was also a journalist, had been married to his high school sweetheart, but that marriage ended in divorce. Early in 1925, Ted moved to Paris to work on the English-language *Paris Times*. He wrote to his father that he had just married for a second time, to nineteen-year-old Mary Beaton. This marriage turned out tragically. Not long after they arrived in Paris, Mary died in childbirth. The baby, a daughter named Mary Louise, after her paternal grandfather, survived. Ted was devastated by the death of his young wife, whom he had adored. He returned to California with his daughter and began a successful career as a movie publicist, but he never remarried.

Two months after L.D.'s 1928 election defeat, his first wife died in an accident in Hollywood. Ted wrote to his father that Annie had been walking on Santa Monica Boulevard and had stepped off the sidewalk in front of an approaching streetcar. At the last moment she had jumped aside into the path of an automobile, which had knocked her down. Severely injured, she lingered in hospital for ten days, then died four days before Christmas. L.D. did not attend the funeral, though he paid for the cremation. In a generous letter to his sons, he blamed himself for the failure of the marriage, saying he had been too much of a loner to be a good husband. "Yes, she was a good mother, and brought you boys up with a hard struggle," he told them. There were no recriminations, and no mention of Annie's drug dependency.[32]

Early in 1929, L.D. left Vancouver for an around-the-world trip, paid for by public subscription from a grateful electorate who might reasonably have supposed that their ex-mayor was sailing off into the sunset. After all, he was a septuagenarian who had recently been on

L.D. with his two sons, Ted (left) and Ken, during one of their visits to B.C. VPL 12601

death's doorstep. He had served more terms as mayor (six) than anyone before or since. He had accomplished in his last terms many of the things he had been advocating since before the War. Surely a peaceful second retirement was the logical ending to a productive career. But if they supposed this, then despite all the years they had been voting for him, they didn't know Louis Taylor at all.

L.D.

A Mayor for the Depression 5

L.D.'s round-the-world excursion lasted several weeks. "He rode rickshaws in China, elephants in India, camels in Egypt and plane from Paris to London. . . . In Rome he was received by the Pope, and in Ireland he took the precaution of kissing the Blarney Stone. In London he had a wonderful time, for there were many prominent people who wished to return the hospitality they had received in Vancouver."[1] Returning home from this hectic schedule of globetrotting, L.D. hardly caught his breath before he set out on another trip, this time a wilderness adventure with his younger son Ken. In July 1929, they were travelling down the Parsnip River in northern B.C. when, for the second time in a year, L.D. had a near-fatal accident. Ken described the incident in a letter to his brother. Accompanied by a sixteen-year-old guide named Bill Fowler, father and son were navigating the river in a 8.5-metre flat-bottomed boat powered by an outboard motor. A strong current swept the boat into the branches of an overhanging tree. Ken, who was standing in the bow wielding a pole, was knocked into the water, and moments later the boat capsized. L.D. managed to hang onto the upturned hull which was carried downstream for half a kilometre before it wedged up against a log jam. Ken and Fowler got to shore and ran along the bank in pursuit of the drifting boat. Fowler reached L.D. first, just as the old man was sinking in the frozen water. He hauled him out and got a fire going to warm everyone. Before too long a Hudson's Bay Company freighter happened by and carried the castaways south to Fort McLeod. Once again, L.D. had cheated death.[2]

Before the year was out, L.D. was away on another trip, this time to his hometown of Ann Arbor, Michigan. In an interview that he gave to the local newspaper there, he said that it was the first time he had been back since he left for Chicago in 1881. The interviewer treated him as something of a celebrity, a "local boy made good," as L.D. reminisced about helping to set type by hand at the *Ann Arbor Courier* when he was a boy, and about working at the university library as a young man. The newspaper made no mention of the circumstances under which he had fled to Canada. L.D. revealed that he was on his way to a family reunion in nearby Lansing where his mother lived for several years before her death. Apparently, within the family, his Chicago indiscretions had been forgiven, overshadowed by the success he had made in his new life.[3]

L.D.

i

L.D. returned from Michigan to a Vancouver that was showing early signs of the deep economic crisis that gripped the world. The stock market crash at the end of October had signalled an end to the prosperity of the twenties. At first it looked like just another recession, but as the international economic system crumbled and the numbers of unemployed multiplied, it dawned on people that something much more serious was going on. British Columbia was particularly vulnerable because its economy relied so heavily on the sale of natural resources to international markets. As the demand for B.C. lumber, minerals, fish, and fruit dried up, local business slowed to a crawl. The first sign of hard times was widespread unemployment in the city. Winter always brought an increase in the number of jobless, but during the winter of 1929–1930 they poured into the city in an unprecedented flood. To the seasonally unemployed were added thousands of transients who left their homes east of the Rockies to look for work and ended up in Vancouver because it was the end of the line. "Vancouver is, of course, the Mecca of the unemployed from the interior of our province and also from the Prairie provinces," a government official wrote. "They are attracted here by milder weather conditions and the prospects of obtaining some kind of work throughout the Winter."[4] Relief offices were besieged by the jobless and bread lines snaked along the sidewalks outside soup kitchens and hostels. Unable to afford accommodation, the truly destitute built

162

Feeding the homeless at one of Vancouver's hobo jungles in 1931. The food was organized by United Church minister Andrew Roddan (standing centre-right in a white hat looking at the camera).

CVA, W.J. MOORE, RE N4.3

their own. Camps of squatters sprang into existence behind the CN train station, underneath the Georgia Viaduct, on the Burrard Inlet waterfront at the foot of Dunlevy and around the False Creek flats. Reverend Andrew Roddan, minister at First United Church, described these "hobo jungles" as "composed of crude shelters, made out of old tins, boards, boxes, disused motorcars, anything and everything, gathered from the dump heap nearby and formed into rough shelters."[5]

A reporter from the *Province* visited one east side jungle where about 100 men had set themselves up next to an automobile dump. The men were using the rusted car bodies as bunkhouses. "One chap has rigged a shelter for himself out of the bodies of two old Ford cars, one turned upside down on top of the other, with a piece of canvas top thrown over to keep off the rain." The reporter saw rats as big as kittens scuffling through the refuse. The men obtained water from stagnant ponds, foraged for food in the dump, and begged for handouts in the downtown streets. When Roddan heard about these places he began making daily visits with donated food and organized a supply of fresh water.[6] "If you could see what I saw!" recalled Shinichi Hara, who arrived in the city in March 1930. "People hungry and dying down on the beach. Three stakes and a sack, that was home for them. You just went down to the foot of Dunlevy Avenue where Hastings Mill used to be, and there were lots of them, both ways. Hungry people. And then the trouble in the city started. People had iron bars, they broke windows at Woodward's and everyone went in and helped themselves. You see, they had no jobs and no food, and the police couldn't do anything with so many – a whole city! And the garbage cans: on Hastings Street, Granville Street, people ate from them. I saw a mother with a baby pull out some chicken bones, set them on the garbage lid and right away three, four kids were standing around eating chicken bones."[7]

If the presence of so many indigents living in such squalor scandalized some people, it panicked police and city officials. They blamed the jobless for a wave of crime that supposedly swept across the city early in 1930. Made desperate by hunger, the unemployed engaged in holdups, housebreaking, and petty thievery. Or so the police maintained. Just as important, authorities worried that Communists were finding fertile ground among the transient jobless for their revolutionary theories. The Unemployed Workers' Association, a Communist-led organization, had an office in the city and its activists began mounting street parades

L.D.

and demonstrations to demand jobs and relief. They were met with stiff resistance from police who alleged that most of the disturbances were led by "agitators" from out-of-province who "want $4.50 a day [i.e., union pay rates] and nothing to do for it."

In mid-December, a group of unemployed occupied the relief office on Cambie Street before holding an unauthorized march through the streets, waving placards that read "Work, Not Sympathy" and "What did we win the war for?" A couple of protesters were arrested, one of whom was held for deportation.[8] Following a brief Christmas break, demonstrations resumed in the New Year. Historian Margaret Ormsby called January 1930 "unlike any previous month in the history of the city" because of the unrest that convulsed the streets.[9] A series of marches and protests culminated in a mass demonstration attended by about 300 people at the Powell Street Grounds (now Oppenheimer Park) on the last Monday of the month. Police chief W.J. Bingham, a former London bobby who had been hired as part of the purge that followed the Lennie report, deployed 120 officers to keep an eye on the demonstration. When protestors began to march out of the grounds in defiance of Bingham's order not to, the police set upon them with whips and truncheons. Justifying his actions, Bingham, who described himself as "a friend of labour, an uncompromising enemy to Communism, and always a champion of the under dog," claimed that the leaders intended to march to Granville Street to smash storefront windows. The police could not be expected "to stand by like a puppy," he said.[10] When the dust settled, seven militants were in custody. Four who were identified as Communists were charged with unlawful assembly and released on bail. The four men faced a possible year in prison if convicted. At their trial in March, they were unrepentant, using their appearance in the witness box to proclaim the plight of the jobless. The jury found all four guilty but recommended mercy, and the judge handed down suspended sentences.

L.D. had inserted himself into the debate early in January when he submitted an article to the *Sun* in which he attacked the Board of Police Commisioners for mismanaging the police force. L.D. was still hurting from the loss handed to him by voters in the previous election. He felt that he had been unfairly blamed for the rot in the police department, that he had been slandered in the press as a friend of the city's crime bosses. He wanted to remind voters that the situation with the police was no better under the new civic administration, perhaps worse. "Too much effort and time have been given to petty vice," he argued, sounding a familiar theme. "Notwithstanding the statements made from time to time at commission meetings that vice has been eradicated, it is far more prevalent now than it ever was, while major crimes are on the increase." L.D. blamed the sinister influence of Gerry McGeer who, *L.D.* because he took such a prominent role in the Lennie hearings, had become something of a *bête noir* for the ex-mayor. McGeer, said L.D., had forced changes on the police force of a type and at a pace that the force could not accommodate. "It has come to a pretty pass when no citizen is safe on our streets." And what about the unemployed protests? Instead of being sympathetic, as his past record would have suggested, L.D. wanted to know who was responsible for allowing parades to be held in defiance of the law.[11] L.D.'s intervention brought a stinging rebuke from the *Province* in an editorial titled "Our Libelled City." Not mentioning him by name, the paper attacked "the old, discredited administration and the old, defeated regime" for spreading misinformation about the police and the local government. Things were much better under Mayor Malkin, asserted the paper, which almost accused L.D. of plotting a civic *coup d'etat*. "It is not good enough, in order that a discredited gang should seize the reins of civic government again, that Vancouver should be placarded throughout the country as the scene of a criminal reign of terror, and it is not good enough that a conscienceless campaign of misrepresentation should succeed."[12]

L.D.'s outburst and the responses to it were a bit of a sideshow. He had the next election in view and was jockeying for political advantage. The main issue was the plight of the poor and jobless in the city. Mayor Malkin was in an unenviable position. His administration was responsible for dispensing relief to the unemployed, but did not have the resources to do so. Public assistance took two forms, either work relief or direct relief. Work relief provided menial labour at different projects around the city in return for a "wage" of two dollars a day for married men, a dollar for single men.[13] (During 1930, the rate fell to seven dollars for a six-day work week regardless of marital status.) This rate of pay was less than half the average daily wage of four dollars for an employed worker, and well below the cost of living. Work relief was very expensive because it encouraged municipalities to embark on public works, thereby placing a heavy burden on their treasuries. Work relief was appealing ideologically – it encouraged honest labour and provided the dignity of a "real" job, even if that job was digging ditches or clearing brush – but by 1932 it had fallen out of favour and direct relief had become the preferred form of public assistance. Direct relief included a cash payment (which varied year to year and depending on marital status and the number of dependents) along with supplements for fuel, rent, and other necessaries. Authorities worried that direct relief sapped the initiative of recipients and encouraged malingering, but the fact of the matter was that it was cheaper than providing jobs on public works.

The cities looked to the senior levels of government to help bear the cost of unemployment relief, but cost-sharing arrangements were a source of antagonism throughout the Depression. Whenever they could, the provincial and federal governments passed the buck. Meeting a delegation of mayors from western cities in February 1930, Prime Minister Mackenzie King told them that unemployment was not really a problem and to the extent that it was, it was their problem, not his. He suggested they approach their provincial governments for help. For King, all the talk of unemployment relief was simply an attempt by his Conservative opponents to embarrass him. In the House of Commons, the prime minister infamously declared that he "would not give a single cent" for relief to any Conservative provincial government. The voters punished King by tossing him out of office in that July's election. The new Conservative government of R.B. Bennett immediately passed an act providing $20 million for the jobless, most of it to be spent on public works. The money was funnelled through the provinces to the municipalities, each of whom was required to top up the fund with its own contribution. But the legislation was administered unfairly and Vancouver, with an estimated ten percent of the country's transient unemployed, received only $220,000.[14] The federal government improved the scheme the next year, but in the meantime the numbers of unemployed continued to grow. By the beginning of 1931, the jobless rate in British Columbia reached twenty-seven percent, the highest in Canada.

L.D.

This was the situation at the end of 1930 as Mayor Malkin's first term of office drew to a close and he prepared to seek a second. L.D. announced that he would challenge Malkin in the election, which was set for December 10. By this time there was no secret about what drove him back onto the campaign trail. He liked being part of the action, he liked the limelight, he was still healthy, he had nothing better to do, and he needed the income. As well, he did not want his career to end on the sour note of the 1928 election with its charges of corruption and incompetence. It had been "a dastardly campaign," he said, and he wanted his revenge.[15]

Surprisingly, the 1930 campaign did not focus on the plight of the unemployed and the state of the city finances, both of which were desperate. Instead, the candidates argued back and forth about transit fares, water meters, a "new system" for organizing city hall, and a variety of other practical matters. Neither man gave any indication that the city was experiencing the worst economic crisis in its history, though Malkin was hurt by revelations earlier in the year that relief officer George Ireland had been taking kick-backs in return for issuing meal tickets to certain city cafes. Ireland went to jail and the incident left the impression that the relief office was poorly administered.[16]

The 1930 campaign was vintage L.D. He kept his opponent off-balance by making allegations which in the heat of the contest never had to be proved. He raised the spectre of big business controlling city hall. He portrayed himself as "a man from the masses and not a corporation man." He avoided dealing with the real issue, except in the most general terms. ("Immediate action on Relief and the Unemployed situation.")[17] And despite his age, the opposition of the local press, and his association with the crime scandals of two years earlier, he won. It was an astonishing result. "Ex-Mayor Taylor's resiliency is astounding," remarked one editorial. "Seemingly, the harder he falls, the higher he bounces."[18] Though the candidates did their best to avoid discussing the economic crisis during the campaign, voters turned out to be dissatisfied enough to think that a change was necessary. At the same time, they returned every alderman and every member of the Parks Board who ran for re-election, indicating that the mood for change was not pervasive. Perhaps L.D.'s advantage was that he offered something new while at the same time being totally familiar.

Not long after L.D. moved back into the mayor's office, police chief Bingham submitted a report on the unemployed agitation. He began by pointing out that the number of jobless on relief did not give an accurate picture of the extent of the problem. Many foreign-born were not applying for assistance, Bingham said, because the Communists had told them that once they identified themselves they would be deported. Many others were managing to subsist on the charity of strangers, either by begging or by taking advantage of free room and board that was being offered at sympathetic hotels and lodging houses. Bingham went on to blame outside agitators for the unrest in the streets.

> While there are a great many social evils that demand the
> very closest attention, it would appear that these agitators
> are simply desirous of fomenting trouble. . . . They demand
> revolution. Their demands for the unemployed have
> at all times been beyond reason. . . . They have offered
> no constructive advice as to how to handle the present
> situation. They merely ridicule all efforts that are made.

Nonetheless, "except for an occasional riot, which the leaders own verbosity demands that they stage at intervals," the chief constable reported that the Communists were making little headway among the unemployed and the police had matters well in hand.[19]

On the same day as he submitted his report, Bingham banned all public meetings and parades without a permit. As if to challenge the chief, the end of January saw another mass demonstration, this one downtown in Victory Square. Originally the site of the provincial courthouse, this urban park was developed in the 1920s using money provided by the Southam family, owners of the *Province*. With the addition of the Cenotaph in 1924, the square became a popular public gathering place and, in the thirties, the focus of unemployed protests. On this occasion, the police waded in with clubs swinging, dispersed the crowd, and arrested ten men. L.D. was unnerved. He released a public statement making clear that protest had its limits.

> It is not the intention of civic authorities that business
> of merchants in any district in the city shall be further

interfered with by congestion . . . caused by parades or demonstrations of any sort. Police have instructions to preserve order and stop all unauthorized gatherings. In this connection I wish to state the authorities are not desirous of suppressing free speech.

L.D.   Anyone wishing to hold a meeting had to apply to the police for a permit. Meetings would be confined to the Powell Street Grounds and "no street parades will be tolerated."[20] Having laid down the gauntlet, L.D. hurried to Victoria to ask the attorney general to provide officers from the B.C. Provincial Police to assist the civic police at all public demonstrations. For as long as he had been in politics, L.D. had identified himself as a friend of "the working man," but the economic crisis was testing the limits of his support. He was sympathetic to the unemployed, but not to the Communist "agitators" who in his opinion were taking advantage of them, and he would not allow the streets and parks of the city to be overrun by protesters. As mayor, his first responsibility was to maintain social order. For once, the *Province* agreed with him.

Citizens of Vancouver will give full support to Mayor Taylor in his stout-hearted attitude on the questions of meetings of unemployed men.

The great majority of these unemployed . . . are, we believe, decent and law-abiding folk, in unfortunate circumstances and eager only to find a job. But there are others, agitators and propagandists, who are exploiting the miseries of the unemployed for their own ends. It is these who are the trouble-makers. It is these who organize the parades and plan the meetings in defiance of constituted authority. It is against these and not against the unemployed as a whole that the mayor has set his face.[21]

In mid-April 1931, a delegation of activists from across the country met with Prime Minister Bennett in Ottawa to present a petition calling for the introduction of an unemployment insurance scheme. "Never," was Bennett's response. Officials from many cities endorsed Bennett's intransigence and called on his government to deport the "Reds." Premier Tolmie wrote to the prime minister encouraging him to deport

L.D. relaxes at his apartment in this photograph by Leonard Frank, taken at Christmas, 1933.

all "foreign agitators" without a hearing of any kind; that is, without actually being convicted of any crime.[22] On August 11, the federal government declared the Communisty Party an illegal organization under the infamous Section 98 of the criminal code. Authorities began arresting leaders and deporting those who were not Canadian citizens. Conservative politicians, bereft of ideas, responded to the crisis by confusing dissent with revolution and suppressing both.

iii

L.D. kept track of these events as best he could from a hospital bed. On July 22, he had attended the official opening of the Vancouver International Airport on Sea Island in Richmond. The new facility was the culmination of a process he had put into motion four years earlier when Charles Lindbergh refused to fly into the city because it lacked a decent landing strip. A site selection committee had considered several possible locations, including the south end of the Second Narrows Bridge, but settled on Sea Island even though it was outside of city limits. Premier Tolmie came over from Victoria to officiate at the opening ceremony. All available aircraft were lined up along the single runway as a brass band played, flags flew, and a congratulatory telegram from the Prince of Wales was read to the crowd of several hundred onlookers. Dignitaries took lunch in one of the two hangars, where L.D. was presented with a diamond pin in honour of his seventy-fourth birthday and his role in getting the facility built. But airports remained unlucky for him. The next day he took to his bed with a mysterious illness. For three weeks he received treatment in his apartment at the Granville Mansions. Then, in the middle of August, he was rushed six blocks to St Paul's Hospital suffering from what was identified at the time as acute arthritis, and he remained in hospital for the entire winter. The attack left him severely weakened, unable to stand, walk, or even write his name. Very gradually his strength returned. In January, he was well enough to officiate at a city council meeting, but he did so from a reclining chair covered with a heavy grey blanket. It was his first appearance in public since he took sick. In a weak voice he swore in six new aldermen and made a short speech, all the time lying flat on his back staring at the ceiling of the council chamber. Twice he had to be revived with smelling salts. It was a sight "unique in civic annals in Canada," thought one reporter. L.D. told his council that doctors had informed him he would be able to start walking within two weeks and he expected to make a full recovery. Then he returned to hospital.[23] Although he began making visits to his office at city hall for a couple of hours a day, it was early May before he was released from St Paul's and even then he used a wheelchair for three more weeks.

While L.D. was away, city council grappled with the problem of the homeless and the unemployed. Early in September 1931, medical officer Dr H.A. McDonald reported a possible case of typhoid in one of the "hobo jungles" on the old Hastings Mill site on the shoreline of Burrard Inlet. McDonald warned that given the unhealthy living conditions in the "jungles," the city was facing a possible epidemic. He described one shantytown under the Georgia Viaduct. "There are about 250 men there. Grounds are filthy and covered with decaying garbage, with open toilets. Flies swarm over everything and on all open food." On behalf of council, Alderman W.C. Atherton fired off a telegram to provincial and federal officials outlining the situation facing the city:

> More than 15,000 registered in city [for relief]. Twenty-five hundred relief families now requiring clothing and rent. Two thousand homeless single men increasing by seventy floaters daily. One thousand men in jungles. . . . Inertness of Dominion Government in failing to control transients and in delaying decision (on relief policy) has paralyzed municipalities. Immediate action imperative.

By "controlling transients," Atherton was referring to the fact that when the city extended assistance of any kind it was immediately "penalized" by an influx of transients attracted by the extra help. Officials in Vancouver were frustrated that they were called upon to assist so many jobless people who were not residents of the city, placing an unsustainable burden on the relief budget. The jungles were particularly aggravating to officials because they provided a ready source of single men to take part in the marches and street protests. So the report of the medical officer provided a handy pretext to take action. Two days after the typhoid alarm was raised, city crews moved into the jungles and destroyed them, setting some shacks on fire and demolishing others with axes and sledge hammers. Inhabitants received tickets providing them with room and board at a hostel for four nights. City officials had hoped to wait until the province had its program of work camps up and running so that the men would have somewhere to go, but the typhoid scare prompted them to take action.[24] Later that fall the first camps did open, more or less taking care of the problem of the transient unemployed as far as civic officials were concerned. At the camps the men were put to work cutting firewood, clearing brush, and making roads and airstrips. In return, they received a bed, food, medical attention, and a cash allowance that began at a dollar a day but gradually was reduced to just twenty cents. British Columbia opened 237 of these camps, more than any other province. (In the winter of 1932–33, they were absorbed into the program of federal work camps administered by the department of national defence.)

L.D.

The opening of the work camps and the destruction of the shantytowns marked an end to the regular street demonstrations that had been taking place in the city since the end of 1929. Marches still took place from time to time, though. Early in March 1932, before L.D. was back on his feet, about 4,000 people staged a "Hunger March" from the Cambie Street Grounds down Hastings Street to protest the fact that single men were denied relief if they did not move into a camp. The march stopped outside city hall, which by this time was located in the Holden Building just east of the B.C. Electric terminus at Carrall. A small delegation went in to confront city council, but it turned out not to be meeting. When police tried to clear a path through the crowd for the streetcar, violence broke out. For forty-five minutes, protestors and police clashed. "As foot police and mounted officers with clubs swinging charged the crowd, the demonstrators fought back vigorously using the standards of their flags and banners as weapons."[25] After peace was restored, the police chief announced that no more permits would be issued for parades in the city.

"1932 and 1933 were the blackest years for Vancouver," recalled theatre manager Ivan Ackery in his memoirs. "Beggars went from house to house, looking for meals or handouts. The streets were filled with people just wandering around in despair, many past even trying to help themselves."[26] In this atmosphere of economic crisis and civil unrest, the business elite responded with its own protest against the way the province was being governed, particularly the growing provincial deficit. In the spring of 1931, a delegation of business leaders from Vancouver and Victoria, led by lumberman H.R. MacMillan, convinced Premier Tolmie that he needed their advice. Reluctantly, Tolmie appointed a five-person, blue-ribbon commission to evaluate the financial performance of the government. The commission was led by George Kidd, former president of B.C. Electric, and included financier W.L. Macken, mine owner Austin Taylor, industrialist R.W. Mayhew, and lawyer A.H. Douglas. By the end of August 1932, they had completed their work and published their report, a stunning and completely unrealistic document. Rejecting any additional taxation, it recommended that the government address the deficit by making deep cuts to expenditures. Among the Kidd Report's many proposals: reduce the size of the legislature almost by half; sell the provincial railway; slash teacher's salaries by one quarter and reduce the salaries of all public servants; stop the provincial grant to UBC, and if the university was unable to function, close it; repeal the minimum wage; reduce the number of students eligible for free high school education; stop all public works except road maintenance; eliminate mothers' allowance. The report was impatient with the messiness of party politics, as business people so often are, and recommended greater power for the lieutenant governor and the creation of a non-partisan coalition government.

Historian Robin Fisher has called the members of the Kidd Commission "Robin Hoods in reverse: they wanted to steal from the poor and give to the rich."[27] The report was roundly condemned by almost all strands of public opinion. While Tolmie was as appalled as the public, and acted on none of its recommendations, the commission was a blow to his administration and contributed to its defeat at the polls the following year. The remedies proposed by Kidd may not have been as extreme as the *British Columbia Financial Times*, which proposed that a benevolent dictatorship replace the existing form of government.[28] Nonetheless, they illustrated just how spooked the business community was by the economic crisis.

There were, of course, issues other than unemployment demanding L.D.'s attention during these troubled years. Chief among them was his own re-election in December 1932. Luckily for him, the opposition was fractured, and three other candidates chose to run. The result of this election, the last one L.D. would win, showed that his traditional support was eroding. He won a minority of the votes cast (forty percent) and his total number of votes was down thirty-four percent from two years earlier. If the popular vote had not been split four ways, L.D. might have lost. On the other hand, he managed to hold onto office in the middle of the worst economic slump the city had ever experienced. If the outcome was not a ringing endorsement for his policies, neither was it an utter rejection.

All through the thirties, the symbol of economic hard times in Vancouver was the British Columbia Hotel. L.D. had broken ground on this CNR-owned project at the corner of Georgia and Burrard in December 1928. But once the depression hit, CN halted work on the hotel. For ten years, the building's unfinished iron skeleton loomed above the city streets, a visible reminder that life had gone out of the local construction industry. (It was May 1939 before the hotel was completed and opened its doors as the third incarnation of the Hotel Vancouver.) Still, the city was not completely moribund during L.D.'s final terms in office. One project that did go ahead was the Burrard Street Bridge, which had been proposed by the Bartholomew Report as a necessary link between the downtown peninsula and the newly-absorbed suburban neighbourhoods of Point Grey. It opened on July 1, 1932. At its south end the bridge set down on land that once was part of the Kitsilano Indian Reserve.

When the first Europeans entered False Creek, they found the waterfront village of Snauq, or Sun'ahk, tucked in behind what came to be called Kitsilano Point. Snauq was home to several dozen Squamish people who fished the waters of the Creek and harvested wildfowl and other game along its marshy shoreline. In 1870, the colonial government granted the Squamish a fifteen-hectare reserve around Snauq, which was enlarged by the Joint Indian Reserve Commission in 1876 to take in most of the point. After the turn of the century, as the city expanded south across False Creek, white residents realized the value of the

Looking south up Burrard Street at the looming iron skeleton of the third Hotel Vancouver in 1931. A symbol of the moribund economic times, it did not open until May 1939. VPL 5695

Kitsilano Reserve and the provincial government put pressure on the original inhabitants to relocate. In 1913, the province made a deal with about two dozen Squamish people who were living at the reserve. Each person received $11,250 in return for moving away from their homes. In total the Squamish received about $218,000 for the reserve. The two negotiators who arranged the deal each received a fee of $39,625.[29]

L.D.

The families were removed on a scow and their homes were burned. Neither the Squamish band nor the federal government endorsed the transaction, and the province failed to obtain the necessary formal land surrender.

Nonetheless, various other parties used the land. In 1928, the province assigned its interest in the reserve to the federal government with the proviso that when Ottawa disposed of the land on behalf of the Squamish it would pay the province $350,000. Soon after, the city approached the federal government about purchasing the reserve so that it could be used as a park. On March 24, 1929, the chiefs of the Squamish band agreed that they would sell the reserve to the city for $750,000, which included the money owed to the province. This was more than the city wanted to pay, plus it hoped to convince the province to waive its $350,000 claim, so the deal was put on hold pending further negotiations. This is where the matter stood when L.D. became mayor, and he had no better luck getting the province to make a decision than his predecessor had. Meanwhile, the Burrard Bridge needed to use a small portion of the reserve. A three-person arbitration board was established, and after hearing representations it concluded that the city should pay $44,966 to the Squamish people for the 3.25 hectares of land required for the bridge, minus expenses of $28,854. Meanwhile, individual non-Aboriginal property owners at the north end of the bridge were paid anywhere up to $125,000 for their properties.[30]

At the official opening of the new bridge, L.D. snipped a ribbon with a pair of golden scissors, then climbed into the first car to cross the span. It was a heady day for a city that had not had much good news of late. "This bridge is the advertisement of Vancouver, to her own people and to all the world, that she has not lost her faith or diminished her pride," declared the *Province*.[31] L.D. reminded his audience, including August Jack Khahtsahlano, who had been born at Snauq fifty-five years previous, that he had first proposed a Burrard Street crossing during the 1911 election. At that time the project had not received much support, Point Grey not having joined the city yet, but L.D. had continued to press for the bridge over the years. (Getting the Indian reserve lands into city hands was a more difficult piece of business, one that was only concluded long after L.D. had retired when the city, in 1966, signed a long-term lease with Ottawa for what is now Vanier Park. The fate of the Kitsilano Reserve was finally resolved in 2000 when the Squamish people voted to accept a $92.5 million settlement with the federal government.)

L.D. played an even more direct role in the completion of the Lions Gate Bridge, the most ambitious construction project in Vancouver during the Depression. The Lions Gate was the brainchild of another Taylor, Fred Taylor, a Victoria-born engineer with ties to wealthy business interests in England. It was Fred Taylor's idea to attract British investment to develop real estate on the slopes of the North Shore mountains in West Vancouver, the future British Properties. As part of his plan, he promoted a bridge across Burrard Inlet at the First Narrows, the "Lions Gate."[32] A First Narrows crossing had been on the public agenda since the mid-1920s when two competing plans received approval from the provincial government. In 1927, during L.D.'s middle terms, the city held a plebiscite asking ratepayers if they approved the construction of a roadway through Stanley Park to provide access to a privately-financed bridge. At this point the public saw no need for a second crossing to a sparsely-populated North Shore (the Second Narrows Bridge had opened two years earlier), and the plebiscite was defeated. But in mid-September 1930, a log barge struck the centre span of the Second Narrows, putting it out of commission for four years. Suddenly Vancouver was cut off from its North Shore suburbs (except for the passenger ferry) and the First Narrows project got new life. By this time the two construction consortiums had merged to form the First Narrows Bridge Company. In London, Fred Taylor and his partners interested the Guinness brewing family in the project. Taylor created British Pacific Properties Ltd to develop about 1,620 hectares of residential real estate in West Vancouver and BPP purchased controlling interest in the bridge company. By the fall of 1933, Taylor had approval for his project from the province and from the North Shore municipalities. But he needed the go-ahead from Vancouver.

A majority of council supported the bridge project, including L.D., but at a stormy council meeting on November 9, two aldermen balked at giving city approval. L.D. was livid. He accused the two of colluding with the CPR to oppose the plan in order to keep up the value of the rail company's Vancouver real estate holdings. In the end, council decided to put the matter to a plebiscite, paid for by the bridge company. During the debate that followed L.D. stumped vigorously for the bridge. Opponents argued that the proposed causeway would ruin Stanley Park, that the bridge would make shipping dangerous by narrowing the entrance to the harbour, that the span was not wide enough, that tolls would line the pockets of the bridge company. An editorial in the *Sun* perfectly captured the contentious nature of the debate when it dismissed these arguments as "frivolous and vexatious, stupid and inconsequential." In the end, city voters overwhelmingly approved the bridge. L.D. hailed the result as a victory for "work, not relief." For him, as for the voters, the bridge meant jobs for the unemployed and a renewed confidence in the future. "The period of dry rot is at an end tonight, I'm sure," he announced.[33]

The Vancouver plebiscite removed the last local roadblock to the First Narrows bridge. But the federal government still had to sign off on the project, and as long as R.B. Bennett was prime minister and under the influence of the CPR, federal approval was held up. Finally, Bennett's government fell in the election of October 23, 1935 and the following April the new, Liberal government endorsed the bridge. Work began on the last day of March 1937, when crews toppled the first trees along the right-of-way for the causeway through Stanley Park. The bridge opened to car traffic in November 1938, and was officially opened on May 26, 1939 when a procession of dignitaries crossed to the British Properties for a small ceremony at the Capilano Golf Club. By this time L.D. was long gone from the mayor's office and his part in the struggle to get the bridge built was mostly forgotten.

Another project that originated during L.D.'s tenure but came to fruition after he was gone was a new city hall. In a string of plebiscites dating back to 1912, ratepayers had shown their inclination to have a purpose-built city hall to replace the original site in the old market building near Hastings and Main. Because successive city councils could not come to an agreement about where to locate a new building, or whether the time was right to build one, the issue remained unresolved. In the 1923 civic election, for example, voters had been asked to approve a bylaw authorizing the purchase of the Tower Building, originally the World Building, so that it could be converted for municipal use.

Ironically, since he had been responsible for constructing the building, L.D. opposed this measure, arguing that renovations would be too costly. The voters agreed and defeated the bylaw. (This episode reflects well on L.D. as a frugal administrator; he must have realized that if he endorsed the Tower site, and it became city hall, it would have been a permanent shrine to his career as mayor.) The market building was too small and threatening to fall down, but year after year nothing was done. With amalgamation in 1929, council agreed to move westward along Hastings Street to leased accommodations in the Holden Building. Named for prominent realtor William Holden, who built it in 1911, this structure, now the Tellier Tower, was located in the heart of the bustling East Hastings business district. It remained the interim city hall into the next decade.

The middle of the Depression seems an unlikely time for the city hall project to get new life, but amalgamation had focussed attention on the need to construct a monumental building that would celebrate the new, enlarged city. In a 1933 plebiscite, voters chose Thornton Park near the CN train station and the head of False Creek as the preferred site.[34] When this location turned out to have serious engineering problems, city council decided to build downtown next door to Victory Square, and another plebiscite during the 1934 civic election approved an expenditure of $630,000 for this site. During the campaign, L.D. opted for a stay-put policy, arguing that the city could not afford an expensive new building. His opponent, Gerry McGeer, insinuated that L.D. was dragging his feet on the issue because his friend William Holden was receiving $30,000 a year in rent. In the end, L.D. lost the election and his opinion did not matter. The newly-elected McGeer moved ahead quickly to win approval for a new city hall in a location that he preferred. He issued bonds to raise money locally for the building and, ignoring previous plebiscites, appointed his own commission to select a site. Not surprisingly, the commission chose Strathcona Park, McGeer's favoured site, across False Creek from downtown on Cambie Street at 12th Avenue. City council endorsed the choice. Once again, the backroom machinations of the CPR were at work. Strathcona Park had never been selected as a site in any of the plebiscites, and the decision sparked a public outcry, but the rail company wanted the site, expecting that it would stimulate the development of its land holdings in South Vancouver, and what the CPR wanted the CPR usually got. Years later, L.D. revealed that during his

A view of the council chambers in the Holden Building when it served as city hall.

last year as mayor a CPR official twice lobbied him to use his influence to make sure that Strathcona Park was the chosen site. "I told him that if the city hall was to be built it would be on a site that the ratepayers decided on and not chosen by the CPR," said L.D.[35] The job of designing the new hall was handed, without competition, to Fred Townley, an old friend of McGeer's. The new mayor had beaten L.D. in a campaign that condemned cronyism and preferential treatment. Yet one of his first acts in office reeked of arrogant favouritism.

V

During the Depression, L.D. was a fierce opponent of the Communists, who he believed were taking advantage of the unemployed. But he remained, in his own eyes, a friend of the working person. At least twice during his second term he used his influence as mayor to intervene in a labour dispute on behalf of the workers. The first occasion was in 1934 when the B.C. Electric Railway Company, which ran the city's streetcar system, announced that it would be cutting wages. In response, the street railway workers decided to go out on strike, but as the deadline approached, a delegation of workers asked L.D. to get involved. The city had an obvious interest in maintaining streetcar service, but also in avoiding any more jobless protestors taking to the streets. He invited BCER president William Murrin to a meeting at his apartment where L.D. revealed that the workers had agreed to stay on the job if the company would postpone the wage cut. According to L.D., he applied a little arm-twisting to the discussion, hinting that if there was an interruption in service the city might legalize jitneys once again and warning that in the event of trouble the police would not be available to protect company property. Murrin agreed to the deal brokered by L.D. and the streetcars kept running.[36]

Later that year, loggers on Vancouver Island went on strike for higher wages. Several hundred of them arrived in Vancouver where their leaders approached L.D. about allowing them to hold a tagday in the city. The mayor gave permission after he got the loggers to promise that no "outside radicals" would take part. The loggers sold tags on the streets and raised $3,700 to help support the members of their union during the strike. When L.D. allowed a second tagday, the B.C. Loggers Association, a group of the largest employers, went on the offensive. It put local journalist and red-baiter Tom MacInnes on the radio to discredit the strikers. But L.D. was sympathetic to the loggers' cause. He booked his own radio time to rebut MacInnes. The next day the strikers raised another $2,700 selling tags, then gave up the fight and went back to the camps to work.[37]

vi

As if L.D. did not have enough on his plate running the city, he decided in the fall of 1933 to run as a candidate in the provincial election called by Premier Tolmie for November 2. Though Duff Pattullo's Liberals were poised to win a landslide victory, and L.D. had been a lifelong supporter of the party, he chose to run as an independent in the northern riding of Omineca, west and northwest of Prince George, where his main opponent was the former Liberal cabinet minister Alex Manson. Taylor stood no chance of winning. He was unknown in the riding, whereas Manson had held the seat in the legislature since 1916. Apparently it was a grudge match. Animosity had built up between the two men during the twenties when L.D. felt that Manson, who was attorney general, was ignoring issues related to the city. L.D. hoped to steal enough votes to deprive Manson of victory. The mayor arrived from Vancouver at his headquarters in Vanderhoof to discover that local campaign organizers had failed to file his nomination papers properly. With twenty minutes to go before the deadline, one of his assistants had to go into the street to ask ten strangers to sign the document. Bruce Hutchison, who was then a young reporter for the *Province*, came to Omineca in the middle of a raging blizzard and left with a vivid impression of the campaign, which he called "the most picturesque fight in the whole election." "They like L.D. up in this country," Hutchison wrote. "They regard him as a big man from the metropolis, a power in the land. But they won't vote for him, at least not many of them." Hutchison attended one of L.D.'s meetings, which was chaired by his campaign manager, "a man more seedy than the rest, unshaved, unwashed, and taciturn, but wearing a greenish bowler hat, his badge of respectability." At campaign gatherings

A Leonard Frank portrait of L.D. in 1933 wearing his trademark red tie and clutching the ubiqui-tous cigar. VPL 12604

in the country, speeches were just an excuse to have a party. Once L.D., whom Hutchison described as "a wizened relic of his early days," was finished, his campaign manager pulled out a concertina from beneath the table and began to play.

L.D.

> He pumped long past midnight, while the audience
> danced, the eminent Mayor of Vancouver forgotten.
> In the pause for supper, assuming that the solitary
> musician must represent the rustic political cunning of the
> hinterland and knew how to elect Taylor, I asked whether
> he had a good chance of winning.
> "Not a snowball's chance in hell," said the campaign
> manager who had been hired to say just the opposite.
> "Then why are you managing his campaign?"
> "Taylor pays good. And it's better than my last job."
> "What was that?"
> "Garbage man at Burns Lake."[38]

True to the campaign manager's prediction, L.D. ran a distant third on election night.

vii

With the election of Pattullo's Liberals came a more sympathetic approach to the municipalities and their attempts to help the jobless. Nevertheless, the unemployment crisis did not relent, nor did the pressure it put on civic finances. (By 1935, the cost of relief in Vancouver was $2.7 million.[39]) At the same time, an alarming number of homeowners were defaulting on their taxes. The properties reverted to the city for sale, but there were not many buyers. In 1934, the city did not even bother to hold a tax sale, so dismal were the prospects of selling any land.[40] This meant that at the same time as need was increasing, tax revenues were in decline. Both Burnaby and North Vancouver (city and district) went bankrupt, their affairs handed over to a provincially-appointed commissioner to manage. The prospect that the same thing might happen to Vancouver seemed very real.

186

During 1934, the unemployed problem worsened. The men who had accepted the government's invitation to go to the relief camps were increasingly unhappy with the treatment they received there. The camps were run on military discipline, the inmates treated like convicts. Men were free to leave, but where would they go and what would they do when they got there? The work was menial and pointless, the living conditions spartan, the pay of twenty cents a day an insult. The whole situation was justly compared to slave labour. No wonder the Relief Camp Workers' Union found it so easy to organize the men in protest. During the year there were 100 disturbances of different kinds in the B.C. camps. These picked up in frequency toward the end of the year as the men prepared to leave the camps and descend on Vancouver. L.D. joined the chorus of voices requesting an investigation into conditions in the camps, feeling that the men had cause for their grievances. But Prime Minister Bennett adamantly refused. As the situation moved toward a crisis, L.D. seemed tired and bereft of ideas. The *Sun* referred to "his inertia, his stagnancy and his hopelessness." "Mr Taylor's career is a lovely old fairy tale. But there is no bread and butter in it for Vancouver's growing families."[41] Never had L.D. seemed as old as he did facing the voters in that December's election.

L.D.'s opponent was Gerry McGeer, one of the best-known politicians in Canada.[42] A Vancouver lawyer, McGeer came to national attention during the 1920s when he represented British Columbia in freight-rate negotiations that resulted in tremendous growth in west coast shipping. He had first clashed with L.D. during the Lennie police inquiry. L.D. blamed him for the outcome of that inquiry, so there was an element of strong personal dislike injected into the civic campaign. During the Depression, McGeer developed his own solution to the economic crisis, which he would publish in 1935 in a book, *The Conquest of Poverty*. Basically, he argued that government should manipulate the supply of money so as to ensure that people had sufficient purchasing power. He blamed the private banking system for restricting the flow of credit and proposed a national bank that would issue money to finance social needs. McGeer believed, quite literally, that his ideas were inspired by God. He predicted that the Depression would be cured in twenty-four hours if government adopted his policies. In the 1933 provincial election, McGeer was elected to the legislature as part of Duff Pattullo's landslide, but to everyone's surprise, especially his own, he was not invited to join Pattullo's cabinet. This brought out another aspect of McGeer's personality. He loved to play the maverick. He turned on Pattullo and was a thorn in the premier's side during his government's first term.

L.D. looked ineffectual in the face of McGeer's eccentric bombast. Demoralized by long years of economic stagnation, the public was ready for big ideas. L.D. had none to offer, while McGeer was a national figure, a friend of Prime Minister King, a supposed authority on banking and finance. There were two big issues in the campaign. The first was the state of the city's finances. McGeer claimed that they were a mess. "The fact of the matter is that Vancouver is bankrupt and the sooner we realize it the quicker we'll be able to deal with the situation."[43] He promised to force a reduction in the interest that the city was paying on its debt. In fact, Vancouver was not bankrupt, as L.D. pointed out, but it did not seem to matter. Voters were drawn to the candidate who promised to do something, even if most of what he proposed was beyond the constitutional power of civic government to accomplish.

The second big issue was crime. It was widely believed, and argued by McGeer, that Vancouver was crime-ridden and that the police were not doing enough to control it. The police force had been a persistent problem for L.D. Early in 1931, Chief Constable Bingham had resigned following a dispute with the police commission. The new chief was C.E. Edgett, with whom L.D. had a volatile relationship. Two years after he was hired, Edgett was suspended by the mayor, allegedly for "inefficiency." The police commission looked into the matter and reported that "vice is rampant in the city." Gambling and illegal drinking went on openly while police looked the other way. Nearly one hundred bawdy houses were operating in the city.[44] The commission supported L.D. and Edgett was fired. A group of the deposed chief's supporters raised the old matter of L.D.'s property qualifications in an attempt to unseat him, but they did not succeed. Edgett's replacement was John Cameron, New Westminster's chief constable, who turned out to be an unfortunate choice. Crime in the downtown continued unabated and Cameron himself was discredited when he was caught socializing with the infamous Joe Celona, the city's leading gangster. (Later, Cameron was charged with conspiracy to corrupt the police force, but he was acquitted.)

L.D. made no attempt to disguise his lenient – he would have said realistic – attitude to vice crimes. "I am proud of this city even if there

L.D.

188

is vice here," he said. "As a matter of fact, there's more or less vice in every city and village and so it has been throughout the ages. Vice may be controlled but it cannot be eradicated. And, I might say, no city was ever run as a Sunday school."[45] Whatever sense this approach might have made as a matter of policy, it was not what the majority of voters wanted to hear. And the more he seemed to be soft on crime, the more L.D. himself was stained with a reputation for corruption. It was widely believed in the city that he had grown too close to the crime bosses who owned the brothels and ran the gambling joints. In his memoirs, Ivan Ackery related a story about L.D. "A musician of the early thirties remembers that Taylor used to take over the Belmont Cabaret every Sunday evening to entertain his friends. Six nights a week the public danced to Les Crane and his orchestra, but the seventh night belonged to His Honor. Joe Salona [i.e., Joe Celona], who dealt in the city's illicit trades in those days, would provide the liquor and the ladies."[46] Celona, who was Vancouver's own Al Capone, was very much in the public eye during the election since he had just been arrested for keeping a "disorderly house" on the top floor of the Maple Hotel on East Hastings. The "vice czar," as he was called in the press, was convicted the next spring and sent to jail for eleven years. When he was released on parole after serving less than half his sentence, there was such a storm of protest from the public that he was sent back to serve out the rest of his term.[47] Whether or not L.D. was as close to Celona as it was sometimes rumoured, he certainly was linked in the public mind with the seamy side of the city and a soft approach to morality enforcement.

McGeer, on the other hand, wanted an all-out war on crime. He drew a vivid picture of a community under seige by the criminal classes. "They don't stay down in the underworld either," he warned; "they come right up into your homes. Your women-folk sit at home trembling when you go out at night, because they don't know who may come knocking at the door." McGeer declared in no uncertain terms: "I intend to expel the gamblers, racketeers and vice-mongers who are making our city a rendezvous for the criminal class."[48] Combined with his proposed solutions to the city's debt crisis, he was the candidate who promised a way out of the doldrums. L.D. just promised more of the same.

Even though most observers would have predicted a McGeer win, the actual result was a stunning surprise. The challenger took close to eighty percent of the popular vote. L.D.'s support had deserted him almost completely. A jubilant McGeer toured the city in a motorcade showing off the green tie he had donned for the occasion. L.D.'s red tie had been a stop light for the city, he quipped, but he was giving a green light to get moving again.[49] L.D. had lost before. His defeat by William Malkin in 1928 had been particularly bitter because it had denied him the chance to be the first mayor of the amalgamated city. But at least that contest had been close. This time he had been buried by a landslide. Would he ever be able to dig himself out? Even his perennial optimism was tested that night as he returned alone to his apartment to think about his future.

L.D.

Conclusions

6

The devastating election loss to Gerry McGeer was the end of L.D.'s political career, though he refused to admit it. He contested four more civic elections, twice for alderman and twice for mayor, losing badly each time. He kept running for office principally because he needed a job. Major Matthews, the city archivist, reported running into L.D. during the 1937 aldermanic campaign. "I've got to run for alderman," L.D. told the major. "I have no money. Nice city, isn't it? Man spends his lifetime and then they let him starve. I haven't enough money to live on." Matthews described the eighty-year-old Taylor: "He is quite feeble on his feet, but made a very fair talk . . . uttered in so low a voice as to be scarcely audible all over the small room – only those near him could guess what he was saying."[1] A few days after the election, prominent defence lawyer Angelo Branca, later a B.C. Supreme Court judge, wrote to L.D.

> Dear LD,
>
> A group of well wishers have decided to place a trust
> account with the Royal Bank of Canada, Hastings and
> Nanaimo Street Branch, and you are kindly requested to
> draw on this account at the rate of $25.00 per week.
> We wish you long life and the comforts that the twilight
> station in life in which you find yourself merits.

This "pension" lasted for the rest of L.D.'s life.[2]

The indefatigable politician was also an indefatigable journalist. In March 1937, he launched another paper, the *New Deal*. It was an eight-page broadsheet, published weekly, a miscellany of reprints from other publications, bits of humour and news, gossip from Hollywood written by his sons, and L.D.'s own commentary on provincial and civic affairs. Mainly it was an opportunity to refight his election loss of 1934. "It will be the aim of the New Deal to be thoroughly impartial and fearless," he wrote in the second issue, calling for the creation of a Peoples Party "free from big or little interests . . . whose aim is A NEW DEAL . . . for all . . . free from the political money which now controls government." As usual, L.D. positioned himself as an outsider battling the establishment, which now included all political parties. For L.D., Gerry McGeer had become the sinister powerbroker manipulating local politics. His intemperate attacks on "Mayor Gerry" recall his bitter feud with Walter Nichol thirty years earlier. "He is OVERBEARING, RUTHLESS, and has NO SYMPATHY with the downtrodden," began one piece. "All his private and public actions are those of a BULLY. . . . He CRAVES the power of a dictator."[3] It is just as well that the *New Deal* ceased publication after twenty-five issues, before McGeer, who by this time was a Member of Parliament, decided to sue.

At the end of December 1938, L.D. received just 429 votes to finish dead last in his twentieth mayoralty campaign. That night he would not speak to reporters when they came to him for a comment and he refused to pose for photographs. Humiliated at the scale of his defeat, he decided finally to retire. George Fitch, his longtime secretary at city hall, had loaned him the money to run. Afterwards he wrote to Fitch:

> I had better have not run – now I know that our people
> do not want me in public life again. I accept. I have made
> my last attempt at a comeback. Yours was the only money
> I had to work with. As to the future I know not what it
> will have in store for me. Too old for a job, have to make
> my own – after 42 years, what have I to show? At least I
> have had the respect and confidence of the people during
> the greater part of that time – and still have, but not for
> public office. However I am not discouraged and will find
> something to occupy my time – at the same time making
> a small living; I am chock full of ambition, too much so for
> my own good. Excuse me for this personal letter but I had

L.D.

192

to talk to someone this morning, so have taken it out on
you – May 1939 be the best year you have had in every way.

Always Your Friend
L.D.[4]

i

While L.D. resigned himself to the sidelines, the Depression played itself
out in the streets of the city. One of McGeer's first acts as mayor was to
declare January 6, 1935, which also happened to be his birthday, a Civic
Day of Prayer. Whatever he was expecting, the collective prayers of
Vancouverites had no noticeable impact on the state of the economy.
Relief camp strikers had been migrating into the city during the winter
and the pace of their arrival picked up with the arrival of spring. By
the beginning of April 1935, there were many hundreds of refugees
from the camps subsisting in the city on public relief and handouts.
Once again the streets filled with protest marches and the parks with
demonstrations. The public was sympathetic to the men, if not to the
socialist rhetoric of their leaders, but McGeer and his council took a hard
line. When the strikers began holding illegal tagdays to raise money, they
were threatened with arrest. On April 23, several thousand strikers and
sympathizers marched through downtown and into the Hudson's Bay
Company store. Attempts to evict them precipitated a free-for-all that
resulted in extensive damage to the store and nineteen arrests. From the
Hudson's Bay Company the strikers moved on to Victory Square where
they were met by several hundred police. The protest was peaceful, and
a delegation was sent down to city hall (then in the Holden Building) to
meet the mayor. McGeer told the men that he could not do anything
for them, and when they left the meeting ten members of the delegation
were arrested for vagrancy. McGeer then drove the three blocks to
Victory Square where, on the advice of his new chief constable, W.W.
Foster, and fearing that the demonstration was the prelude to some sort
of Communist insurgency, he stood on the cenotaph and, in a quiet
voice, read the Riot Act ordering everyone to disperse. At this point
the crowd marched away, but matters did not end there. In the evening

police raided the Cordova and Hastings Street meeting rooms of the strikers, seizing two vanloads of printed material. In response, strikers and their sympathizers began gathering at Carrall and Hastings and at midnight police again descended on the area to break up the protest and make arrests. The time had come for stern measures, warned Chief Foster. (By an interesting coincidence, on that same day former police chief John Cameron was in court attempting to explain his close relationship with gangster Joe Celona. Some officers came directly from testifying in the corruption trial of their one-time boss to do battle with the unemployed in Victory Square.)

Defiant demonstrations continued for another five weeks as McGeer tried to convince the federal government to improve conditions in the camps and help the city cope with the influx of protestors. His pleas fell on deaf ears, so eventually strike leaders decided to take their message directly to Ottawa. Early in June, the men boarded CPR freight trains and headed "On To Ottawa." Their departure brought only temporary relief to the troubled labour scene in the city. On June 18, a two-week-old longshoremen's strike flared into violence on the waterfront. Angry at the use of non-union stevedores to keep the port open, about a thousand strikers marched on Ballantyne Pier where they were met by a combined force of city police and RCMP armed with guns, tear gas and batons. When marchers refused to turn back, the infamous "Battle of Ballantyne Pier" broke out. By the time peace was restored, twenty-eight people were being treated for injuries and twenty-four others were in police custody. Later that year the strike ended in defeat for the union.

Despite all the turmoil in the streets, Vancouver celebrated its Golden Jubilee in high style in 1936. McGeer planned a summer-long series of festive events, ranging from fireworks and military parades to hula dancers and concerts in the parks. Two lasting monuments built for the fiftieth birthday were the fountain in Lost Lagoon and the statue of Captain Vancouver at city hall. McGeer invited a steady flow of dignitaries to add distinction to the occasion, including the Lord Mayor of London and the Governor General, Lord Tweedsmuir, better known as the novelist John Buchan. The upbeat mood of the Jubilee celebrations seemed to indicate that the worst of the Depression was over. And so it was, for many people. But not for the unemployed men in government work camps. In the spring of 1938, Ottawa began closing the camps and once again the streets of Vancouver filled with transients who supported

L.D.

themselves by doing odd jobs and begging. When Mayor George Miller (McGeer had not run for a second term at city hall, deciding to concentrate on his job as a Member of Parliament) banned panhandling, the militant unemployed reacted by sitting in at the art gallery, the post office, and the Georgia Hotel. After ten days, the men in the hotel agreed to leave, but the others stayed on for another month. Finally, in the early hours of June 19, "Bloody Sunday," police surrounded the gallery and the post office and ordered the protestors out. At the gallery the evacuation went peacefully, but at the post office the men began damaging the building and the RCMP drove them into the streets with whips, clubs, and teargas. A furious mob stormed through downtown, breaking store windows. That afternoon 10,000 people gathered at the Powell Street Grounds to protest police behaviour and to demand Premier Pattullo's resignation. Eventually federal and provincial governments worked out a scheme to disperse the unemployed back across the country. This was a temporary solution to the lingering problem of unemployment. The war solved it permanently.

Historian Margaret Ormsby calculated that Vancouver was "more scarred by the depression than any other city in Canada."[5] While he was in office, L.D. had not been able to do much to alleviate the suffering, but neither had his successors. The city was the victim of simple arithmetic: too many unemployed, too few resources to deal with them. As Andrew Roddan had observed, the city was "a blamed summer resort for all the hoboes in Canada." While senior levels of government dithered about who was responsible and how best to address the problem, the city had to cope with the reality of hungry families and homeless men. Civic authorities were sitting on a powderkeg, without the ability to defuse it. When resentment and frustration and anger at government inaction boiled over, it was the city that suffered the fallout.

ii

As Depression gave way to war, L.D. continued to live alone in his apartment at the Granville Mansions, acquiring a reputation as a recluse. Alan Morley, in his history of the city, described a "penniless" L.D. "barricaded in his flat . . . opening only to a secret knock" and "convinced of the ingratitude of the city he had loved."[6] However, this portrait seems overdrawn. The series of articles by Ronald Kenvyn reveals that the old man was not the embittered hermit Morley made him out to be. "I have had a lot of grief and a lot of fun," he told Kenvyn. "I have made enemies but made more friends. I feel that I have accomplished something for my beloved adopted city."[7] L.D. kept in touch by mail with his sons, Ken and Ted, and in the fall of 1941 he went down to California to see them. Ted wanted his father to move south to live permanently with him and his daughter Mary, but L.D. declined, claiming he did not want to be a burden. He sent money to the boys from time to time, indicating that he was not as destitute as people supposed.

In August 1943, L.D. had a serious nosebleed in the middle of the night. He managed to alert one of the other tenants in the building, who sent for a doctor. L.D. was diagnosed with high blood pressure, but otherwise seemed to be as fit as could be expected for a man his age. Old age and inactivity were a burden to him. He complained in a letter to Ted of being tired and of leading a dull life. He died in St Paul's Hospital after a brief illness on June 4, 1946, six weeks short of his eighty-ninth birthday. His funeral was thronged by hundreds of people who stood outside the service to catch a glimpse of the casket, topped with a wreath of red carnations, as it was driven away to Mountainview Cemetery for cremation.

iii

Posterity has not been kind to L.D. The consensus of opinion seems to be that he was a lightweight. "L.D. was perhaps never a great mayor," said the *Province* at his death. "But he was a competent and enterprising mayor and had the city's best interests always at heart and the years gave him vast experience."[8] Faint praise, and typical of the fog of condescension that settled over his career. In his history of the city, Alan Morley described L.D.'s "reputation for deep and sometimes unscrupulous intrigue," and continued: "A slight and quiet man with little timbre to his voice and no gift of oratory, it was a tribute to his dogged personality that he made so great an impression on the electors."[9] Gerry McGeer's biographer, David Ricardo Williams, wrote that L.D. was "weak-willed" and "easily led by underworld figures" and that during the Depression he and his council were "a group of nonentities."[10] This underestimation of L.D.'s abilities continues down to the present, when he is more or less forgotten in the city that he governed for so many years.

Both Morley and Williams hint at the odour of corruption that has tainted L.D.'s reputation. He is considered, when he is considered at all, to have been a politician who allowed the criminal element to flourish. During his career he faced accusations that he purchased support for his political campaigns, that he used his position as mayor to obtain favours in his business life, and that he was suspiciously soft on crime. These stories began with his failed attempts to keep his newspaper solvent, and were strengthened during the Lennie inquiry into the police department in 1928 and the charges that were flung about during his 1934 election contest with McGeer. L.D.'s very success worked against him. His experience began to seem like shrewdness; his hold on office suggested connections of the wrong kind. He was linked with the idea of the "open city," which his opponents claimed to mean a city that was wide open to criminal elements. Unlike many of his rivals on the hustings, L.D. did not engage in self-righteous moralizing. He did not believe in cracking down hard on morality crimes such as gambling, drinking, and prostitution. As a politician he appealed to a working-class constituency and saw no need to deny the people their harmless pastimes. He believed in regulating vice crimes and confining them to certain areas of the city. As a result he was often the target of moral reform elements who organized to shut down the bawdy houses, gambling dens, and drinking holes. Nevertheless, no incidents of actual corruption were ever proved against him. If he did have a close relationship with any crime figures, it was not a profitable one for him. Even his opponents recognized that he did not profit personally from his years in office. In 1915, he lost his newspaper to bankruptcy and thereafter he was chronically short of money. He had no gangland patrons. Indeed, one of the distinctive things about L.D. was that he had no patrons of any kind. He began his newspaper with support from the Liberal Party, but his independent streak soon cost him. He had no financial backing from the political or financial elites in the province. As mayor he was invariably opposed by the major newspapers in the city, likewise by the various reformist leagues and associations that organized elite opinion from time to time around particular issues. He was a classic outsider who was disdained by the elites for being morally suspect, a bit pushy, dangerously radical in his politics, and unconnected by family or business to the city's dominant social circles. The fact that he lived openly with Alice Berry for several years without being married to her may have been another factor in shaping this reputation; at the least it was unusual behaviour for a respectable community leader.

L.D.

On the other hand, L.D. had something better than patrons; he had the consistent support of a large number of voters. Although his adversaries sometimes accused him of it, L.D. was not a demagogue. At times he came close; for example, when he inflamed public opinion against Asian immigration. But he had neither the personal charisma nor the bombastic rhetoric of the true demagogue. It is more accurate to call him a populist. He presented himself as a representative of "the people," opposed to the large corporations which threatened the public interest. "I am in thorough sympathy with the man who earns his living with his hands," he once told a journalist. "He is the backbone of the country."[11] He appealed to voters because he supported causes of immediate practical importance to them. His opponents labelled him a "socialist," but most voters recognized he was nothing of the kind. L.D. was a middle-class reformer, trying to make things better for workers and small business people like himself, "an ordinary man representing ordinary folk."[12] His reformist impulse was more pronounced early in his career when he campaigned on "dinner pail" issues and seemed to be a voice for the disadvantaged in society. When L.D. came into office in 1910, he was impatient to get things done. Following the election, the very first meeting of city council enacted the eight-hour work day for civic employees. Another example was the creation of a Juvenile Court. In January 1909, ratepayers had authorized by plebiscite the expenditure of $5,000 to establish a home for delinquent youths, including the province's first court expressly for juvenile offenders, but council had dragged its feet, much to the annoyance of youth workers in the city. L.D., on the other hand, lost no time in appointing a committee to arrange the details and the court was up and running within six months of his election. When it appeared that there was not enough money in the budget, he turned over $3,000 of his $5,000 mayor's salary to fund the project.[13] Women's suffrage and tax reform were two other reformist measures that he championed during his first terms.

By the middle years of his career during the 1920s, L.D. presented himself less as the voice of reform than the voice of experience. Some of his most significant accomplishments date from this period: the town planning commission, the first airport, amalgamation of city and suburbs, to name three. His opponents no longer accused him of socialism. Even in their eyes, L.D. had made the transition from radical to moderate, from innovator to administrator. His last two terms, during the 1930s, were the least productive. His health and energy were failing. He seemed to have grown more cantankerous with age. To be fair, it was easier to accomplish things during his early terms. In 1910, when he was mayor for the first time, Vancouver had a population of about 100,000 people and the civic government spent just over $2 million. It was a place where everyone knew everyone else and a politician could get a lot done with a smile and a handshake. By 1934, his last year in office, the population had grown by 150 percent and the city spent close to $1.5 million on relief and social service costs alone. Total spending was $7.8 million, almost four times as much as it had been twenty-five years earlier.[14] Government was more complicated, and made more complicated still by the Depression. The time had passed when L.D. could be the kind of activist mayor he liked to be.

L.D. knew how to accept defeat graciously – he had a lot of practice at it – but he also knew how to nurse a grudge. The three great enemies of his career were Walter Nichol, Joseph Martin, and Gerry McGeer. All three had humiliated him publicly, Nichol by belittling his talents as a publisher, Martin by accusing him of taking bribes, and McGeer by delivering the worst drubbing of his political life. He forgave none of them and expended a great deal of energy feuding with each one. His quarrels with McGeer and Nichol in particular went far beyond the usual political differences. L.D. could not stand feeling that he had been made a fool of in public. It unhinged him, and he lashed out vituperatively. On these occasions, the resentment that he felt against the condescension of the city's establishment, and that he usually kept bottled up, would burst to the surface and he would embarrass himself with a flood of angry recriminations.

L.D.'s was the type of Horatio Alger story so beloved by his generation. He fit the pattern of the "little guy" from a humble background who achieves success through hard work and the force of his own energy and personality. This is the narrative of his life that he presented over the years. L.D. also embodied the classic immigrant story of someone who moves to a new place and reinvents himself. He never revealed the truth of his Chicago experience to anyone in Vancouver. His life was divided into two halves. When the traumatic break came in 1896 and he was forced to flee to Canada, he made up a plausible story to account for his arrival. He left family, friends, and career behind and, with hardly a dollar to his name, managed to start over in a new country and make a success of himself. His humble background was part of his appeal as a politician. At the same time, his brush with the law in Chicago left a lasting impact on his personality. He was humiliated by the experience and blamed the powerful business interests who had denied him the help he needed to survive. For the rest of his life he struggled to achieve the success that had been stolen from him in Chicago, and for the rest of his life he railed against the special interests — "those people" he used to call them — who he thought conspired against him and, by extension, the public good.

L.D.

While not a visionary mayor, L.D. had an understanding of Vancouver's character. He recognized from soon after his arrival that the city could not be confined to its downtown peninsula, but would inevitably absorb the surrounding suburbs. It was not his fault that this took two decades to accomplish. He supported the kinds of infrastructure projects that linked the city to its hinterland: bridges across False Creek and Burrard Inlet, transcontinental train connections, and an international airport. He believed in the city's destiny as a regional metropolis and did what he could to help realize it. During his first term as mayor in 1910, an interurban train line linked the downtown via New Westminster to Chilliwack, putting the whole of the Fraser Valley within an easy tram ride of every Vancouverite. Almost thirty years later, the completion of the Lions Gate Bridge might be taken as the culmination of his career, reaching as it did out from the small peninsula that contained the city toward a wider future.

On the other hand, L.D. failed to understand an important implication of being a Pacific port city. Because of his own racial prejudice, he did not recognize that all ports must be open to the world, with the racial mixing that implies. Along with so many other civic and provincial leaders, he vainly tried to stop this process by ghettoizing the Asian population. In his defence, it can only be said that he possessed the prejudices of his time and ethnic background.

At his death, the *Sun* published an editorial regretting that L.D. had been allowed to slip away with so little public recognition. "L.D. served

L.D. was a fervent supporter of the Lions Gate Bridge, completed in November 1938 and officially opened the following May. VPL 3036

Vancouver well," it concluded, "better than Vancouver served him." In terms of public recognition for his years of service, this is true enough. On the other hand, the city served L.D. extremely well. He arrived as an accused embezzler on the run from the law. Vancouver gave him the opportunity to remake himself. When he arrived, the city was barely a decade old. Opportunities were plentiful. It was the perfect place for him to lose his old identity and begin again. Much as he complained about the powerful elites, they were not strongly enough established to deny an outsider like himself the success he craved. L.D. and Vancouver were perfectly suited to one another. As newspaper publisher and mayor, he made important contributions to the growth of the city. At the same time, that growth gave him the chance to indulge his restless ambition and to gain redemption for his past failures. In other words, to become L.D.

Appendices

Chronology of
Louis Taylor's Life

1857	July 22	born in Ann Arbor, Michigan. His parents were Gustavus Adolphus Taylor and Amy Denison Taylor.
1891		moves to Chicago to work for the Wabash Railroad.
1892	May 26	marries Annie Louise Pierce, the daughter of architect O.J. Pierce and his wife Catherine.
1896	August	when his bank fails he is sued by creditors and jailed. Released on bail, he flees to Canada.
	September 6	arrives in Vancouver.
1897	July	goes to work for the CPR in Revelstoke.
1898	February	returns to Vancouver from Revelstoke to prepare to go prospecting. In May he heads up the Stikine Trail. In the fall he returns, broke, to Vancouver.
1899		takes over circulation for the *Province* newspaper.

1900		naturalized a Canadian.
1901		in the spring his wife Annie and their son Ted join him in Vancouver. They move into a house on the Fairview Slopes.

L.D.

1902	January 9	wins his first election, for license commissioner.
1903	January 8	defeated in his attempt to be re-elected license commissioner.
1905	May	buys the *World* newspaper.
1906		separates with Annie; she moves to Los Angeles with their two sons.
1909	January 14	makes his first, unsuccessful, attempt to win election as mayor.
1910	January 13	wins mayoralty for the first time.
1911	January 12	re-elected mayor.
1912	January 11	loses mayoralty election. the World Building opens; at the time it is the tallest building in the British Empire.
	March 28	loses attempt to win the Rossland riding in the provincial election.
1914	January 8	fails again to get elected mayor.
1915	January 14	re-elected mayor for a third term.
	April	forced by creditors to sell the *World*.

206

1916	May	divorces Annie.
	June 8	marries Alice Berry.
1917		works as editor of the *B.C. Mining News.*
		Publishes *The Critic.*
1919	November 23	his second wife, Alice, dies.
1922	January 12	runs for mayor again, unsuccessfully.
1924	December 10	wins the first of four consecutive terms as mayor.
1928	July 23	is struck by an airplane propeller at the airport; his life is saved by emergency surgery.
	October 17	loses mayoralty to W. H. Malkin.
	December 21	his first wife Annie dies from injuries sustained when she is struck by a car in Hollywood.
1929	January	leaves for an around-the-world holiday paid for by public subscription.
	July	almost drowns in the Parsnip River in northern B.C. on a boating excursion with his son Ken.
1930	December 10	re-elected to the first of two consecutive two-year terms as mayor.
1931	July	takes ill at the opening ceremonies for the Sea Island Airport and is hospitalized for much of the following twelve months.
1933	November 3	runs unsuccessfully in the provincial election as an independent in the riding of Omineca.

1934	December 12		loses mayoralty election to Gerry McGeer. Despite subsequent attempts to win election as mayor and alderman, he never serves on council again.

1937	March 26		the inaugural issue of his new paper, the *New Deal*.
1938	December 14		contests his final election for mayor, finishing last behind five other candidates, getting just 429 votes.
1939	February–March		a series of articles reviewing his life appears in the *Province*.
1946	December 14		dies at St Paul's Hospital, age 88.

Civic Election Results

1902	January 9	license commissioner (two elected)	
	E.B. Morgan	1,273
	L.D. Taylor	**1,153**
	H.H. Layfield	980
	D.S. Wallbridge	812
	Samuel Gothard	282
	Robert Todd	165
	Wm. McGivor	152
	G. Molaro	130
1903	January 8	license commissioner (two elected)
	Wm. Hunt	925
	Hugh McKee	760
	John McLennan	700
	L.D. Taylor	**582**
	Sam Gothard	292
	Herbert Hewke	251
	R.E. Green	240
	Wm. Cartwright	124

1904	January 14	Ward 6 alderman (two elected)
	William Hodson	198
	Francis Williams	181
	L.D. Taylor	**127**
	T.H. Larney	88
L.D.	T.T. Richardson	84

1905	January 12	Ward 6 alderman (two elected)
	C.G. Johnson	294
	Francis Williams	194
	L.D. Taylor	**182**
	S.J. Macey	143

1909	January 14	mayor
	C.S. Douglas	2,029
	L.D. Taylor	**1,393**
	Edward Odlum	1,024
	D. M. Stewart	647
	Walter Hepburn	197

1910	January 13	mayor
	L.D. Taylor	**3,188**
	C.S. Douglas	2,915

1911	January 12	mayor
	L.D. Taylor	**4,582**
	Alexander Morrison	2,899

1912	January 11	mayor
	James Findlay	5,727
	L.D. Taylor	**4,413**

1914	January 8	mayor	
	T.S. Baxter	6,504	
	L.D. Taylor	**4,653**	

1915	January 14	mayor	
	L.D. Taylor	**4,549**	
	T.S. Baxter	3,863	
	Joseph Martin	3,066	
	C.S. Douglas	2,239	

Civic Election Results

1915	March 13	mayor	
	L.D. Taylor	**5,839**	
	Walter Hepburn	4,656	
	William Whiteway	85	

1922	January 12	mayor	
		(Preferential ballot in use. The following are first-ballot results.)	
	Charles Tisdall	3,555	
	J.J. McRae	3,127	
	L.D. Taylor	**1,975**	
	Thomas Kirk	1,632	
	Leon Lotzkar	139	

1922	December 13	mayor	
		(This is the last election using the preferential ballot.)	
	Charles Tisdall	4,049	
	L.D. Taylor	**3,795**	
	J.J. McRae	2,325	
	Arthur Fawcett	48	

	1923	December 12	mayor
		W.R. Owen	5,670
		L.D. Taylor	**5,617**
		Parm Pettipiece	2,459
L.D.	1924	December 10	mayor
		L.D. Taylor	**7,778**
		W.R. Owen	7,131
	1925	December 9	mayor
		L.D. Taylor	**9,859**
		Louis Rubinowitz	1,131
	1926	December 8	mayor
			(This election is for the first two-year term.)
		L.D. Taylor	**11,251**
		G.H. Worthington	4,524
		Louis Rubinowitz	197
	1928	October 17	mayor
		William Malkin	19,331
		L.D. Taylor	**17,242**
		Louis Rubinowitz	236
	1930	December 30	mayor
		L.D. Taylor	**22,797**
		William Malkin	17,568

212

1932	December 14	mayor
	L.D. Taylor	**14,924**
	Fred Crone	10,209
	Thomas Fletcher	8,326
	John Bennett	3,225
1934	December 12	mayor
	Gerry McGeer	34,521
	L.D. Taylor	**8,978**
1935	December 11	Ward 5 alderman
	Louis McDonald	1,225
	L.D. Taylor	**374**
	Thomas Irvine	284
1936	December 9	mayor
	George Miller	16,041
	Louis McDonald	12,363
	Charles Thompson	6,150
	L.D. Taylor	**3,994**

*Civic
Election
Results*

1937	December 8	alderman (four elected at large)	
	Henry Corey	12,501	
	Thomas Kirk	12,167	
	Helena Gutteridge	11,613	
L.D.	H.J. DeGraves	10,736	
	Parm Pettipiece	10,689	
	Alfred Hurry	10,408	
	Wm. Offer	7,940	
	Lilette Mahon	6,308	
	Ernest Robinson	6,223	
	Archibald Cowan	5,276	
	L.D. Taylor	**4,751**	
	Alexander Fordyce	3,981	
1938	December 14	mayor	
	Lyle Telford	17,004	
	George Miller	14,859	
	Nelson Spencer	8,388	
	T.H. Kirk	914	
	Arthur Barton	778	
	L.D. Taylor	**429**	

214

Notes

Chapter One

1. *World,* 6 May 1911.
2. Biographical memo in Major Matthews Collection, Vancouver City
   Archives.
3. *Province,* 16 March 1939.
4. Taylor to Pierce, 21 October 1905, Werbel Collection.
5. Kate Cooley to Annie Taylor, 8 May 1915, Werbel Collection.
6. *Province,* 27 February 1939.
7. *Chicago Tribune,* 12 August 1896.
8. *Ibid.*
9. These accounts are in *Vancouver Historical Journal,* Archives Society of Vancouver
   (January 1958): pp 50−53.
10. McGregor, *The British Columbia Magazine,* vol VII, no 6 (June 1911), p 467.
11. Ethel Wilson, *The Innocent Traveller,* (Toronto: McClelland and Stewart, 1949).
12. L.D. to Pierce, 9 September 1896, Werbel Collection.
13. L.D. to Pierce, 10 September 1896, Werbel Collection.
14. L.D. to Pierce, n.d., Werbel Collection.
15. L.D. to Amy Taylor, 10 November 1896, Werbel Collection.
16. J. Herbert Welch, "The Prospector Who Became Vancouver's Mayor,"
    Opportunities, vol II, no 6 (December 1910), p II.
17. L.D. to O.J. Pierce, 9 September 1896, Werbel Collection.
18. L.D. to Pierce, 20 September 1896, Werbel Collection.
19. J.S. Matthews, *Early Vancouver,* vol 2 (Vancouver: Brock Webber Printing,
    1932); L.D. to Pierce, 11 November 1897, Werbel Collection.

20. *News-Advertiser*, 12 September 1896.

21. Letter from CPR superintendent, Revelstoke, 21 February 1898, Werbel Collection.

22. Robert D. Turner, *The Pacific Empresses* (Victoria: Sono Nis Press, 1981), pp 48–51.

23. Brereton Greenhous, *Guarding the Goldfields: The Story of the Yukon Field Force* (Toronto: Dundurn Press, 1987).

24. *Daily Province*, 27 February 1939.

25. D.A. McGregor, "Adventures of Vancouver Newspapers: 1892–1926," *British Columbia Historical Quarterly*, vol x, no 2 (April 1946), p 102.

26. *Province*, 28 February 1939.

27. *Ibid*, 2 March 1939.

28. Robert A.J. McDonald, *Making Vancouver: 1863–1913* (Vancouver: UBC Press, 1996), p 117.

29. *World*, 1 October 1901.

30. M. Allerdale Grainger, *Woodsmen of the West* (Toronto: McClelland and Stewart, 1964), p 15; originally published 1908.

31. Robert A. Campbell, *Demon Rum or Easy Money: Government Control of Liquor in British Columbia from Prohibition to Privatization* (Ottawa: Carleton University Press, 1991), p 18.

32. Joe Swan, *A Century of Service: The Vancouver Police, 1886–1986* (Vancouver: Vancouver Police Historical Society, 1986), p 20.

33. *World*, 6 January 1902.

34. *Province*, 3 January 1902.

35. *World*, 8 January 1902.

36. *Ibid*, 7 January 1902.

37. *Ibid*, 10 January 1902.

38. *Province*, 8 December 1902.

39. *Ibid*, 9 January 1903.

40. *World*, 7 January 1903.

L.D.

Chapter Two

1. For Sara McLagan, see John A. Cherrington, *Vancouver at the Dawn* (Madeira Park: Harbour Publishing, 1997). Also Marjory Lang and Linda Hale, "Women of *The World* and other dailies: The lives and times of Vancouver newspaperwomen in the first quarter of the twentieth century," *BC Studies*, no 85 (Spring 1990), pp 3–23.

2. D.A. McGregor, "Adventures of Vancouver Newspapers: 1892–1926," *British Columbia Historical Quarterly*, vol x, no 2 (April 1946), p 113.

3. *Province*, 28 February 1939.

4. 5 May 1905, Werbel Collection.

5. City of Vancouver Archives, J.S. Matthews Collection, 504-B-5, file 97.

6. *Ibid,* 505-D-1, file 10.

7. *Province*, 28 February 1939.

8. McGregor, p 114.

9. *Province*, 13 May 1952.

10. Minko Sotiron, *From Politics to Profits: The Commercialization of Canadian Daily Newspapers, 1890–1920* (Montreal: McGill-Queen's University Press, 1997), p 22.

11. Paul Rutherford, *The Making of the Canadian Media* (Toronto: McGraw-Hill Ryerson Ltd., 1978), p 38.

12. W.H. Kesterton, *A History of Journalism in Canada* (Toronto: McClelland and Stewart Ltd., 1967), pp 69–70.

13. Henry Ewert, *The Story of the B.C. Electric Railway Company* (North Vancouver: Whitecap, 1986), pp 22–24.

14. *Province*, 21 September 1907.

15. Winnifred Pierce to her parents, 28 July 1901, Werbel Collection.

16. Roy Werbel, personal communication, 17 August 2000.

17. L.D. to O.J. Pierce, 8 October 1905, Werbel Collection.

18. L.D. to O.J. Pierce, 21 October 1905, Werbel Collection.

19. O.J. Pierce to L.D., 2 November 1905, Werbel Collection.

20. Biography of Alice Berry in E.O.S. Scholefield and F.W. Howay, *British Columbia from Earliest Times to the Present* (Vancouver: S.J. Clarke, 1914), vol 4, pp 621–23.

21. M.E. Nichols, *(CP) The Story of the Canadian Press* (Toronto: The Ryerson Press, 1948), pp 20 *ff*.

22. *Province*, 1 March 1939.

23. Nichols, p 105.

24. *Ibid*, p 107.

25. McGregor, p 105.

26. *Ibid*, p 98.

27. *Province*, 28 April 1905.

28. *Ibid*, 12 July 1907.

29. *Saturday Sunset*, 13 July 1907.

L. D.

30. *Province*, 1 March 1939.

31. *World*, 22 March 1913.

32. Kay J. Anderson, *Vancouver's Chinatown: Racial Discourse in Canada, 1875–1980* (Montreal: McGill-Queen's University Press, 1991), p 67.

33. See Anderson; W. Peter Ward, *White Canada Forever: Popular Attitudes and Public Policy Toward Orientals in British Columbia* (Montreal: McGill-Queen's University Press, 1978); and Patricia Roy, *A White Man's Province: British Columbia Politicians and Chinese and Japanese Immigrants, 1858–1914* (Vancouver: UBC Press, 1989).

34. *World*, 1 September 1906.

35. *Saturday Sunset*, 6 July 1907.

36. Quoted in Peter Ward, p 66.

37. *World*, 20 July 1907.

38. *Ibid*, 22 July 1907.

39. Patricia Roy, pp 193–94.

40. *World*, 10 September 1907.

41. *Ibid*, 11 September 1907.

42. *Ibid*, 8 October 1907.

43. *Vancouver Province*, 10 March 1908.

44. The most thorough account of this episode is Hugh Johnston, *The Voyage of the Komagata Maru* (Vancouver: UBC Press, rev. ed. 1989).

45. *World*, 23 May 1914.

46. *Ibid*, 24 June 1914.

47. *New Deal*, 26 March 1937.

48. *World*, 9 December 1908.

49. *Province*, 13 January 1909.

50. *Ibid*, 19 December 1908.

51. *Province*, 7 January 1910; *World*, 3 January 1910; 6 January 1910; 7 January 1910.

52. Robert K. Burkinshaw, *False Creek* (Vancouver: City of Vancouver Archives, 1984), p 20.

53. *Ibid*, p 32.

54. *World*, 12 January 1910.

55. *Province*, 11 January 1910; *Province*, 12 January 1910; *World*, 11 January 1910.

56. *World*, 8 January 1910; *Province*, 10 January 1910.

57. *World*, 14 January 1910; *Province*, 14 January 1910.

58. City of Vancouver Archives, City Council Minutes, 17 January 1910, vol 16, p 577.

59. *World*, 31 May 1910.

60. *Province*, 21 June 1910.

61. *World*, 27 June 1910.

62. *Province*, 28 June 1910.

63. *Ibid*, 3 March 1939.

64. *Ibid*, 14 January 1911.

65. *World*, 13 December 1910; *Province*, 3 January 1911.

66. *Province*, 7 January 1911.

67. *Province*, 13 January 1911.

68. *Ibid*, 29 August 1911.

69. *World*, 6 May 1911.

70. *World*, 31 May 1910; *News-Advertiser*, 6 November 1910.

71. For the context of George and other American reformers, see John L. Thomas, *Alternative America: Henry George, Edward Bellamy, Henry Demarest Lloyd and the Adversary Tradition* (Cambridge, MA: Harvard University Press, 1983).

72. Gregory Levine, "The Single Tax in Montreal and Toronto, 1880–1920," *American Journal of Economics and Sociology*, vol 52, no 4 (October 1993), p 425.

73. Allen Mills, "Single Tax, Socialism and the Independent Labour Party of Manitoba," *Labour/Le Travailleur*, no 5 (Spring 1980), pp 38–39.

74. *Single Tax Review*, vol 11, no 3 (May–June, 1911), p 15; *World*, 7 October 1911; 11 October 1911.

75. *World*, 29 September 1911.

76. *Province*, 28 November 1911; *World*, 29 November 1911.

77. Richard Wilbur, *H.H. Stevens* (Toronto: University of Toronto Press, 1977), pp 17–18.

78. *Province*, 5 January 1912.

79. These events are described in Mark Leier, "Solidarity on Occasion: The Vancouver Free Speech Fights of 1909 and 1912," *Labour/Le Travail*, no 23 (Spring 1989), pp 39–66.

80. *World*, 6 January 1912.

81. *World*, 12 January 1912; *Province*, 12 January 1912.

82. The most complete description of these events is in Leier.

83. *World*, 29 January 1912.

84. *Ibid*, 31 January 1912.

Chapter Three

1. *Sun*, 1 November 1918.
2. See Deborah Nilsen, "The 'Social Evil': Prostitution in Vancouver, 1900–1920," *In Her Own Right: Selected Essays on Women's History in British Columbia*, Barbara Latham and Cathy Kess, eds (Victoria: Camosun College, 1980), pp 215 *ff*; City of Vancouver Archives, Board of Police Commissioners, series 181, minutes, 5 December 1912.
3. Cited in Nilsen, p 212.
4. Mayor's secretary to John Moncreiff, managing editor, *Winnipeg Tribune*, 30 November 1910, Werbel Collection.
5. *World*, 28 March 1912.
6. *Federationist*, 22 June 1912.
7. See Kay J. Anderson, *Vancouver's Chinatown: Racial Discourse in Canada, 1875–1980* (Montreal: McGill-Queen's University Press, 1991), pp 92 *ff*.
8. Emily Murphy, *The Black Candle* (Toronto: Thomas Allen, 1922), p 29.
9. *World*, 10 February 1912.
10. *Sun*, 11 November, 27 November, 2 December, 3 December 1912.
11. *World*, 4 December 1912.
12. *World*, 9 December 1913.
13. *World*, 16 December 1913; *Province*, 22 December 1913.
14. *World*, 2 January 1914; *Sun*, 2 January 1914.
15. *Sun*, 5 January 1914; *World*, 6 January 1914; 9 January 1914.
16. *Province*, 15 January 1910.
17. Alan Morley, *Vancouver: From Milltown to Metropolis* (Vancouver: Mitchell Press, 1961), p 114.
18. J.A. Hobson, *Canada Today*, (London: T.F. Unwin, 1906).
19. J. Herbert Welch, "The Prospector Who Became Vancouver's Mayor," *Opportunities*, vol 2, no 6 (December 1910), p 12.
20. McDonald, *Making Vancouver*, p 141.
21. *World*, 13 October 1914.
22. Rutherford, *The Making of the Canadian Media*, p 51.
23. McGregor, pp 122–23.
24. *Province*, 30 July 1914.
25. *Ibid*, 4 January 1915.
26. *World*, 6 January 1915; 8 January 1915; 11 January 1915.
27. *Province*, 15 January 1915; *World*, 15 January 1915.
28. *Ibid*, 15 January 1915, p 5; 16 March 1915.

L.D.

29. *World*, 17 March 1915.

30. Martin Robin, *The Rush for Spoils: The Company Province, 1871–1933* (Toronto: McClelland and Stewart, 1972), p 135.

31. Sotiron, p 37.

32. *Province*, 7 April 1915.

33. *Province*, 4 March 1939; *World*, 18 February 1915.

34. *Province*, 4 March 1915; 8 March 1915.

35. *World*, 12 March 1915; 15 March 1915.

36. *Ibid*, 15 March 1915.

37. L.D. to Annie Taylor, 19 April 1915, Werbel Collection.

38. Annie Taylor to Clarence Chapman, 16 May 1915, Werbel Collection.

39. Chapman to Annie Taylor, 18 May 1915, Werbel Collection.

40. Kate Cooley to Annie Taylor, 8 May 1915.

41. L.D. to Caroline Pierce, 1 June 1915, Werbel Collection.

42. Annie Taylor to Clarence Chapman, 9 August 1915, Werbel Collection.

43. Chapman to Annie Taylor, 26 August 1915, Werbel Collection.

44. *World*, 27 March 1915.

45. Henry Ewert, *The Story of the B.C. Electric Railway Company* (North Vancouver: Whitecap Books, 1986), pp 127–28, 136–39; Patricia Roy, "The Fine Arts of Lobbying and Persuading: The Case of the B.C. Electric Railway, 1897–1917" in *Canadian Business History: Selected Studies, 1497–1971*, David S. Macmillan, ed (Toronto: McClelland and Stewart, 1972), pp 246–49; see also Roy's *The British Columbia Electric Railway Company, 1897–1928: A British Company in British Columbia* (Vancouver: PhD thesis, UBC, 1970), p 213.

46. *World*, 19 July 1915; *Sun*, 19 July 1915; *Province*, 7 March 1939.

47. Diane L. Matters, "Public Welfare Vancouver Style, 1910–1920," *Journal of Canadian Studies*, vol 14, no 1 (Spring 1979), p 5.

48. Eleanor A. Bartlett, "Real Wages and the Standard of Living in Vancouver, 1901–1929," *BC Studies*, no 51 (Autumn 1981), pp 8–10, 59.

49. Patricia Roy, "Vancouver: 'The Mecca of the Unemployed,' 1907–1929," *Town and City*, A.F.J. Artibise, ed (Regina: Canadian Plains Research Centre, University of Regina, 1981), p 399; Matters, p 5.

50. *Province*, 7 April 1915; 8 April 1915; 9 April 1915.

51. City of Vancouver Archives, City Council minutes, 30 June 1915, p 643; 19 July 1915, p 671; *Province*, 29 June 1915.

52. *Sun*, 18 January 1916.

Chapter Four

1. Margaret Andrews, "Epidemic and Public Health: Influenza in Vancouver, 1918–1919," *BC Studies*, no 34 (Summer 1977), pp 21–44.

2. *Province,* 3 January 1922.

3. Eleanor Bartlett, p 10.

L.D.   4. See The Working Lives Collective, *Working Lives: Vancouver, 1886–1986* (Vancouver: New Star Books, 1985), p 171.

5. Daphne Marlatt and Carole Itter, eds, *Opening Doors: Vancouver's East End* (Province of British Columbia: Sound Heritage Series, vol XIII, nos 1–2, Victoria, 1979), p 20.

6. *Victoria Colonist,* 15 November 1922.

7. The best account of the Janet Smith case is Edward Starkins, *Who Killed Janet Smith?* (Toronto: McMillan, 1984).

8. *Province,* 14 December 1922; 6 March 1939.

9. *Ibid,* 13 December 1923.

10. *Province,* 6 December 1924; 8 December 1924; 9 December 1924; 10 December 1924; *Sun,* 11 December 1924.

11. L.D. to Ted Taylor, 7 September 1925, Werbel Collection.

12. *Province,* 9 December 1926.

13. Patricia Roy, *Vancouver: An Illustrated History* (Toronto: James Lorimer, 1980), p 117.

14. *Province,* 3 December 1926.

15. David C. Corbett and Eleanor Toren, *A Survey of Metropolitan Governments: A Report to the Metropolitan Joint Committee* (Vancouver, 1958), pp 24–27.

16. Thomas H. Mawson, "Civic Art and Vancouver's Opportunity," *Canadian Club of Vancouver. Addresses and Proceedings* (Vancouver, 1911–12), pp 39–46.

17. See John C. Weaver, "The Property Industry and Land Use Controls: The Vancouver Experience, 1910–1945," Peter Ward and R.A.J. McDonald, eds, *British Columbia: Historical Readings* (Vancouver: Douglas & McIntyre, 1981), pp 436–39; Graeme Wynn and Timothy Oke, eds, *Vancouver and Its Regions* (Vancouver: UBC Press, 1992), pp 118–21.

18. Harland Bartholomew and Associates, *A Plan for the City of Vancouver* (Vancouver: Town Planning Commission, 1929).

19. Louis P. Cain, "Water and Sanitation Services in Vancouver: An Historical Perspective," *BC Studies*, no 30 (Summer 1976), pp 27–43. See also Will Koop, *Wake Up Vancouver!: an historical outline of the policies and administration, including some of the debates, circumstances, and controversies, of the Greater Vancouver watersheds* (Vancouver, 1993) and James Morton, *Capilano: The Story of a River* (Toronto: McClelland and Stewart, 1970).

20. A. Scott Berg, *Lindbergh* (New York: G.P Putnam's Sons, 1998), p 170.

21. *Province*, 7 March 1939.

22. *Province*, 7 March 1929; T.M. McGrath, *History of Canadian Airports* (Ottawa: Lugus Publications, 1992), p 242.

23. *Province*, 20 November 1926; 8 March 1939.

24. *Province*, 8 May 1928; see City of Vancouver Archives, Vancouver Police enquiry report of R.S. Lennie, Commissioner.

25. For example, *Province*, 2 December 1924.

26. *Opening Doors*, pp 61–2.

27. Emily Murphy, *The Black Candle* (Toronto: Thomas Allen, 1922), pp 169, 188.

28. *Opening Doors*, pp 32, 51.

29. *Ibid*, p 104.

30. *Sun*, 5 March 1958.

31. *Province*, 11 October 1928.

32. L.D. to his sons, 4 January 1929, Werbel Collection.

Chapter Five

1. *Province*, 8 March 1939.

2. Ken Taylor to Ted Taylor, July 1929, Werbel Collection.

3. *Ann Arbor Daily News*, 25 November 1929, clipping in Werbel Collection.

4. Quoted in Roy, *Vancouver: An Illustrated History*, p 99.

5. Andrew Roddan, *God in the Jungles* (Vancouver: First United Church, 1932), p 10.

6. *Ibid*, p 54–55.

7. *Opening Doors*, p 123.

8. *Province*, 18 December 1929, 20 December 1929.

9. Margaret Ormsby, *British Columbia: A History* (Toronto: MacMillan Company of Canada, 1958), p 442–443.

10. *Province*, 19 February 1930.

11. *Sun*, 10 January 1930.

L.D.

12. *Province*, 15 February 1930.

13. John Belshaw, *The Administration of Relief to the Unemployed in Vancouver During the Great Depression* (Vancovuer: MA thesis, Simon Fraser University, 1982), pp 104–05.

14. *Ibid*, p 96.

15. *Province*, 4 December 1930.

16. Belshaw, p 126.

17. *Province*, 5 December 1930; 9 December 1930; 11 December 1930.

18. *Ibid*, 11 December 1930.

19. City of Vancouver Archives, "Report of Chief Constable Bingham to police commission re. Unemployed situation and agitation," Board of Police Commissioners, Series 181, 21 January 1931, 75-C-4, file 18.

20. *Province*, 25 January 1931.

21. *Ibid*, 26 January 1931.

22. Lita-Rose Betcherman, *The Little Band* (Ottawa: Deneau Publishers, 1982), p 154.

23. *Province*, 6 January 1932.

24. *Ibid*, 4 September 1931; 6 September 1931.

25. *Ibid*, 4 March 1932.

26. Ivan Ackery, *Fifty Years on Theatre Row* (Vancouver: Hancock House, 1980), p 107.

27. Robin Fisher, *Duff Pattullo of British Columbia* (Toronto: University of Toronto Press, 1991), p 222.

28. *Ibid*, p 224.

29. City of Vancouver Archives, J.S. Matthews Collection, "Kitsilano Indian Reserve," 506-A-2, file 19A.

30. City of Vancouver Archives, Mayors' Papers, series 483, 33-A-5, files 5, 10, 12; 33-A-6, file 5.

31. *Province*, 2 July 1932.

32. The best work on the Lions Gate Bridge is Lilia D'Acres and Donald Luxton, *Lions Gate* (Vancouver: Talonbooks, 1999).

33. *Sun*, 7 December 1933; 14 December 1933.

34. A summary of the city hall issue is in David Monteyne, "'From Canvas to Concrete in Fifty Years,' The Construction of Vancouver City Hall, 1935–6," *BC Studies*, no 124 (Winter 1999/2000), pp 41–68.

35. *New Deal*, 28 May 1937.

36. *Province*, 14 March 1939.

37. *Ibid*.

224

38. *Province*, 26 October 1933; Bruce Hutchison, *The Far Side of the Street* (Toronto: Macmillan of Canada, 1976), p 94.

39. Ormsby, p 463.

40. Roy, p 112.

41. *Sun*, 4 December 1934.

42. See David Ricardo Williams, *Mayor Gerry: The Remarkable Gerald Gratten McGeer* (Vancouver: Douglas & McIntyre, 1986).

43. *Province*, 6 December 1934.

44. *Ibid*, 7 February 1933.

45. *Ibid*, 27 November 1934.

46. Ackery, p 108.

47. *Sun*, 5 March 1958.

48. *Ibid*, 10 December 1934.

49. Williams, p 171.

Chapter Six

1. City of Vancouver Archives, J.S. Matthews Collection, 505-D-1, file 10.

2. Angelo Branca to L.D., 24 December 1937, Werbel Collection.

3. *New Deal*, 2 April 1937, 27 August 1937.

4. *Province*, 23 August 1958.

5. Ormsby, p 469.

6. Morley, p 180.

7. *Province*, 16 March 1939.

8. *Ibid,* 5 June 1946.

9. Morley, pp 164–65.

10. Williams, pp 169, 221. For a more even-handed assessment, see Robert McDonald, chapter 7.

11. J. Herbert Welch, "The Prospector Who Became Vancouver's Mayor," *Opportunities,* vol 11, no 6 (December 1910), p 12.

12. McDonald, p 179.

13. City of Vancouver Archives, City Clerk Papers, Series 20, "Juvenile Court 1909–10," 10-D-4, file 11.

14. Annual Reports, Corporation of the City of Vancouver, 1911, 1935.

Sources

I Primary

Werbel Collection
    The private collection of papers in the possession of Roy Denison Werbel.
City of Vancouver Archives
    J.S. Matthews Collection
    City Council minutes
    City Clerk papers
    Mayors papers
    Board of Police Commissioners
Newspapers
    Chicago Tribune (August–September 1896)
    Saturday Sunset (1907)
    The New Deal (1937)
    Vancouver Daily Province
    Vancouver World
    Vancouver Sun

II Secondary

Ackery, Ivan. *Fifty Years on Theatre Row*. Vancouver: Hancock House, 1980.
Anderson, Kay J. *Vancouver's Chinatown: Racial Discourse in Canada, 1875–1980*.
    Montreal: McGill-Queen's University Press, 1991.

Andrews, Margaret W. "Epidemic and Public Health: Influenza in Vancouver, 1918–1919." *BC Studies,* no 34 (Summer 1977): 21–44.

Barman, Jean. "Neighbourhood and Community in Interwar Vancouver: Residential Differentiation and Civic Voting Behaviour." *BC Studies,* 69–70 (Spring/Summer 1986): 97–141.

──────────. *The West Beyond the West: A History of British Columbia.* Toronto: University of Toronto Press, 1991.

Bartholomew, Harland & Associates. *A Plan for the City of Vancouver, including Point Grey and South Vancouver and a general plan of the region.* Vancouver: Town Planning Commission, 1929.

Bartlett, Eleanor A. "Real Wages and the Standard of Living in Vancouver, 1901–1929." *BC Studies,* no 51 (Autumn 1981): 3–62.

Belshaw, John. "The Administration of Relief to the Unemployed in Vancouver During the Great Depression." MA thesis, Simon Fraser University, 1982.

Berg, A. Scott. *Lindbergh.* New York: G.P Putnam's Sons, 1998.

Berton, Pierre. *Klondike.* Toronto, McClelland and Stewart, rev. ed. 1972 (orig. pub. 1958).

──────────. "Magic in Their Souls." *British Columbia Digest,* July 1946, pp 88–95.

Betcherman, Lita-Rose. *The Little Band.* Ottawa: Deneau Publishers, 1982.

Bottomley, John. "Ideology, Planning and the Landscape: The Business Community, Urban Reform and the Establishment of Town Planning in Vancouver." PhD thesis, University of British Columbia, 1977.

Burkinshaw, Robert K. *False Creek: History, Images and Research Sources.* Vancouver: City of Vancouver Archives, Occasional Paper #2, 1984.

Campbell, Robert A. *Demon Rum or Easy Money: Government Control of Liquor in British Columbia from Prohibition to Privatization.* Ottawa: Carleton University Press, 1991.

──────────. *Sit Down and Drink Your Beer: Regulating Vancouver's Beer Parlours, 1925–54.* Toronto: University of Toronto Press, 2001.

Cherrington, John A. *Vancouver at the Dawn: A Turn-of-the-Century Portrait.* Madeira Park: Harbour Publishing, 1997.

Conley, James. "'Open Shop' Means Closed to Union Men: Carpenters and the 1911 Vancouver Building Trades General Strike." *BC Studies,* nos 91–92 (Autumn 1991–Winter 1991-92): 127–151.

Corbett, David C. with Eleanor Toren. *A Survey of Metropolitan Governments.* Vancouver: Report to the Metropolitan Joint Committee, September 1958.

L.D.

228

D'Acres, Lilia and Donald Luxton. *Lions Gate*. Vancouver: Talonbooks, 1999.

Davis, Chuck, ed. *The Greater Vancouver Book*. Vancouver: The Linkman Press, 1997.

Ewert, Henry. *The Story of the B.C. Electric Railway Company*. Vancouver: Whitecap, 1986.

Fetherling, Douglas. *The Rise of the Canadian Newspaper*. Toronto: Oxford University Press, 1990.

Fisher, Robin. *Duff Pattullo of British Columbia*. Toronto: University of Toronto Press, 1991.

Francis, Daniel. "The Secret Life of a Public Man." *The Beaver*, vol 83, no 2 (April/May 2003): 26–31.

Grainger, M. Allerdale. *Woodsmen of the West*. Toronto: McClelland and Stewart, 1964 (orig. pub. 1908).

Greenhous, Brereton. *Guarding the Goldfields: The Story of the Yukon Field Force*. Toronto: Dundurn Press, 1987.

Gutstein, Donald. *Vancouver Ltd*. Vancouver: 1975.

Hillam, Walter A. "The Magic of Single Tax." *The British Columbia Magazine*, vol VII, no 4 (April 1911): 303–305.

Howard, Irene. *The Struggle for Social Justice in British Columbia: Helena Gutteridge, the Unknown Reformer*. Vancouver: UBC Press, 1992.

Hutchison, Bruce. *The Far Side of the Street*. Toronto: Macmillan of Canada, 1976.

Johnston, Hugh. *The Voyage of the Komagata Maru*. Vancouver: UBC Press, rev. ed. 1989.

Keller, Betty. *On the Shady Side: Vancouver, 1886–1914*. Ganges: Horsdal & Schubart, 1986.

Kesterton, W.H. *A History of Journalism in Canada*. Ottawa: McClelland and Stewart, Carleton Library Series, 1967.

"Kitsilano Indian Reserve: Documentary Reprints." *Vancouver History* (August 1979): 16–31.

Kluckner, Michael. *Vancouver, The Way It Was*. Vancouver: Whitecap Books, 1984.

——————. *Vanishing Vancouver*. Vancouver: Whitecap Books, 1990.

—————— and John Atkin. *Heritage Walks Around Vancouver*. Vancouver: Whitecap Books, 1992.

Koop, Will. *Wake Up Vancouver!: an historical outline of the policies and administration, including some of the debates, circumstances, and controversies, of the Greater Vancouver watersheds*. Vancouver: 1993.

Lamb, Bessie. "From 'Tickler' to 'Telegram': Notes on Early Vancouver Newspapers." *British Columbia Historical Quarterly*, vol IX, no 3 (July 1945): 175–199.

Lang, Marjory and Linda Hale. "Women of *The World* and other dailies: The lives and times of Vancouver newspaperwomen in the first quarter of the twentieth century." *BC Studies*, no 85 (Spring 1990): 3–23.

Leier, Mark. "Solidarity on Occasion: The Vancouver Free Speech Fights of 1909 and 1912." *Labour/Le Travail*, no 23 (Spring 1989): 39–66.

_____. *Where the Fraser River Flows: The Industrial Workers of the World in British Columbia*. Vancouver: New Star Books, 1990.

Levine, Gregory J. "The Single Tax in Montreal and Toronto, 1880 to 1920." *American Journal of Economics and Sociology*, vol 52, no 4 (October 1993): 417–432.

Lewis, A.H. *South Vancouver: Past and Present*. Vancouver: Western Publishing Bureau, 1920.

Loosmore, Thomas R. "The British Columbia Labour Movement and Political Action, 1879–1906." MA thesis, University of British Columbia, 1954.

McCann, L.D. "Urban Growth in a Staple Economy: The Emergence of Vancouver as a Regional Metropolis, 1886–1914." L.J. Evenden, ed. *Vancouver: A Regional Metropolis*. Victoria: Camosun College, 1978: 17–41.

MacDonald, Norbert. "A Critical Growth Cycle for Vancouver, 1900–1914." Gilbert Stetler and Alan Artibise, eds. *The Canadian City: Essays in Urban History*. Ottawa: McClelland and Stewart, Carleton Library Series, 1977, pp 142–59.

_____. "CPR Town: The City-Building Process in Vancouver, 1860–1914." Gilbert Stelter and Alan Artibise, eds. *Shaping the Urban Landscape*.

_____. *Distant Neighbours: A Comparative History of Seattle and Vancouver*. Lincoln, NE: University of Nebraska Press, 1987.

McDonald, Robert A.J. "Business Leaders in Early Vancouver, 1886–1914." PhD thesis, University of British Columbia, 1977.

_____. "Victoria, Vancouver, and the Economic Development of British Columbia, 1886–1914." Peter Ward and R.A.J. McDonald, eds. *British Columbia: Historical Readings*. Vancouver: Douglas & McIntyre, 1981: 369–395.

_____. "The Business Elite and Municipal Politics in Vancouver." *Urban History Review*, 11 (February 1983): 1–14.

_____. "'Holy Retreat' or 'Practical Breathing Spot'?: Class Perceptions of Vancouver's Stanley Park, 1910–1913." *Canadian Historical Review*, vol LXV, no 2 (June 1984): 127–153.

_____. "Working Class Vancouver, 1886–1914: Urbanism and Class in British Columbia." Jean Barman and R.A.J. McDonald, eds. *Vancouver Past: Essays in Social History*. Vancouver: UBC Press, 1986: 33–69.

L. D.

_____. *Making Vancouver: Class, Status and Social Boundaries, 1863–1913.*
Vancouver: UBC Press, 1996.

McFaul, D. "Louis D. Taylor." *Vancouver History*, vol 18, no 4 (August 1979): 12–16.

McGrath, T.M. *History of Canadian Airports.* Ottawa: Lugus Publications, 1992.

McGregor, Donald A. "The Marvel of Vancouver." *The British Columbia Magazine*,
vol VII, no 6 (June 1911): 457–472.

_____. "Adventures of Vancouver Newspapers: 1892–1926." *British
Columbia Historical Quarterly*, vol x, no 2 (April 1946): 89–142.

Marlatt, Daphne and Carole Itter, eds. *Opening Doors: Vancouver's East End.* Victoria:
Ministry of Provincial Secretary and Government Services, Sound
Heritage, 1979.

Marquis, Greg. "Vancouver Vice: The Police and the Negotiation of Morality,
1904–1935." Hamar Foster and John McLaren, eds. *Essays in the History of
Canadian Law. vol vi: B.C. and the Yukon.* Toronto: University of Toronto Press,
1995: 242–273.

Matters, Diane L. "Public Welfare Vancouver Style, 1910–1920." *Journal of Canadian
Studies*, vol 14, no 1 (Spring 1979): 3–15.

Matthews, J.S., ed. *Early Vancouver: Narratives of Pioneers of Vancouver.* 2 vols.
Vancouver: Brock Webler, 1932.

Mawson, Thomas H. "Civic Art and Vancouver's Opportunity." *Addresses and
Proceedings.* Canadian Club of Vancouver, 1911–12: 39–46.

Miller, Donald L. *City of the Century: The Epic of Chicago and the Making of America.*
New York: Simon & Schuster, 1996.

Mills, Allen. "Single Tax, Socialism and the Independent Labour Party in
Manitoba: The Political Ideas of F.J. Dixon and S.J. Farmer." *Labour/Le
Travail*, no 5 (Spring 1980): 33–56.

Monteyne, David. "'From Canvas to Concrete in Fifty Years,' The Construction
of Vancouver City Hall, 1935–6." *BC Studies*, no 124 (Winter 1999/2000):
41–68.

Morley, Alan. *Vancouver: From Milltown to Metropolis.* Vancouver: Mitchell Press, 1961.

Morton, James. *Capilano: The Story of a River.* Toronto: McClelland and Stewart,
1970.

Murphy, Emily. *The Black Candle.* Toronto: Thomas Allen, 1922.

Nichols, M.E. *(CP): The Story of the Canadian Press.* Toronto: The Ryerson Press,
1948.

Nilsen, Deborah. "The 'Social Evil': Prostitution in Vancouver, 1900–1920."
Barbara Latham and Cathy Kess, eds. *In Her Own Right: Selected Essays on
Women's History in British Columbia.* Victoria: Camosun College, 1980: 205–227.

Odlum, Roger. *Victor Odlum: A Memoir*. West Vancouver: Petrokle-Tor Publications, 1995.

O'Keefe, Betty and Ian Macdonald. *Merchant Prince: The Story of Alexander Duncan McRae*. Surrey: Heritage House, 2001.

Ormsby, Margaret. *British Columbia: A History*. Toronto: Macmillan, 1958.

Rawson, Mary. "Eight Times Mayor of Vancouver." *BC Historical News*, vol 34, no 1 (Winter 2000/2001): 22–26.

Roddan, Andrew. *God in the Jungles*. Vancouver: First United Church, 1932.

Robertson, Angus E. "The Pursuit of Power, Profit and Privacy: A Study of Vancouver's West End Elite, 1886–1914." MA thesis, University of British Columbia, 1977.

Robin, Martin. *The Rush for Spoils: The Company Province, 1871–1933*. Toronto: McClelland and Stewart, 1972.

Roy, Patricia. "The British Columbia Electric Railway Company, 1897–1928: A British Company in British Columbia." PhD thesis, University of British Columbia, 1970.

_____. "The Fine Arts of Lobbying and Persuading: The Case of the B.C. Electric Railway, 1897–1917". David S. Macmillan, ed. *Canadian Business History: Selected Studies, 1497–1971*. Toronto: McClelland and Stewart, 1972.

_____. *Vancouver: An Illustrated History*. Toronto: James Lorimer and Co. and National Museum of Man, 1980.

_____. "Vancouver: 'The Mecca of the Unemployed,' 1907–1929." A.F.J. Artibise, ed. *Town and City*. Regina: Canadian Plains Research Centre, University of Regina, 1981: 393–413.

_____. *A White Man's Province: British Columbia Politicians and Chinese and Japanese Immigrants, 1858–1914*. Vancouver: UBC Press, 1989.

Rutherford, Paul. *A Victorian Authority: The Daily Press in Late Nineteenth-Century Canada*. Toronto: University of Toronto Press, 1982.

Scholefield, E.O.S. and F.W. Howay. "Mrs Alice H. Berry." *British Columbia from Earliest Times to the Present*, vol 4. Vancouver: S.J. Clarke, 1914.

Shaw, Charles Lugrin. "Mayor Taylor." *Maclean's Magazine*, 15 March 1934, p 28.

Single Tax Review, vol 11, no 3 (May–June 1911): special issue devoted to Vancouver.

Smith, Andrea. "The Origins of the NPA: A Study in Vancouver Politics, 1930–40." MA thesis, University of British Columbia, 1981.

_____. "The CCF, NPA and Civic Change: Provincial Forces Behind Vancouver Politics, 1930–40." *BC Studies*, no 53 (Spring 1982): 45–65.

Sotiron, Minko. *From Politics to Profit: The Commercialization of Canadian Daily Newspapers, 1890–1920*. Montreal: McGill-Queen's University Press, 1997.

L.D.

Spinney, Robert G. *City of Big Shoulders: A History of Chicago.* Dekalb, IL.: Northern Illinois University Press, 2000.

Starkins, Edward. *Who Killed Janet Smith?* Toronto: MacMillan, 1984.

Swan, Joe. *A Century of Service: The Vancouver Police, 1886–1986.* Vancouver: Vancouver Police Historical Society, 1986.

Tennant, Paul. "Vancouver City Politics, 1929–1980." *BC Studies,* no 46 (Spring 1980): 3–27.

Thomas, John L. *Alternative America: Henry George, Edward Bellamy, Henry Demarest Lloyd and the Adversary Tradition.* Cambridge, MA: Harvard University Press, 1983.

Tinkess, Robert G. "The Failure of Civic Structural Reform Movements in Vancouver: 1907–1916." Honour's essay, Dept of History, University of British Columbia, 1981.

Turner, Robert D. *The Pacific Empresses: An Illustrated History of Canadian Pacific Railway's Empress Liners on the Pacific Ocean.* Victoria: Sono Nis Press, 1981.

Van Nus, Walter. "The Fate of City Beautiful Thought in Canada, 1893–1930." Gilbert Stetler and Alan Artibise, eds. *The Canadian City: Essays in Urban History.* Ottawa: Carleton University Press, Carleton Library Series, 1977, pp 162–185.

Vancouver Historical Journal, January 1958: nos 1–3 (1958–1960).

Wade, Jill. *Houses for All: The Struggle for Social Housing in Vancouver, 1919–50.* Vancouver: UBC Press, 1994.

Walker, J. Alexander. "Town Planning in Vancouver." *The Municipal Review of Canada,* vol 31, no 6 (June 1935): 5–10.

Ward, W. Peter. *White Canada Forever: Popular Attitudes and Public Policy Toward Orientals in British Columbia.* Montreal: McGill-Queen's University Press, 1978.

Weaver, John C. "The Property Industry and Land Use Controls: The Vancouver Experience, 1910–1945." Peter Ward and R.A.J. McDonald, eds., *British Columbia: Historical Readings.* Vancouver: Douglas & McIntyre, 1981.

Welch, J. Herbert. "The Prospector Who Became Vancouver's Mayor." *Opportunities,* vol 11, no 6 (December 1910): 11–13.

Wilbur, Richard. *H.H. Stevens, 1878–1973.* Toronto: University of Toronto Press, 1977.

Williams, David Ricardo. *Mayor Gerry: The Remarkable Gerald Grattan McGeer.* Vancouver: Douglas & McIntyre, 1986.

Wilson, Ethel. *The Innocent Traveller.* Toronto: McClelland and Stewart, 1949.

Working Lives Collective. *Working Lives: Vancouver 1886–1986.* Vancouver: New Star Books, 1985.

Wynn, Graeme and Timothy Oke, eds. *Vancouver and Its Region.* Vancouver: UBC Press, 1992.

Index

L.D.

L. D.

Daniel Francis is a historian and the author/editor of more than fifteen books, including *National Dreams*, *The Imaginary Indian*, and *Imagining Ourselves*. His other books include *Copying People: Photographing British Columbia First Nations 1860-1940*, *The Great Chase: A History of World Whaling*, and *New Beginnings: A Social History of Canada*. His most recent project was the popular *Encyclopedia of British Columbia*. He lives in North Vancouver.